TSQ Transgender Studies Quarterly

Volume 9 ∗ Number 3 ∗ August 2022

Trans-Exclusionary Feminisms and the Global New Right

Edited by Serena Bassi and Greta LaFleur

RESISTING TRANS-EXCLUSIONARY FEMINISMS: A DISCUSSION FORUM

TRANSLATION

Introduction

TERFs, Gender-Critical Movements, and Postfascist Feminisms

SERENA BASSI and GRETA LAFLEUR

I n October 2018, the *New York Times* leaked a United States Department of
Health and Human Services memo that sought to redefine "sex" as "a biological, immutable condition determined by genitalia at birth" (Hanssmann
2018). To experts of contemporary right-wing movements, this memo marked
yet another moment during Trump's presidency when the administration sought
to curry favor with its electorate by attempting to codify into administrative
law and policy an anti-trans—or, in the words of some of its proponents, an
"anti-gender"—position. This attempt to legally redefine "sex" clearly reads as
a bureaucratic rewriting of the online refrain "there are only two genders!,"
which can be found across platforms in the "conservative blogosphere" in a
number of semiotic genres: from YouTube right-wing comedy shows and Men's
Rights memes to white-nationalist Twitter (Cole 2018). Of course, neither grassroots conservative transphobia nor its party-political retrievals are unexpected
recent occurrences. However, what seems worth investigating further about twenty-
first-century varietals of transphobia is the gesture of framing trans exclusion not so
much via the well-worn trope of an impending culture war, but as "a global battle
of ideas" (Kuhar and Paternotte 2017b: 10) traveling under the banner of "gender-
critical" politics. In all its multiple manifestations, gender-critical discourse ostensibly takes issue with the feminist theoretical notion that sex and gender are
social and cultural inventions (Scott 2016: 300) and, crucially, with the attendant
trans political vision for a world where a multitude of lives beyond the gender
binary are both imaginable and rendered materially possible. But the simplistic
vignette of a clash of progressive feminist versus conservative anti-feminist ideas
fails to capture the complexities of our current cultural moment, one in which
much of what is under contestation is the meaning attributed to feminism itself.

TSQ: Transgender Studies Quarterly ∗ Volume 9, Number 3 ∗ August 2022   **311**
DOI 10.1215/23289252-9836008   © 2022 Duke University Press

Take, for example, the recent political vicissitudes of the Gender Recognition Act (GRA) in Britain. After the British Parliament held an inquiry in 2015 into transgender equality—which led to their recommendation to reform GRA to democratize trans people's ability to access medical transition—the gender-critical trans-exclusionary feminist movement organized against the proposed changes to the act, causing the reform process to stall (Pearce, Erikainen, and Vincent 2020: 678–79). As is well known, the focus of the campaign that defeated the trans movement's attempt to rethink GRA was the argument—presented as a vehemently feminist position—that the right to self-determine one's own gender identity would endanger women in everyday single-sex spaces like public bathrooms (Jones and Slater 2020). In turn, this argument was backed up by the idea that "gender" is an ideological tool of deflection away from the everyday politics of "real" women's lives and the multiple forms of oppression they face due more or less exclusively to their embodiment (Lewis 2019). Thus, gender critical thinking gets articulated, in some instances, as a classic conservative call to return to an imagined "golden age where everything was simpler and genders were what they looked like" (Kuhar and Paternotte 2017b: 14) and, in others, as a timely piece of feminist militancy grounded on an essentialist story of womanhood as always already under threat: in danger, at risk, and in need of protection. Moreover, a number of conservative gender-critical activists are advocating their position speaking emphatically as women: for example, popular European Catholic personalities like the German pro-life sociologist Gabriele Kuby (Kovats and Peto 2017: 117–18), the Italian blogger and chick-lit writer Costanza Miriano (Evolvi 2022), and the Belgian theologian and thinker Marguerite Peeters (Bracke, Dupont, and Paternotte 2017: 41) all present the word *gender* as a shorthand for a currently unfolding anthropological revolution that—if not stopped in time—will eventually erase all differences between the sexes, depriving women, in particular, of their right to fulfill their biological destiny and pursue happiness (Garbagnoli 2017: 154).

In both the avowedly feminist and the explicitly conservative articulations of gender-critical thinking, mobilization relies, in great part, on the ability of the addressee to identify politically and culturally as an "authentic woman," which is itself a particular gender identification. In fact, gender-critical movements at large bear similarities with strands of liberal feminism centered on the primacy of gender over other vectors of power, authentic womanhood, embodied vulnerability, and individualizing notions of happiness and empowerment. For this reason, even the self-described conservative section of the gender-critical movement should not be seen simply as an anti-feminist project at a time of conspicuous rise of the Far Right on a global scale, as scholars typically view it (Corredor 2019). The driving objective of this special issue is to start a collective conversation on the gender-critical movement as a whole by engaging it as an increasingly successful attempt to initiate something that, we propose, should be understood as a distinctively postfascist feminism. In this introduction, we firstly situate contemporary trans exclusion in our particular political juncture—one in which fascist movements, ideologies, and imaginaries that had been hastily declared defunct after 1945 seem to be having something of a powerful afterlife (Eco 1995). To frame the multiple stakes of this special issue, we go on to trace the contemporary retrievals of transphobic tropes like the notion of a singular, biologically determined womanhood and, critically, we do so by building on several decades' worth of critique from woman-of-color, Third World, and Black feminisms surrounding the question of what "feminism" may accrue in different cultural moments. Ultimately, we argue that, in our specific moment, eschewing celebratory narratives of feminism as an incontrovertible political good—as we urgently rethink the boundaries between what we normally imagine as "feminist" and "anti-feminist" movements—is a *conditio sine qua non* for any kind of antifascist trans feminist political and critical intervention.

Understanding Postfascist Feminism: Anti-Gender and TERFism

This special issue tells the story of two political projects that are simultaneously deploying transphobia, and transmisogyny in particular, as part of a call to return to a melancholically mourned "authentic womanhood" that has allegedly been lost. The trans-exclusionary feminist (TERF) movement (Pearce, Erikainen, and Vincent 2020; Hines 2020) and the so-called anti-gender movement (Bracke and Paternotte 2016; Graff, Kapur, and Walters 2019) are only rarely distinguished as movements with distinct constitutions and aims, and when distinguished are only sometimes discussed alongside one another, even though the parallels are multiple. TERFism is typically described as an originally fringe group of Anglophone—largely American, British, and Australian—1970s cultural feminism that has grown exponentially over the past decade partially due to heightened media exposure. In the past decade or so, the shorthand "TERF" has traveled globally through online spaces: highly visible TERFs like the theorist Sheila Jeffreys, the journalist Julie Bindel, and the popular writer J. K. Rowling articulate the movement's brand of transphobia by claiming that trans womanhood is a patriarchal invention aimed at infiltrating women's spaces and undermining feminist movement building from within (Pearce, Erikainen, and Vincent 2020; Hines 2020). Trans politics of all kinds, according to this story, pose a threat to both lesbianism and womanhood, supposedly resulting in the radical erasure of the political power of both. Drawing out the contrapuntal paranoia with which much TERF rhetoric hums, the broader gender-critical movement rails against "Gender Theory," which it identifies as a US American ideology that, under the pretense of fighting for social justice, seeks to create a New Human that is neither male nor female (Bernini 2018). If this story sounds like far-right conspiracy theorizing, that is because it is familiar to and has long been promulgated by right-wing pundits and movements across old and new media platforms alike. As Kuhar and Paternotte (2017b) explain, since the late 1990s, the right-wing self-described "anti-gender" movement has been organizing across Europe and parts of Latin America (Careaga-Pérez 2016) against transgender people's rights and against a number of queer and feminist political projects including reproductive rights, legislation against gender violence, and anti-LGBT+ bullying initiatives, to name just a few.

Gender-critical movements often reemploy the well-known right-wing populist opposition between "the corrupt global elites" and "the people" (Wodak 2015: 46)—imagined, as part of populist rhetoric, through the figurations of "hardworking families" and "concerned citizens" (Villa 2017)—by tweaking it slightly. In anti-gender discourse, the corrupt global elites cast as the enemy of "normal everyday people" are the "genderists," a vaguely defined collectivity that includes visible transgender celebrities and athletes; pro-choice and reproductive rights activists; scholars of women, gender, and sexuality studies; and supranational organizations like the European Union and liberal-leaning private foundations like the Open Society (Kuhar and Paternotte 2017b: 15). In fact, although the targets of the anti-gender movement are remarkably diverse, "transgender" as a broad set of experiences that may offer an alternative to binary gender roles and the heteronormative family is arguably the chief figuration against which anti-gender coalitions organize. Moreover, in entering what they frame as a global battle of ideas, the anti-gender movement references and repackages a number of often contradictory and incompatible ideologies and theories, derived from sources as far-flung as Catholic theology, anthropology, colonial-era ethnography, far-right anti-Americanism, and scientific racism, as well as decontextualized references to postcolonial feminist thought (Graff and Korolczuk 2018). Indeed, in this special issue, Jenny Andrine Madsen Evang provides tools for reading the tangled rhetoric of the anti-gender movement, insisting on the critical importance of understanding how it works and foregrounding its attempt to appropriate and redefine postcolonial feminist analyses in service of its white-supremacist project. To critically interrogate the overlaps among varietals of trans-exclusionary feminism and the wider gender-critical movement, the articles in this special issue expose a number of understudied recent or contemporary transphobic alliances: between second-wave US feminists and Zionism, online atheist groups and TERFs, and French theorists of materialist feminism and European religious conservatives.

What these articles showcase, we argue, is a particular manifestation of what Enzo Traverso (2019) describes as "postfascism," a broad, open-ended and uneven cultural moment of political and cultural transition in which tropes and rhetorical fragments echoing pre-1945 fascist projects intersect heterogeneously with the current political culture of neoliberalism. An example of how fascist imaginations and neoliberal *dispositifs* may intersect can be found in routinely deployed arguments about trans rights and the supposed attack on women's safety. Think, for example, of the transphobic point mentioned above that transgender identities allegedly offer an excuse for "predators" to infiltrate women's spaces. In this instance, gender critical discourse attempts to juxtapose a vulnerable and silenced homogenous mass of "real women" to pathological individuals who are neither authentically female nor male. Importantly, both trans and cis womanhood are here rendered in highly ideological ways: the former as an example of individual behavior that is perverted and deviant and the latter as an ontological state whose normativity derives from its putative naturalness. As is well-known, in Fascist Italy and Nazi Germany, the entangled figurations of perversion, degeneracy, and crisis were key mechanisms employed to surveil, control, and curb both organized and everyday political dissent (Mosse 1985; Benadusi 2012). As Chang (2015) explains, in Fascist Italy in particular, a coherent figure—the crisis-woman—emerged that served to transform widely consumed liberal feminist narratives of the Euro-American "new woman" into fear-mongering devices aimed at making women conform to state-sanctioned femininities deemed natural, chiefly that of the fascist housewife and mother. The crisis-woman was deployed as a stand in for the degeneracy of modern society and, particularly, its increasingly androgynous gender roles that posed a threat to the binary gender system and heteronormative reproductive futurity.

In contemporary mainstream transphobia, then, we may be witnessing the postfascist resurfacing of the "crisis-woman" via representations of trans womanhood as a site of ominous danger and individualized risk. In fact, in the widely rehearsed trans-exclusionary argument mentioned above, the postfascist anxiety that degeneracy may lurk around the corner, always uncomfortably and unsafely adjacent to normalcy (and therefore constantly on the verge of corrupting, infecting, or sabotaging it) is coupled with a typically neoliberal sensibility that frames social issues like gender violence as matters of individual risk produced by a diffused cultural climate of insecurity. We do not, however, wish to present the emergent alliances that the contributors to this special issue are examining—in which supposed ideological antagonists collectively shape new trans-exclusionary imaginaries for the twenty-first century—as a unique historical development demonstrating a special, late modern tendency wherein even ideologies centered on fixity, uniformity, and homogeneity like fascism morph, hybridize, and adapt. Rather, our thinking is indebted to Ernst Bloch's ([1935] 1977: 5) pioneering insight that fascism entered the political arena, in the very first instance, as a "powerful cultural synthesis" of a variety of conservative, liberal, and even progressive formations, the same "heterogenous surprise" (27) that today forces us to attend to the syncretic soldering of the fascist "crisis-woman" to the neoliberal "at-risk" woman (Banet-Weiser 2015) and, as we have argued, even to particular varietals of liberal feminism.

Even as it is making a number of overtures to liberal feminism (mired as these may be in ambivalence and contradiction), the kind of postfascist feminism we are examining here explicitly promotes the renaturalization of the heteronormative sexual order and of the gendered division of labor between men and women (Garbagnoli 2016: 190). Importantly and unsurprisingly, national and racial formations are also woven through the normative sexual and gender formations that the anti-gender movement sees itself as defending. Alongside its obvious anti-Semitic undertones, for example, the key anti-gender charge that gender ideology is yet another "world program" unleashed by "global elites" on "normal families," encodes demographic anxieties and fears about reproduction and ethnonational decline (Kuhar and Paternotte 2018). Similarly, the call to citizenry to resist the translation of a morally suspect theory into European languages in particular makes implicit reference to well-worn colonial tropes of Europe as "the standard-bearer of civilization" (Kuhar and Paternotte 2017a: 268). If, as Finchelstein (2019: 97) has suggested, today's right-wing movements that act within democratic national contexts are indeed engaged in a systematic "postfascist attempt to redefine democratic theory," the anti-gender movement shows that that redefinition is occurring through the transformation of a number of terms, among them *gender, sexuality, nation, race, women,* and, crucially, *transgender*. In their multiple references to liberal feminism, religious conservatism, colonialism, historical fascist imaginations, and even a highly reappropriated and reconfigured version of postcolonial feminist theory, gendercritical movements demand that we carefully attend to trans exclusion as a complex palimpsest and avoid reducing it to an easily dismissible brand of reactionary thought.

A Postfascist Feminism of the 99 Percent?

To be clear, while we are here presenting twenty-first-century gender-critical trans-exclusionary discourses as highly syncretic yet distinctly postfascist palimpsests, we do not think it useful to engage in something like a game of "spot the present-day fascist!" with either TERFs or anti-gender activists. As Bray et al. (2020: 3) remind us, the "post" in Traverso's "postfascism" should be read neither temporally (as a straightforward aftermath of historical fascism), nor as negating any kind of world-historical frame, but rather as drawing out the entrenched "fascist potential" in supposedly democratic presents. Building on work on the postfascist times we are living through, then, this special issue asks what aspects of feminist history and thought may participate in or collude with projects ultimately fostering a violent right-wing cultural hegemony and diffusing and bolstering the fascist potential in our gendered imaginations, even when these are presented as feminist. In fact, the gender-critical politicization of a true womanhood under threat by trans politics is not only genealogically coherent with multiple conservative moral panics and resilient fascist tropes but also with the *longue durée* of liberal, bourgeois, white feminist exclusions perpetrated along racial and class lines. The authors of the contributions in this special issue collectively invite us to rethink the distinction between feminist anti-trans projects and anti-feminist anti-trans movements, such that we may be able to redefine trans exclusion cogently and capaciously.

The process of repackaging "gender" as postfascist politics involves a variety of social agents: from parent groups to neofascist youth organizations, from Catholic intellectuals to far-right publishers and pro-life activists, from infotainment personalities and online content creators to national political leaders. As Mickey Elster explains in this special issue, today proponents of trans exclusion are more likely to use what the author calls a strategy of "insidious concern" than a straightforward moral indictment of transness. In fact, from the outset, the first anti-gender thinkers were keen to not present themselves simply as reacting to queer and feminist social advancements, attempting instead to utilize the latter as opportunities to establish something of an alternative conceptual laboratory. In the late 1990s, for example, French priest and psychoanalyst Tony Anatrella (1998) published *La différence interdite: Sexualité, éducation, violence trente ans après Mai 68*. In it, Anatrella argued that the same Western societies that eagerly "celebrate diversity" in all its forms are waging a cultural war against the physical, psychological, and ontological differences between men and women (Stambolis-Ruhstorfer and Tricou 2017: 84). In Anatrella's account—which is accidentally strikingly similar to what a number of extremely active far-right women content creators also argue today in explicitly white supremacist online spaces (Tebaldi 2021)—secular institutions and markets see sexual difference as a hindrance to economic progress, and, as he goes on to argue, it is women who pay the highest price for this late-capitalist twofold economic and anthropological restructuring. What is being articulated here is a distinctively right-wing anticapitalism which casts heteronormative cis women as the ultimate losers of modernization and, therefore, the potential vanguard in the resistance against it.

In the many national iterations of the gender-critical movement beyond the Anglophone world, the word *gender* is kept in English and presented as untranslatable (Kuhar and Paternotte 2017b: 14). As we will explain, we interpret this as another distinctively postfascist strategy that, by framing "gender theory" as suspiciously "fashionable" imported knowledge, affectively binds it with fears of foreign contagion. For example, in Germany the slogan "Geisteskrankheit namens Gendermainstreaming" (A mental illness named gender-mainstreaming), first advanced in 2014 by the openly Islamophobic far-right group Patriotische Europäer gegen die Islamisierung des Abendlandes (Patriotic Europeans against the Islamicization of the Occident) (Haller and Holt 2019: 1677), has reappeared in widely respected newspapers, magazines, and TV as part of the increasing circulation in mainstream media of gender-critical soundbites and talking points (von Redecker 2016). While non-Anglophone speakers might not be able to ascribe an exact meaning to the phrase "Gendermainstreaming," they will be familiar enough with English as the idiom of global popular culture for the phrase to elicit an interpretation and an emotional response. Thus, anti-gender activism does not simply reproduce English words like *gender* in languages other than English. It takes these terminologies out of context and attempts to recontextualize them within a right-wing bid for cultural and affective hegemony that wields power productively rather than simply reactively or repressively. Much like the assemblage of fascist and neoliberal gendered figurations we have examined so far, the supposed untranslatability of *gender* is an easily recognizable postfascist rhetorical device: this is because refusing the possibility that a particular concept can be hybridized and rephrased in national languages other than English implicitly articulates the vision of a world made out of sovereign, linguistically and culturally uniform protectionist nations that will not bow down and assimilate putatively "foreign" theories of human experience. In spite of its own self-image as embattled against the feminist global traffic of meaning about gender and the body, the gender-critical movement has nonetheless managed to translate, popularize, and fundamentally reframe within public debate long-standing intellectual conversations about "sex" and "gender" as epistemological categories. In fact, as we have tried to show here, gender-critical activism functions itself as a large-scale translation process through which particular counter-theories and concepts are formulated and released into circulation. In turn, these new concepts and counter-theories can be described as articulating something which we name "a postfascist feminism of the 99 percent."

In the early 2000s, the Pontifical Council for the Family (2006) published the volume *Lexicon: Ambiguous and Debatable Terms Regarding Family Life and Ethical Questions*—a dictionary that lays bare the "new forms of manipulation" that hide beneath apparently innocent terms and phrases such as *homophobia, reproductive health, pro-choice, discrimination*, and, in an entry titled "An Ideology of Gender: Dangers and Scope," *gender* (Garbagnoli 2017: 153). The dictionary officially opened what the Pontifical Council for the Family called "a semantic battle." The metaphor of a fight over meaning powerfully implies that, for the

Vatican, winning this particular war of position may mean contributing to redefining some of the basic terminologies regulating citizenship and belonging in democratic contexts, while reasserting the gender-binary system in an avowed attempt to stand with cis women—understood here as one monolithic and bio-logically overdetermined population—against the supposed attack on their very nature encapsulated by the word *gender* (Garbagnoli 2016; Case 2016). Drawing from the history of gender-critical thinking and its multiple current manifes-tations, we suggest that this ideological and political position can be cast as a postfascist feminism of the 99 percent insofar as what gender-critical actors consistently invoke is an injured mass defined by their ontologically under-stood gendered identification. Importantly, this imagined 99 percent of women oppressed by the corrupt "genderist" elites is fully stripped of the classed con-notations of other kinds of mass feminist mobilization—chiefly, socialist femi-nism. Here, in fact, feminist working-class solidarity seems to be replaced by the idea that what should instead bring women together is a shared self-definition as biologically overdetermined and authentically gendered subjects—in other words, "normal women." This postfascist variation on a feminism of the 99 percent is certainly both problematically essentialist and highly paternalistic, but, as we will see more clearly in the next section, it may not, in fact, be any less feminist for that, as it is also perfectly in line with a particular Euro-American genealogy of liberal feminism.

The Nature of Feminism

If trans-exclusionary politics of various kinds—including a generalized rhetoric voicing supposed concern over the well-being of people who might be referred to as "women"—have been folded seamlessly into global right-wing movements, this is not, in some ways, a new or even necessarily recent phenomenon.[1] So how is it that it has garnered the sustained attention of scholars only over the past decade or so?

Part of the problem—not all of it, granted, but certainly part of it—may be that it has taken until the last decade, at least in the United States, for main-stream feminisms to experience a paradigm-shifting reckoning with the ambiv-alent character of feminist activism and politics, even as this reckoning had long been called for and has been unevenly absorbed. This is not to say, of course, that the many varietals of thinking about gender that have traveled under the name of feminism over the past 150 years have not each had their critics. Indeed, the rise of liberal feminism in the United States—perhaps most obviously embodied by the movement for women's suffrage, which spanned from the mid-nineteenth-century through 1919—is in fact perfectly coeval with the first criticisms of the US American feminist movement, as Black women (among many others) immediately recognized that those liberal prerogatives would mean functionally nothing for the Black women and men who still lived under enslavement and the constant threat of white supremacist violence.[2] The tradition of critique of liberal feminism, which is these days more or less coterminous with what is referred to as "white feminism," has always insisted on offering a clear-eyed account of its use-value for the ends of white supremacy, in part owing to what liberal feminism necessarily shares with liberalism itself.[3] Rarely do these critiques ask whether feminism itself is the problem, focusing instead on how to make feminism better: more anti-racist, more responsive to both structural and localized injustices, less hegemonic. The project of doing feminism better, we worry, has obscured a host of sobering but absolutely critical questions about how we understand feminism itself.

Feminism is not, of course, one thing. There are endless varietals of feminist activism, theorizing, politics, and praxis. Critics of, for example, liberal feminism would not necessarily wage the same critiques of, say, many materialist feminisms (although materialist feminisms have their own critics).[4] Feminism has many histories and, we hope, many futures. Recognizing that *feminism* is a word that refers to a multiplicity of political tactics, frameworks, and histories is also a critical starting point for the development of a more nuanced and importantly unromantic understanding of what *feminism* might and does mean right now. There is no stability of meaning that might be attributed to the term *feminist politics*. While this will be an obvious statement to anyone who has spent even the most minimal time thinking about feminism and its discontents, somehow the self-evident nature of this idea has not, at least to our mind, been sufficiently absorbed into our understanding of trans-exclusionary feminisms, gender-critical feminisms, or other veins of feminist thinking that could broadly be characterized by an enduring concern with refuting the womanhood of trans women and contesting the legitimacy of trans experience as a whole. Critiques of how feminism has, today and in earlier times, been invoked in service of a wide range of pernicious and anti-liberationist ends have somehow not yet spurred a careful enough reckoning with the enduringly ambivalent character of feminism.

We received many proposals for this special issue that made arguments that went like something like this: "Trans-exclusionary feminisms and gender-critical feminisms are not, in fact, feminisms. Actually, they're X." We do not intend this statement as a call-out of the authors of these submissions, all of whom were seeking to engage closely and carefully with trans-exclusionary feminisms. But the volume of this genre of submissions illustrates, to our mind, the problem: there is still a persistent sense, especially among white Americans or other scholars situated in the global North, that feminism is an incontrovertible political good that, while perhaps requiring some tweaks, needs to be saved from those supposedly feminist bad actors that speak, without legitimation, in its name. This position requires a belief in something akin to a reform politics, and in turn it suffers from all the predictable liabilities of reform projects more generally, namely, an inability (or unwillingness) to see the problems that inhere in the structure itself, choosing instead to focus on fixing the smaller manifestations of the deeper-seated issues.

While we believe that there are situations in which reforms can be strategic, reforms can nonetheless only be strategic when embarked on with a clear-eyed understanding of the bigger problems. To state it clearly, this special issue is organized around the notion that trans-exclusionary feminisms, gender-critical feminisms, and all other problematic—if we dare use such an innocuous term, which these politics absolutely do not deserve—feminisms are, in fact, iterations of feminism. That the Seneca Falls Women's Rights Convention in 1848 identified a set of priorities for women that were almost entirely unresponsive to the condition of Black and Native women does not mean it was not a feminist effort. White supremacist feminisms—think of Charlotte Perkins Gilman, Margaret Sanger, and other self-avowed feminists who advocated for racial eugenics, among other ideas—are feminisms. Imperialist feminisms—think of feminist global interventionism, histories of "white women saving brown women from brown men," as Lila Abu-Lughod (1998: 14), riffing on Gayatri Chakravarty Spivak, once put it[5]—are feminisms. To suggest that trans-exclusionary or gender-critical feminisms are somehow the first movement to call themselves feminist while working against the ends of gender liberation but are not feminist movements flies in the face of the very real and very complicated histories of feminism across the globe. This special issue, then, proceeds from the assumption that trans-exclusionary and gender-critical feminisms are feminisms and thus demand careful historicization, analysis, and contextualization as a recent (but not in any way new) formation of feminism that has gained terrifying traction on a global scale over the last fifty or so years.

But why linger with this question, which seems, in itself, perhaps merely semantic? Well, there are a few reasons, and because we find each of them so important, we elaborate them here. First, to insist on the idea that feminism cannot accommodate oppressive politics is to commit to a kind of historical revisionism and present-day refusal of reality that bespeaks a will to ignore or even conceal the harm that is done in the name of feminism. If we want to develop a righteous, critical feminism that will remain handy in the fight against gender-based oppressions of all kinds, the first step to getting there is necessarily taking a long, hard look at the many ways that feminisms have previously failed in the fight for justice.

Second, and related, the impulse to understand feminism as an incontrovertible political good is a form of purity politics that—apart from being a clichéd hallmark, in our current moment, of a particular cadre of the white Left—refuses to engage the pressing problem of ambivalence.[6] On an individual or highly localized level, a politics of purity understands harm that one causes— intentionally, knowingly, recklessly, or negligently, to invoke one of the foundational logics of mainstream feminism's most darling allies, American criminal law—as an extension of one's identity. To cause harm is to be bad. This is, of course, a bad take on the condition of living in the world with other people; all of us will wound, and be wounded by, others. But what we are referring to as a politics of purity insists on the bind between identity and action, which in turn makes taking responsibility almost impossible. Under this framework, if acknowledging that one caused harm means that one is a bad person, it is difficult to account for the harm one causes because it means acquiescing not to a bad act but to a bad identity. The same principle can be, we think, abstracted into an understanding of what a larger-scale logic of purity looks like: if feminism is understood to have one unified character that is broadly if imperfectly beneficent, any indictment of feminism for the many elaborate harms perpetrated in its name becomes an attack on feminism as a whole, rather than an attack on what feminism is used to announce or enact. A careful accounting for the promises and liabilities of any set of politics seems more promising as a means of engaging the complexities of the world around us.

Finally, we linger on the reality of complicit or downright fascist feminisms in order to offer historical and contextual scaffolding in this discussion of a movement we have witnessed gain an intimidating traction over even just the last decade. Trans-exclusionary feminisms—in their manifold, quicksilver iterations— represent a rising tide of conservative feminism, a movement increasingly hailed by its proponents as something like a feminism of the 99 percent from a distinctively right-wing perspective. It is a movement—indeed, a *feminism*—that points to the existence, or even an apotheosis, of a coalitional and longstanding global Far Right imagination that has been decades in the making. That some feminists seem reluctant to recognize it as such speaks to the need for better and more widely available vocabularies, frameworks, and analyses for how to anatomize the multivalent fortunes of feminist politics in the twenty-first century.

The structuring economic conditions under which we currently live— neoliberalism—also demand incredible deftness in the face of ambivalence and complexity. Indeed, as Inderpal Grewal, Lisa Duggan, Nancy Fraser, Michelle Murphy, Rahila Gupta, and many others have argued, one of the particularly pernicious tactics of neoliberal economization—the effort to convert activism into profit, ideas into brands, and movements into markets—has been to parrot or even absorb feminist frameworks toward the production of capital.[7] One of the hallmarks of what we might call this *style* of neoliberal economics is precisely its emphasis on flexibility, which manifests at times as an incredibly absorptive capacity, a tendency to take the shape of the political container it fills. It can mold capitalism into feminism, for example—think of Sheryl Sandberg's *Lean In* feminism and note, too, that bell hooks (2013) argued that "lean in feminism" is not a feminism but a "faux feminism"—or present a company that exclusively employs independent contractors to undermine decades-old labor organizing by taxi drivers as the only safe transportation option for trans people.[8] This is simply to say that to deny the ambivalent character of feminism, in this particular moment, is also to voice a dangerous willingness to ignore how feminism, in particular, has been so successfully wielded in the service of racism, capital and labor exploitation, and imperialism, to name just a few of its harms—and, of course, transphobia and transmisogyny.

We are thus lucky, in this special issue, to have a piece in our forum—an eclectic assemblage of shorter meditations on the same topic as the special issue as a whole—by Sophie Lewis and Asa Seresin that does exactly the work we call for here, contextualizing the unfortunate but very real sympathies that have historically existed between fascisms and feminisms. Lewis and Seresin's "Fascist Feminism: A Dialogue" presents a conversation between two theorists and critics of feminist movements, their promises, and their failures. In so doing, they join a conversation that has flourished over the last several years in particular on the use-value of gender-critical feminism, critiques of "gender ideology" and "genderism," and trans-exclusionary radical feminism for the aims of fascism. As Judith Butler argued in a piece published in October 2021 in the *Guardian*,

> Anti-gender movements are not just reactionary but *fascist* trends, the kind that support increasingly authoritarian governments. The inconsistency of their arguments and their equal opportunity approach to rhetorical strategies of the left and right, produce a confusing discourse for some, a compelling one for others. But they are typical of fascist movements that twist rationality to suit hypernationalist claims. . . . The anti-gender movement is not a conservative position with a clear set of principles. No, as a fascist trend, it mobilizes a range of rhetorical strategies from across the political spectrum to maximize the fear of infiltration and destruction that comes from a diverse set of economic and social forces. It does not strive for consistency, for its incoherence is part of its power.[9]

Of course, here Butler is embarking on a project slightly different from that of Lewis and Seresin; while Butler is interested in the terrifying potential of anti-gender rhetoric—both that which travels under the name of feminism and that which does not—to set the table for the rise of fascist or otherwise totalitarian politics, Lewis and Seresin's discussion is organized around, among other things, the oft-ignored histories of how feminist politics have been used in service of folding women into fascist structures of governance. What these pieces share, however, is an understanding of the labile political potential of feminism, and especially feminisms that understand themselves as broadly politics "about" women, rather than wide-ranging lateral efforts to build solidarity in movements organized against gender-based oppression.

One of the many sources of feminism's political versatility in a range of both left- and right-wing projects is the fact that the notion of feminism has accrued an almost impossible capaciousness over the last century and a half. But one common tenet—not universal, but common—of many feminisms is the importance of sustained attention to how embodied experience is accounted for, and frequently hierarchized, in structures of power, including but not limited to epistemologies like medicine and law, the organization of family and kin, and statecraft more broadly. In some contexts this attention to embodied difference has been a vital site of resistance to, for example, racist violence and hegemony. Think, for example, of Ida Wells's critiques of white women's complicity in the proliferation of lynching and other white supremacist violence against Black men at the end of the nineteenth century and into the twentieth; Sandy Stone's 1993 call for a "posttranssexual" politics that neither exacts a vow of secrecy nor requires gender-affirming medical treatments from trans people in exchange for being treated with dignity and respect; or Brittney Cooper's 2017 call for a feminist politics that neither takes genital morphology as its universalizing foundation nor ignores histories of the deprioritization of Black people's reproductive health, especially people whose bodies house a vagina, uterus, and ovaries.[10] But in other contexts rallying calls that identify feminism as a natural outgrowth of an embodied politics of womanhood themselves become hegemonic, working distinctions between having a penis or not, having a vagina or not, or being able to gestate or not, among others, into benchmarks adjudicating whether a person or group of people and their attendant political priorities belong under the umbrella of women or feminism. This latter approach also assumes women to be the subject of feminism, and womanhood to be an easily delineated category that includes most cis women and excludes most trans people, including—or especially—trans women. This is, of course, a quick and flat rendering of a wide swath of feminisms that, while not all explicitly trans exclusionary, lean that way simply by virtue of relying on a restricted understanding of what might be indicated by *woman*.

Importantly, this latter approach to feminist politics is typically and profoundly committed to the assumption of a coterminousness between womanhood and vulnerability—especially sexual vulnerability. While we do not, of course, want to undermine the very real and very pressing threat that sexual violence represents for people of all genders—and we know that those who do not adhere to white supremacist and cisheterosexist gender norms are often disproportionately affected by its ubiquity—here we want to focus on the rhetorical force of

claims of vulnerability to violence. Butler's focus, above, on the ideological incoherence of the claims of those who criticize "genderism" or the existence of trans
positive services or accommodations is certainly right, but political fearmongering
about the threat that gender diversity poses to the political and social order
frequently returns to invocations of the putative threat to "women" and children that these politics bear. This is not just an effort to pathologize trans people,
and especially trans women and feminine people, by representing trans people as
wolves in sheep's clothing, foxes in the proverbial henhouses of feminism and
women's spaces. Rather, it is that, but it is just as much an effort to consolidate
a sense of cis womanhood as ontologically defined by a particular relationship
to victimization, the incursion of trans and otherwise gender-affirming politics
being only the most recent perpetrator thereof. Think, for example, of Abigail
Shrier's 2020 *Irreversible Damage: The Transgender Craze Seducing Our Daughters*,
or writer Tristan Fox's article "A Butch Eradication, Serviced with a Progressive
Smile," which appeared on AfterEllen.com in 2019, whose original title, it should
be noted, was not "A Butch Eradication" but "A Butch Genocide," riffing on the
white nationalist conspiracy theory of "white genocide." Both of these recent anti-
trans polemics present trans experience as a threat to putatively cis women
(although *butch* as a formation is often understood by both those who so identify,
as well as scholars of gender and sexual cultures, as sitting on the transgender or
nonbinary spectrum), but, equally important, they imagine the status of being
endangered as fundamental to the experience of cis girlhood (in Shrier's case)
and women (in Fox's, although again, the assumption that *butch* is a word for cis
women or lesbians is, for many, an inappropriate one).[11]

We invoke these examples to illustrate how trans-exclusionary feminisms
deploy the rhetorical flashpoints of victimization and endangerment as part of
an ongoing effort to forge and consolidate a new vision of cis womanhood rising
from the ashes of a theory of sexual vulnerability rooted in a profoundly racialized
and cissexist understanding of embodiment. As rhetorical postures, ringing the
alarm around the putative victimization and endangerment of individual cis
women draws on an age-old strategy, at least in the context of North American
feminisms, and one that has historically walked neatly in step with white supremacy
and nativism. To frame trans women as a threat to cis girls and women—and often
as specifically a threat to sexual safety, as advocates for trans-exclusionary bathroom bills have been wont to do—is to insist on the exchangeability of *woman*
and *cis woman*, and simultaneously bears two seemingly innocuous effects.
First, positing cis womanhood, as a putative experience, as under attack by trans
people appeals to those who would call themselves feminists while also invoking
older and more paternalistic and protective approaches to womanhood. It drafts
those who would seek to protect "women" into transphobic and transmisogynist

projects, and makes it easy to do so, for who is *against* protecting women? And second, insofar as this rhetorical posture travels in step with a variety of mainstream feminist common sense, it functionally inoculates transphobic calls for the protection of cis women from critique. Think, for example, of *Soule v. CIAC*, a case emerging from Connecticut in which two (then eventually four) cis high school girls, all runners, three of them white and all of them affluent, sued the Connecticut Interscholastic Athletic Conference under Title IX—a federal civil rights law protecting equity in education and sport—for having been "made" to compete against two high school trans girls, both Black and from less affluent areas. When their lawsuit—filed by the Alliance Defending Freedom (ADF), a conservative impact litigation organization—did not convince a federal judge, who dismissed their complaint for lack of standing, one of the girls worked with the ADF to place a number of first-person articles about her own experience, one of which appeared on a billboard just down the road from us in Connecticut, where I-95 meets a number of other highways near Bridgeport. Featuring Chelsea Mitchell, one of the original plaintiffs who is now on a running scholarship at the College of William and Mary, a Division I school, the billboard read, "I was the fastest girl in Connecticut, until I was forced to compete with biological males [*sic*]."

This is exactly the kind of invocation of vulnerability we want to highlight, here; Mitchell admits that she is actually a very successful runner who has beat transgender girls in high school races many times, including Terry Miller, one of the trans girls named in the *Soule* lawsuit who Mitchell and her cis girl co-complainants claim was the source of such disadvantage to them. But these facts clearly have not been as effective as simply invoking the specter of trans girl runners as the harbingers of the future downfall of all women's sports; Mitchell's (2021) first-person article (carefully placed on yahoo.com), "I Was the Fastest Girl in Connecticut. But Transgender Athletes Made It an Unfair Fight," contains a subhead that simply exhorts "Don't Eliminate Women's Sports," as if that was ever on the table in her case or anyone else's. Here we can see the neat alignment between the interests of trans-exclusionary radical feminists and those of conservative litigators: through the recourse to the rhetoric of victimization or sheer elimination, they present trans people, and especially trans women, as an endemic threat to both feminism and womanhood more broadly. These issues are taken up by the authors of two of the articles in this special issue, political scientist C. Heike Schotten and religious studies scholar C. Libby, who remind us, as Libby does by way of Emi Koyama's (2020) work, that white female vulnerability is frequently used to argue against transgender rights. Even the argument by trans-exclusionary radical feminists that the term *TERF* (an acronym for "trans-exclusionary radical feminist") is a "slur"—rather than a description of a particular approach to politics—leans on a "politics of injury" that distances itself from the real and very harmful work trans-exclusionary radical feminism is doing in the world. The consistent recourse to the language of vulnerability and extinction—"butch genocide," cis women's vulnerability in bathrooms, the end of women's sports, the list could go on forever—"foregrounds 'the concept of harm' as 'central both to the feminist understanding of women's experience in patriarchy, and to the optimal approach of feminism to law.'"[12] It is also, it should be said, an effort to reify the political innocence of women (well, cis women, and even then, only certain cis women) and feminism by defining those terms through a framework of phantasmatic vulnerability to trans people and politics without any account-ability for the aggressive political harm they have also been used to effect.

To be clear, in this special issue we are not advocating for an abdication of feminist politics, nor are we asserting that the political potential of feminism has been evacuated. Particular feminist political traditions have been both formative and transformative for both of us in different ways. Rather, this special issue joins ongoing efforts to think about the emergence of trans-exclusionary politics, and trans-exclusionary feminist politics in particular, and to track how they have been increasingly folded into the broader landscape of conservative, authoritarian and totalitarian, and otherwise right-wing politics across the globe. It is also an effort to reckon with the memory of trans exclusion within the history of feminism, a history that has at times been flattened into easy narratives that lean in one clear direction or the other (e.g., all "second-wave" feminists were trans exclusionary; no "second-wave" feminists were trans exclusionary); the transphobic imperative to consistently frame transness through the lens of novelty undergirds trans-exclusionary feminist claims to the historical endurance of their beliefs.[13] As the authors of essays in this special issue demonstrate, however, trans-exclusionary positions have emerged most loudly at moments when feminist movements have insisted on the centrality of trans liberation to their cause. If trans-exclusionary feminisms are at least fifty years old in the United States, for example, then the importance of trans people to feminist political liberation, as scholars such as Emma Heaney and Jules Gill-Peterson have demonstrated, is even more enduring.

Furthermore, if we think about trans-exclusionary feminisms as part of an ongoing litigation surrounding what constitutes legitimate womanhood, which has been consistently conscripted into the service of forms of structural power that we would do well to work against—white supremacy, xenophobia and nativism, ableism and eugenics—we may well end up being able to tell a clearer and more canny story about the rise of trans-exclusionary feminisms in our immediate pasts and presents and to try to short-circuit the warm welcome they have received in both right-wing and liberal movements at home and abroad. Trans-exclusionary politics within feminism have also become a veritable crucible for what we under-stand feminism to be and to do, and they point importantly to the different femi-nist horizons that are delimited or made possible by different visions of the feminist political. For example, to return to the issue of how conservative litigators have cited Title IX in complaints seeking to bar trans girls from participating in high school and college sports, we could frame the questions that trans girl athletes present in a couple of ways. We could ask, What makes a "girl" or a "woman" athlete, and what measures must we take to protect that category within state-sponsored athletics? Or, we could ask, Is dividing sports participation into supposed "sex" categories really the best way to create equity for young athletes? To what degree might heavily biologized understandings of what "girls'" and "women's" bodies are capable of be as restrictive as they are protective? Are there other means of organizing athletes for competition (weight and height classes, etc.) that might create more equity and opportunities for participation? The first set of questions voice a feminist intervention on behalf of girls and women; the second set voice a feminist intervention on behalf of gender-based equity more broadly, asking how or whether moving away from the category of girls and women—assumed, too often, to also mean *cis*—might actually be of greater benefit to all who identify as girls and women, as well as participants of all other genders, too.

Like all edited projects, the special issue that is the product of our and our contributors' work is a very different vision of the project than that which we had first imagined. We had imagined a collection of essays from writers in many different countries, written in many languages and translated to ensure their reach. We had imagined a special issue that connected geographies through the trans-exclusionary movement networks there: Poland to Brazil, through Catholicism, or the United States to Nigeria and to China through the shared strength of gender-critical writing circulating among evangelicals. The essays that we received, however, tended to cluster around a host of fairly well-studied sites, relative to this phenomenon, primarily the United States and England, although the issue also contains essays from writers discussing trans-exclusionary politics in Japan and France. While this is probably due at least in part to a mix of an overlapping Anglophone readership and the fact that conversations on trans-exclusionary feminisms have more or less exploded over the last five years in US American and British scholarly communities, we emphasize that even an issue full of essays showcasing distinct regions, languages, religious traditions, and political milieux would nonetheless never be able to offer a comprehensive account of the growing importance of trans-exclusionary politics to a vast range of right-wing movements. Trans-exclusionary politics is an increasing and increasingly complex phenomenon that has contributed to both the strength of right-wing movements and the strength of cultures of transphobia. This special issue, then, offers no definitive conclusions, but hopefully some productive foundations for future scholarship, movement, and careful thinking about how to more effectively fight both of these dangers.

Serena Bassi is assistant professor of Italian studies at Yale University. Their work interrogates modern racial, gendered, and sexual formations by focusing on literature in translation. They have published in journals including *Translation Studies*, *Comparative Literature Studies*, and *Signs*.

Greta LaFleur is associate professor of American studies at Yale University. They are the author of *The Natural History of Sexuality in Early America* (2018) and coeditor of *Trans Historical: Gender Plurality before the Modern* (2021) and "The Science of Sex Itself," a forthcoming special issue of *GLQ*.

Notes

1. Black feminists have been criticizing the racial and class hegemony of the putatively universal category of woman since at least the nineteenth century. For a discussion of this tradition, see Carby 1987. For a very recent approach to the issue of white feminism and its racial exclusions, see Zakaria 2021.

2. Note that the 1848 women's convention was held at a time when slavery was legal in most states and a major structuring condition of US American domestic production and its economic landscape more broadly.

3. Black, woman-of-color, and Third World feminist movements have all, albeit differently, identified and attempted to correct the strong liberal foundations of many US feminisms. Some of the thinkers central to these movements have also identified feminism as *inseparable* from the liberal tradition and suggested frameworks for theorizing gender justice that are not feminisms; womanism, for example, is distinguished by some thinkers as a political philosophy distinct from feminism (see Collins 1996). In the last five years a slate of articles have been published that also ask about the relationship between womanism and feminism, specifically asking whether womanism is a type of feminism or whether it is in fact a distinct political approach to the racialization of gender. For one such article, see Bowen 2021.

4. For just one example of a critique of Marxism and materialist feminism, see MacKinnon 1989.

5. Here, Abu-Lughod is riffing on Spivak's (1988) oft-cited "Can the Subaltern Speak?"

6. On purity politics, see Shotwell 2016.

7. On the co-option of liberation politics as a strategy of neoliberal economics, see Duggan 2004; Grewal 2005; Fraser 2009; Gupta 2012; Murphy 2017; and Rottenberg 2018, among others.

8. During the fiftieth anniversary of the Stonewall Riots, Uber ran a series of ads in New York City featuring well-known local trans artists, activists, and performers, as part of the rollout of their "Right to Move" campaign, which Uber describes as follows: "Uber believes that everyone has the right to move freely, safely, and without fear. And that, not only in the month of June but year-round, everyone has a right to pride. This year, we're committing to helping empower a better experience for our LGBTQIA+ community, and particularly the transgender community. It takes everyone, and we're starting with us." Safety and mobility are unquestionably major concerns for many if not most trans people, but Uber has, by most accounts, only exacerbated those concerns while revising their brand to capitalize on the attention to trans people and politics wrought by New

York's promotion of the fiftieth anniversary of the Stonewall riots as an opportunity for tourism industry profits. Uber has been the subject of long-standing complaints by trans and nonbinary drivers—who Uber has worked hard to keep classified as "independent contractors" to whom they owe few employee protections and whom they can thus prevent from unionizing—who have argued that Uber uses hiring practices that discriminate against trans and nonbinary people. On criticisms of Uber by trans employees and applicants, see Hussain 2022. On Uber's "Right to Move" campaign, see Uber n.d.

9.   Butler continues, "In his well-known list of the elements of fascism, Umberto Eco writes, 'the fascist game can be played in many forms,' for fascism is 'a collage . . . a beehive of contradictions.' Indeed, this perfectly describes anti-gender ideology today. It is a reactionary incitement, an incendiary bundle of contradictory and incoherent claims and accusations. They feast off the very instability they promise to contain, and their own discourse only delivers more chaos. Through a spate of inconsistent and hyperbolic claims, they concoct a world of multiple imminent threats to make the case for authoritarian rule and censorship. This form of fascism manifests instability even as it seeks to ward off the 'destabilization' of the social order brought about by progressive politics. As a fascist trend, the anti-gender movement supports ever strengthening forms of authoritarianism. Its tactics encourage state powers to intervene in university programs, to censor art and television programming, to forbid trans people in their legal rights, to ban LGBTQI people from public spaces, to undermine reproductive freedom and the struggle against violence directed at women, children, and LGBTQI people. It threatens violence against those, including migrants, who have been cast as demonic forces and whose suppression or expulsion promises to restore a national order under duress."

10. On Ida Wells's anti-lynching campaigns, see Feimster 2011; Wells 1892; Wells 1895; Stone (1987) 1993; and Cooper 2017.

11. Leslie Feinberg (1992), Susan Stryker (2006), Joanne Meyerowitz (2004), among others, all have included "butch" as a gender identity that can be collected under the umbrella of transgender or nonbinary experience.

12. Here Libby cites Halley 2005.

13. Many transgender studies scholars have offered critiques of the persistent tendency of nontransgender writers or commentator and transphobic or otherwise politically hegemonic frameworks to portray trans people as a "new" phenomenon. For just one recent work that discusses this tendency, see Gill-Peterson 2018.

References

Abu-Lughod, Lila. 1998. *Remaking Women: Feminism and Modernity in the Middle East*. Princeton, NJ: Princeton University Press.

Anatrella, Tony. 1998. *La différence interdite: Sexualité, éducation, violence trente ans après Mai 68*. Paris: Flammarion.

Banet-Weiser, Sarah. 2015. "'Confidence You Can Carry!': Girls in Crisis and the Market for Girls' Empowerment Organizations." *Continuum* 29, no. 2: 182–93.

Benadusi, Lorenzo. 2012. *The Enemy of the New Man: Homosexuality in Fascist Italy*. Madison: University of Wisconsin Press.

Bernini, Lorenzo. 2018. "The 'Teoria del Gender' in Italy: A Partisan Essay on a Floating Signifier." *Revista psicologia política* 18, no. 43: 543–56.

Bloch, Ernst. (1935) 1977. "Nonsynchronism and the Obligation to Its Dialectics." *New German Critique* 11: 22–38.

Bowen, Angela. 2021. "Calling the Question: Is Womanism Feminism?" *Journal of International Women's Studies* 22, no. 8. https://vc.bridgew.edu/jiws/vol22/iss8/41.

Bracke, Sarah, Wannes Dupont, and David Paternotte. 2017. "'No Prophet Is Accepted in His Own Country': Catholic Anti-Gender Activism in Belgium." In *Anti-Gender Campaigns in Europe: Mobilizing against Equality*, edited by Roman Kuhar and David Paternotte, 41–58. London: Rowman and Littlefield.

Bracke, Sarah, and David Paternotte. 2016. "Unpacking the Sin of Gender." *Religion and Gender* 6, no. 2: 143–54.

Bray, Mark, Jessica Namakkal, Giulia Riccò, and Eric Roubinek. 2020. "Editors' Introduction." *Radical History Review*, no. 138: 1–9.

Butler, Judith. 2021. "Why Is the Idea of 'Gender' Provoking Backlash the World Over?" *Guardian*, October 23. https://www.theguardian.com/us-news/commentisfree/2021/oct/23/judith-butler-gender-ideology-backlash.

Carby, Hazel. 1987. *Reconstructing Womanhood: The Emergence of the Afro-American Woman Novelist*. New York: Oxford University Press.

Careaga-Pérez, Gloria. 2016. "Moral Panic and Gender Ideology in Latin America." *Religion and Gender* 6, no. 2: 251–55.

Case, Mary Ann. 2016. "The Role of the Popes in the Invention of Complementarity and the Vatican's Anathematization of Gender." *Religion and Gender* 6, no. 2: 155–72.

Chang, Natasha. 2015. *The Crisis-Woman: Body Politics and the Modern Woman in Fascist Italy*. Toronto: University of Toronto Press.

Cole, Mike. 2018. *Trump, the Alt-Right and Public Pedagogies of Hate and for Fascism*. London: Routledge.

Collins, Patricia H. 1996. "What's in a Name? Womanism, Black Feminism, and Beyond." *Black Scholar* 26, no. 1: 9–17.

Cooper, Brittney. 2017. "Pussy Don't Fail Me Now: The Place of Vaginas in Black Feminist Theory and Organizing." Crunk Feminist Collective, January 23. https://www.crunkfeminist collective.com/2017/01/23/pussy-dont-fail-me-now-the-place-of-vaginas-in-black-feminist-theory-organizing/.

Corredor, Elizabeth. 2019. "Unpacking 'Gender Ideology' and the Global Right's Antigender Countermovement." *Signs* 44, no. 3: 613–38.

Duggan, Lisa. 2004. *The Twilight of Equality? Neoliberalism, Cultural Politics, and the Attack on Democracy*. Boston: Beacon.

Eco, Umberto. 1995. "Ur-Fascism." *New York Review of Books*, June 22.

Evolvi, Giulia. 2022. "The Theory of Hypermediation: Anti-Gender Christian Groups and Digital Religion." *Journal of Media and Religion* 21, no. 2: 69–88.

Feimster, Crystal. 2011. *Southern Horrors: Women and the Politics of Rape and Lynching*. Cambridge, MA: Harvard University Press.

Feinberg, Leslie. 1992. *Transgender Liberation: A Movement Whose Time Has Come*. New York: World View Forum.

Finchelstein, Federico. 2019. *From Fascism to Populism in History*. Oakland: University of California Press.

Fox, Tristan. 2019. "A Butch Eradication, Served with a Progressive Smile." AfterEllen, April 26.

Fraser, Nancy. 2009. "Feminism, Capitalism, and the Cunning of History." *New Left Review*, no. 56: 97–117.

Garbagnoli, Sara. 2016. "Against the Heresy of Immanence: Vatican's 'Gender' as a New Rhetorical Device against the Denaturalization of the Sexual Order." *Religion and Gender* 6, no. 2: 187–204.

Garbagnoli, Sara. 2017. "Italy as a Lighthouse: The Anti-Gender Protests between the 'Anthropological Question' and 'National Identity.'" In *Anti-Gender Campaigns in Europe: Mobilizing against Equality*, edited by Roman Kuhar and David Paternotte, 151–74. London: Rowman and Littlefield.

Gill-Peterson, Jules. 2018. *Histories of the Transgender Child*. Minneapolis: University of Minnesota Press.

Graff, Agnieszka, Ratna Kapur, and Suzanna Danuta Walters. 2019. "Introduction: Gender and the Rise of the Global Right." *Signs* 44, no. 3: 541–60.

Grewal, Inderpal. 2005. *Transnational America: Feminisms, Diasporas, Neoliberalisms*. Durham, NC: Duke University Press.

Gupta, Rahila. 2012. "Has Neoliberalism Knocked Feminism Sideways?" Open Democracy, January 4. https://www.opendemocracy.net/en/5050/has-neoliberalism-knocked-feminism -sideways/.

Haller, André, and Kristoffer Holt. 2019. "Paradoxical Populism: How PEGIDA Relates to Mainstream and Alternative Media." *Information, Communication, and Society* 22, no. 12.

Halley, Janet. 2005. "The Politics of Injury: A Review of Robin West's Caring for Justice." *Unbound* 1: 65–92.

Hanssmann, Cristoph. 2018. "Trump's Anti-Trans Memo Opens Door to Escalating State Surveillance." *Truthout*, October 27. https://truthout.org/articles/trumps-anti-trans-memo -opens-door-to-escalating-state-surveillance/.

Hines, Sally. 2020. "Sex Wars and (Trans) Gender Panics: Identity and Body Politics in Contemporary UK Feminism." *Sociological Review* 68, no. 4: 699–717.

hooks, bell. 2013. "Dig Deep: Beyond Lean In." *Feminist Wire*, October 28. https://thefeministwire .com/2013/10/17973/.

Hussain, Suhauna. 2022. "Uber Faces 'Serious Questions' over Trangender Drivers' Treatment after Times Report." *Los Angeles Times*, February 2. https://www.latimes.com/business /story/2022-02-02/california-city-attorneys-uber-transgender-drivers-blocked-accounts.

Jones, Charlotte, and Jen Slater. 2020. "The Toilet Debate: Stalling Trans Possibilities and Defending 'Women's Protected Spaces.'" *Sociological Review* 68, no. 4: 834–51.

Korolczuk, Elżbieta, and Agnieszka Graff. 2018. "Gender as 'Ebola from Brussels': The Anticolonial Frame and the Rise of Illiberal Populism." *Signs* 43, no. 4: 797–821.

Kovats, Eszter, and Andrea Peto. 2017. "Anti-Gender Discourse in Hungary: A Discourse without a Movement?" In *Anti-Gender Campaigns in Europe: Mobilizing against Equality*, edited by Roman Kuhar and David Paternotte, 117–32. London: Rowman and Littlefield.

Koyama, Emi. 2020. "Whose Feminism Is It Anyway? The Unspoken Racism of the Trans Inclusion Debate." *Sociological Review* 68, no. 4: 735–44.

Kuhar, Roman, and David Paternotte. 2017a. "The Anti-Gender Movement in Comparative Perspective." In *Anti-Gender Campaigns in Europe: Mobilizing against Equality*, edited by Roman Kuhar and David Paternotte, 253–72. London: Rowman and Littlefield.

Kuhar, Roman, and David Paternotte. 2017b. "'Gender Ideology' in Movement: Introduction." In *Anti-Gender Campaigns in Europe: Mobilizing against Equality*, edited by Roman Kuhar and David Paternotte, 1–22. London: Rowman and Littlefield.

Kuhar, Roman, and David Paternotte. 2018. "Disentangling and Locating the 'Global Right': Anti-Gender Campaigns in Europe." *Politics and Governance* 6, no. 3: 6–19.

Lewis, Sophie. 2019. "How British Feminism Became Anti-Trans." *New York Times*, February 7. https://www.nytimes.com/2019/02/07/opinion/terf-trans-women-britain.html.

MacKinnon, Catherine. 1989. *Toward a Feminist Theory of the State*. Cambridge, MA: Harvard University Press.

Meyerowitz, Joanne. 2004. *How Sex Changed: A History of Transsexuality in the United States*. Cambridge, MA: Harvard University Press.

Mitchell, Chelsea. 2021. "I Was the Fastest Girl in Connecticut. But Transgender Athletes Made It an Unfair Fight." *Yahoo! News*, May 25. https://news.yahoo.com/fastest-girl-connecticut -transgender-athletes-110054181.html.

Mosse, George. 1985. *Nationalism and Sexuality: Middle-Class Morality and Sexual Norms in Modern Europe*. Madison: University of Wisconsin Press.

Murphy, Michelle. 2017. *The Economization of Life*. Durham, NC: Duke University Press.

Pearce, Ruth, Sonja Erikainen, and Ben Vincent. 2020. "TERF Wars: An Introduction." *Sociological Review* 68, no. 4: 677–98.

Pontifical Council for the Family. 2006. *Lexicon: Ambiguous and Debatable Terms Regarding Family Life and Ethical Questions*. Front Royal, VA: Human Life International.

Rottenberg, Catherine. 2018. *The Rise of Neoliberal Feminism*. New York: Oxford University Press.

Scott, Joan. 2016. "Gender and the Vatican." *Religion and Gender* 6, no. 2: 300–301.

Shotwell, Alexis. 2016. *Against Purity: Living Ethically in Compromised Times*. Minneapolis: University of Minnesota Press.

Spivak, Gayatri Chakravarty. 1988. "Can the Subaltern Speak?" In *Marxism and the Interpretation of Culture*, edited by Cary Nelson and Lawrence Grossberg, 271–313. Urbana: University of Illinois Press.

Stambolis-Ruhstorfer, Michael, and Josselin Tricou. 2017. "Resisting 'Gender Theory' in France: A Fulcrum for Religious Action in a Secular Society." In *Anti-Gender Campaigns in Europe: Mobilizing against Equality*, edited by Roman Kuhar and David Paternotte, 79–98. London: Rowman and Littlefield.

Stone, Sandy. (1987) 1993. "The *Empire* Strikes Back: A Posttranssexual Manifesto." https://uberty .org/wp-content/uploads/2015/06/trans-manifesto.pdf.

Stryker, Susan. 2006. "(De)Subjugated Knowledges: An Introduction to Transgender Studies." In *The Transgender Studies Reader*, edited by Susan Stryker and Stephen Whittle, 1–17. New York: Routledge.

Traverso, Enzo. *The New Faces of Fascism: Populism and the Far Right*. London: Verso.

Uber. n.d. "Right to Move." https://www.uber.com/us/en/pride/ (accessed February 1, 2022).

Villa, Paula Irene. 2017. "Anti-Genderismus: German Angst?" In *Anti-Gender Campaigns in Europe: Mobilizing against Equality*, edited by Roman Kuhar and David Paternotte, 99– 116. London: Rowman and Littlefield.

Von Redecker, Eva. 2016. "Anti-Genderismus and Right-Wing Hegemony." *Radical Philosophy*, no. 198: 2–7.

Wells, Ida B. 1892. *Southern Horrors: Lynch Law in All Its Phases*. New York: New York Age Print.

Wells, Ida B. 1895. *The Red Record: Tabulated Statistics and Alleged Causes of Lynching in the United States*. Chicago: Donohue and Henneberry.

Wodak, Ruth. 2015. *The Politics of Fear: What Right-Wing Populist Discourses Mean*. London: Sage.

Zakaria, Rafia. 2021. *Against White Feminism: Notes on Disruption*. New York: Norton.

TERFism, Zionism, and Right-Wing Annihilationism

Toward an Internationalist Genealogy of Extinction Phobia

C. HEIKE SCHOTTEN

Abstract This article traces the emergence of what the author calls predation TERFism to the development of US Jewish-identified feminism and, in particular, Zionist lesbian separatism. This historical connection is reflected in the rhetorical and ideological similarities between predation TERFism and Zionism, both of which are defined by an "extinction phobia" that confuses oppressor and oppressed, presenting the subordinate party as capable of eliminating the dominant one. This extinction phobia transforms into "right-wing annihilationism" via a dehumanization of the subordinate party as innately harmful and therefore requiring elimination; hence the hallmark predation TERF abjection of trans women as rapists of cis women and the Zionist abjection of Palestinians as "savage" and/or "terrorist." These connections can be obscured by the siloization of social justice movement work in the United States, wherein anti-colonial and anti-imperial organizing is often separated from organizing for gender and reproductive justice and sexual freedom. Recognizing the continuities, however — whether historical, material, or ideological — between predation TERFism and Zionism offers useful lessons for understanding not only the power of the contemporary global anti-trans resurgence, but also how we might build solidaristic, anti-colonial movements to defeat it.
Keywords TERFism, Zionism, US feminism, lesbian separatism, Jewish feminism

The pronounced rise of trans-exclusionary radical feminism (TERFism) around the world in the last half-century is indisputable. Widely imagined (or hoped) to be a political perspective that would die off with its progenitors, 1970s American and British radical and lesbian feminists, TERFism has found new allies in right-wing Catholic and Evangelical researchers, scholars, activists, and figureheads, reinventing itself as "gender critical" feminism that casts doubt on "gender ideology" (Greenesmith 2020a; Martínez and Rojas 2021). Despite the new terminology, however, this TERFism is both eerily reminiscent of and actually dependent on the founding views of that same small group of white second-wave lesbian and radical

TSQ: Transgender Studies Quarterly ★ Volume 9, Number 3 ★ August 2022
DOI 10.1215/23289252-9836022 © 2022 Duke University Press

feminists. This tiny number of people (Chapman and Du Plessis 1997: 174) have exerted outsized influence not simply on US feminism and its global reception but also, increasingly, on the broader right wing of which it has become a part.[1]

It nevertheless remains controversial to observe that TERFism is a reactionary or right-wing political position. This is due, at least in part, to its association with feminism, a movement to end sexist oppression (hooks 1984). The trickiness of this overlapping association occurs variously across multiple issues, but nowhere so unambiguously as at another, seemingly unrelated, site of vexed political contestation: Zionism and anti-Semitism. Just as critics are reticent to point out the reactionary character of TERFism because of its proximity to an oppressed group, women, and their movement for liberation, feminism, so too are critics reticent to point out the reactionary character of Zionism, or Jewish nationalism, due to its proximity to a historically oppressed group, Jewish people, and what has been cast as its liberation movement, Zionism (Cable 2022).

The connections between TERFism and Zionism are not simply rhetorical, however. They are also historical, insofar as the "classic" TERF analyses are themselves implicated in Zionist commitments and presuppositions. In contrast with the standard explanation that Catholicism or Catholic theology lie at the root of feminist transphobia (given that its primary US exponents, Mary Daly and Janice Raymond, are Catholic theologians and ethicists), I instead trace the genealogy of US TERFism through the advent of Jewish-identified feminism and, in particular, Zionist lesbian separatism. This genealogy reveals that the significant factor in TERF analysis is not actually religion so much as what Lynne Stahl (2021) calls "extinction phobia." Extinction phobias are existential beleaguerment narratives that cast political opponents as threats to survival, describing those opponents in objectified and dehumanizing terms that characterize them as innately threatening evil or "savage." Elsewhere, I have argued that extinction phobias are a version of Nietzschean slave morality (Schotten forthcoming, 2016); one can also recognize elements of moral panic, as theorized by Gayle Rubin (1984), at work here. Whether described as slave moralities or moral panics, however, extinction phobias are reactionary because they are ideological: they obscure the actual functioning of power by reversing hierarchy's material realities. In other words, rather than recognize their own power or position of superiority in relation to the political enemy they identify, exponents of extinction phobias instead insist on their own marginalization and victimization, instrumentalizing claims of oppression in order to wield them against their actually marginalized political opponents, whom they objectify and dehumanize as innately threatening.[2] The version of TERFism I identify in this article, which I call predation TERFism, is an extinction phobia to be sure. But so too is the Zionism that coexists alongside TERFism's historical emergence and also serves as one of predation TERFism's ideological resources. Rereading the history of US Jewish-identified feminism, which is developing at the exact same time as TERFism and has as one of its offshoots the remarkable development of Zionist lesbian separatism, offers a strikingly clear articulation of an extinction phobia that overlaps, informs, and facilitates the development of predation TERFism. It is here, I argue, that we should look for the origins of predation TERFism and its reactionary character.

The connections between these two seemingly unrelated ideologies—TERFism and Zionism—can be obscured by the siloization of progressive/Left social movement work in the United States. Indeed, there is a real divide between those parts of the Left that prioritize anti-imperialism and anti-colonialism and those that focus on ostensibly more "domestic" or "cultural" issues of gender justice, reproductive justice, and sexual freedom. Similarly, right-wing watchdog groups do not always make the necessary connections between white Christian nationalism (which includes Christian Zionism) and the Jewish Zionist lobby, neoconservatism, and the Islamophobia network (Ali et al. 2011; Duss et al. 2015). While contemporary TERFism may be funded in large part by the Evangelical and Catholic Right and Zionism by the neoconservative (and largely, but not entirely, Jewish) Right, the continuity in their arguments—specifically on the existential question of survival itself—suggests not only that these different parts of the Right have more in common than it may initially seem, but also the importance of understanding and taking imperialism and colonialism seriously in US social justice movement work. This hitherto unexplored link is thus significant in its own right and offers useful lessons for understanding the power of the contemporary anti-trans resurgence and its continuing ability to stymie and confuse otherwise well-meaning and progressive people about the legitimacy of trans people's existence and resistance—not to mention the continuing legitimacy of the existence and resistance of the Palestinian people.

I. Predation TERFism and Extinction Phobia

TERFism takes at least two different positions on the basis of women's oppression.[3] For more Marxist- or socialist-minded TERFs, the basis of women's oppression is the exploitation of specifically female-sexed bodies in the forms of (forced) childbearing, child-rearing, sterilization, prostitution and sex work, and so forth, and forms of physical violence or abuse that are (claimed to be) specific to female-sexed bodies, for example, (vaginal) rape, sexual harassment, (father-daughter or brother-sister) incest, and (once again) prostitution and sex work. These feminists view this analysis as "more radical" than socialism alone because it recognizes the oppression of women by men, rather than the oppression of labor by capital, as the primary social antagonism and the foundation on which capitalist exploitation is built. These socialist-minded TERFs argue that gender transition, while necessary or important for many people, is an individual choice, not a collective action, and thus not a political solution to the problem of women's oppression. Moreover, gender transition does not alter the terms of "gender" itself, which these feminists view as a counterproductive term because it obscures the basis of women's oppression—biological sex, which in their view cannot be changed— and potentially colludes with that oppression insofar as it appears to subscribe to and thus perpetuate binary "sex roles" (their term for gender). As the 2013 open statement from radical feminists puts it, "We look forward to freedom *from* gender," not flexibility to move between its two options (Hanisch et al. 2013).

By contrast, the more famous version of classical TERFism, exemplified by figurehead Janice Raymond and her book *The Transsexual Empire* (albeit not limited to her or this text alone), argues a bit differently. For these TERFs, the basis of women's oppression is the behavior and, perhaps more precisely, simply the very nature of people assigned male at birth: these feminists hold the penis itself to be the root of and reason for women's oppression. Sheila Jeffreys—in some ways Raymond's British counterpart and a near contemporary—explicitly names this theory "penile imperialism," which she defines as "the rule and control over women under male dominance through the wielding of the penis" (Engle 2006). It is evidenced throughout her anti-trans screed, *Gender Hurts* (Jeffreys 2014), wherein the presence of "complete" or "intact" male genitalia is considered sufficient to convey if not also enact violence and harm to (cis) women. And some radical feminist and lesbian separatist analyses (Cowan 1978; Gorgons 1978; Gutter Dyke Collective [1973] 1988) attribute all violence, racism, war, and environmental degradation to the doings of men, understood as persons with "prick power" (Gorgons 1978: 396). As Jennifer Earles (2018: 247) notes, these TERF analyses "conflate bodies with gender so that the penis became a symbol of patriarchy, male socialization, and unwanted heterosexuality."

Both TERF views agree that so-called women's space should be preserved solely for cis women because they also agree that trans women are not women. However, trans women's exclusion from "women's space" takes a different character in each view. For socialist-leaning TERFs, trans women are simply irrelevant to the problem of women's oppression. They are not "real" women, so they are not subject to women's—that is, female, that is, biological sex–based—oppression. Trans women can therefore be legitimately excluded from "women's spaces" not because they are a threat or problem but simply because they are not women or oppressed as women, and it is the right of oppressed people to gather and forge community absent the external constraints of the oppressors, whose world they seek to undo.

By contrast, for predation TERFs, trans women are agents of (cis) women's oppression and constitute active threats to (cis) women by their very existence.

This is based on the premise that, like "gay men, fetishists, transvestites, trans-sexuals, bisexuals, sado-masochists, necrophiliacs, scatologists, pederasts, [and] those who practice bestiality" (not to mention drag and butch/femme), trans women are simply "extensions of the sexual objectification/power/dominance way that men in this society relate to everything" (Alice et al. [1973] 1988: 392). As the latest ingenuity of patriarchal ideology, in other words, trans women represent yet one more male stratagem to infiltrate, undermine, divide, and destroy (cis) women, lesbians, and feminism. This claim may seem at odds with the predation TERF focus on the penis as the emblem and agent of patriarchal oppression. But it is easily resolved via the additional TERF assertion that removal of male genitalia and/or taking female hormones is insufficient to "make" a (cis) woman (see, e.g., Cowan and House 1977b: 34; Marty et al. 1983a: 344; Raymond [1979] 1994: 104; Raymond 1977: 13). In other words, trans women are men in predation TERF analysis.

Raymond agrees with these views, which is how and why she can conclude that trans women are in fact rapists of (cis) women. Since trans women, by their very existence, both constitute and enable a patriarchal takeover of the female body, they are therefore innately threatening to cis women. This assertion is typically considered Raymond's ([1979] 1994) distinctive contribution to predation TERFism. It is the most notorious of the many incendiary claims she makes in *The Transsexual Empire*; the passages wherein she asserts it (104, 118) are among its most repudiated and most reproduced. Too frequently overlooked, however, is Raymond's argument that trans women portend not simply the rape of cis women and lesbians but also their actual elimination. This is made abundantly clear in Raymond's cheap, trite, and solely rhetorical association between trans women and Nazis, or the "transsexual empire" (i.e., the medical establishment) and Nazi doctors. Raymond acknowledges the cheapness and triteness of this very association, noting that "the example of the Nazi camps has often been cited in ethical arguments that attempt to sensationalize and disparage opposing views" and "throw sand in people's eyes about such issues as abortion and euthanasia." However, she proceeds to do just this, excusing her reliance on this hackneyed rhetorical tactic by denying it is a "direct" comparison between "transsexual surgery" and "what went on in the camps but rather" a demonstration that "what did go on there can be of value in surveying the ethics of transsexualism" (148).[4]

Raymond's "argument" here is twofold: 1) referencing Thomas Szasz, Raymond claims that the medical establishment undertaking the treatment and care of trans people "is a science at the service of a patriarchal ideology of sex-role conformity in the same way that breeding for blond hair and blue eyes became a so-called science at the service of Nordic racial conformity" (149); and 2) the commodified search for scientific knowledge incentivizes trans medical treatment, which is otherwise "unnecessary surgery, performed in part because of the 'objective' knowledge that it offers to researchers and technicians on a subject that is not knowable from other sources" (150). Trans health care, in other words, is a kind of gender eugenics driven by an insatiable scientific will to knowledge. The rest of this section purports to substantiate these claims via a series of bizarre allusions and circumstantial associations, including factoids such as the first person to perform "sex-conversion surgery" was German; Magnus Hirschfield's Institute of Sexual Sciences studied "transvestitism (and probably transsexualism before it was named as such)"; Magnus Hirschfield was . . . German. Despite these cited incidents predating the Nazi regime, Raymond nevertheless goes on to allege that "one transsexual operation was done in the camps," which she confusingly uses as evidence to claim that such medical practice originates with Nazism and, to return to her first point (she does not make the connection herself), this consequently means that transsexual surgery is a eugenics program intended (via a comparison that is not, remember, a direct comparison) to eliminate or weed out cis women entirely ("in the same way that breeding for blond hair and blue eyes became a so-called science at the service of Nordic racial conformity").[5]

As Susan Stryker (2017: 107) aptly notes, this is one of the "more lurid yet logically incoherent sections" of *The Transsexual Empire*, relying on "a string of false syllogisms, inferences, and analogies that work to associate transsexuality with Nazism without actually asserting that transsexuals are Nazis or Nazi collaborators." Not only this, but if we were to take Raymond's noncomparative comparison seriously and hold it to some sort of consistency, we would be forced to conclude that, in this bizarre scenario wherein "the doctors" are "the Nazis," trans people electing surgical care would be "the Jews" insofar as they are "the victims" of the doctors' "medical experimentation." Yet Raymond doesn't actually argue this, of course; her claim is rather that trans women are the agents (i.e., "the Nazis") of a patriarchal medical and scientific edifice (Nazism?) that is bent on destroying (cis) lesbians, feminism, and lesbian feminism.

Underappreciated is how much of this and other of Raymond's hallmark "analyses" are present in the work of her mentor and PhD dissertation director Mary Daly (Kelly 2016).[6] Indeed, Raymond's focus on the medical establishment may very well derive from Daly's singular focus on gynecologists "of both body and mind" as the distinctly American face of patriarchal gynocide. Most significant for my purposes is the fact that both use Nazism as the relevant model or comparison to illustrate the harms done to (cis) women by "the transsexual empire" (Raymond) or "gynecological gynocide" (Daly 1978: 305). As we have seen, Raymond puts equivocal qualifiers on her own use of this rhetorical tactic. By contrast, Daly is much less restrained. Referencing Hannah Arendt ([1963] 1994), Daly (1978: 304–5) notes that the "banality of evil" is not an unfamiliar theme to women struggling to refuse all of patriarchy's bad medicine. . . . We have seen gynocidal practices and operations become acceptable to and accepted by women who are filled with self-loathing, and who are unable to bond with the loathed mirror-images of their decaying selves. Such fashioned and fashionable women are not caked with mud and feces [as Nazi death camp prisoners were], but are encrusted in the mold of man-made femininity.

If readers are taken aback by this graphic comparison of American women's suffering with those of Nazi death camp prisoners, Daly concludes this is because of a refusal to accord the horrors of both American gynocide and the Nazi Holocaust their proper due:

> Nowhere does the mechanism of banalizing of evil function more smoothly and insidiously than in gynecology. A symptom of this is the predictable re-action of outrage at an analysis which dares to expose the common roots and similarities between Nazi medical atrocities and American gynecological practice. Since the degradation of women is as commonplace and acceptable as the neighborhood drug store, this is perceived—if it is perceived at all—as minimally offensive. By contrast, the Nazi atrocities are recognized *as atrocities*. Yet the latter *are* belittled in the sense that they are seen as isolated events. Since their radical origin in patriarchal myth and social reality is not acknowledged, their deep roots are not eradicated. It is precisely the isolation of those genocidal atrocities from the reality of patriarchal gynocide, particularly in its most lethal modern manifestations, which should elicit outrage, for it minimizes the horror of the Holocaust, allowing its uneradicated roots to grow unnoticed, to sprout again elsewhere. This resistance to seeing connections, this scorn for integrity of vision re-presents/re-enforces the triumph of the banality of evil. (306)

In short, what happened to Jews in 1940s Europe is happening to American women right now (i.e., in 1978). This is because Nazism is in fact an offshoot of the depravities of medical (mal[e])practice: "patriarchal gynocide . . . is the root and paradigm for genocide" (298). But if Nazism is a by-product of patriarchal gynocide, it is difficult not to conclude that the end goal of male domination, whether it is called "gynocide" or "the transsexual empire," is the elimination of (cis) women, just as the aim of Nazism was the extinction of the Jews.

To my knowledge, Jeffreys does not invoke either Nazism or the Holocaust to describe trans people or the medical establishment, but she does repeatedly assert that the existence of trans people portends the eradication of (cis) women and lesbians. In this sense, her work is an update on Raymond's, who limits her analysis to trans women only, alleging without evidence that most trans people are trans women. By contrast, Jeffreys (2003: 122) asserts (also without evidence) that there is a new "epidemic" of trans men that constitutes an "emergency for lesbian politics." The emergency, however, is actually just the same old crisis, since, for Jeffreys, the existence of trans men also results in the elimination of (cis) women and lesbians, since, in trans surgery, "lesbians are physically destroyed . . . and their lesbianism is removed along with female body parts" (122). Although removal of the penis was insufficient to "create" a (cis) woman for predation TERFism, removal of breasts or the uterus is now apparently sufficient to "create" a [cis?] man. And a straight man no less: validating the old subcultural lesbian TERF chestnut that "all the butches are becoming men," Jeffreys goes so far as to claim that if the trans man is partnered, two lesbians are "eliminated" via surgery, because one transition results in two heterosexual people (chap. 6). This inconsistency depends not on any clear definition(s) of sex or gender in predation TERF analysis, but rather and solely on extinction phobia: regardless of which trans gender is under consideration, the end result is always the same—the patriarchal elimination of cis women/lesbians—because cis women's extinction is both the premise and the conclusion of predation TERF analysis.

The invocation of Nazism and the Holocaust to situate and explain the threat posed to (cis) women by trans people is not simply a particularly outrageous (if also banal) rhetorical tactic. It is also distinctly revelatory of a defining aspect of predation TERF analysis that Stahl (2021) identifies as "extinction phobia," an ideological and psychological phenomenon that exceeds the bounds of mere antipathy or xenophobia. It is instead a terrified anxiety about the ability of the demonized other to eradicate oneself and one's people. What renders it reactionary is its reversal of the relationship of oppressor and oppressed, presenting the weaker or more marginalized party as capable of eliminating the oppressor. This reversal is facilitated by the essentialization and dehumanization of the more marginal party as inherently predatory and incapable of anything other than violence, destruction, and harm by their very nature. Thus the flip side of extinction phobia is a kind of counterdiscourse that I call right-wing annihilationism. If, in fact, trans people pose an existential threat to cis women and lesbians owing to their inherently invasive and predatory nature, then safety requires their eradication—the elimination of the would-be eliminators. Therefore, as Raymond ([1979] 1994: 178) famously argues, the best response to transsexuality is to "morally mandate it out of existence." She claims this is neither as authoritarian as it sounds nor a kind of lawfare. It includes "First Cause legislation" (e.g., mandating nonsexist public school education [179–80]) to alleviate sex-role conditioning and consciousness-raising-based therapeutic treatment for trans people. Although these proposals may not sound annihilatory, in an article version of *The Transsexual Empire* published in *Chrysalis* about two years prior, Raymond (1977) lists questions she believes should animate "consciousness-raising counseling" for trans women. While they all appear wholly rhetorical in nature, the last one is particularly pointed: "Is transsexual surgery a male-defined, male-perpetuated, and male-legitimated mode of happiness? . . . Can one then view the transsexual 'solution' as the beginning of a world where men not only dominate women but become women—and perhaps even try to eliminate and surpass us?" (22). The correct answer to this question, and the extinction phobia underpinning it, are of course obvious. Although Raymond (2014) consistently complains that she is unfairly misconstrued as advocating the "elimination" of transsexuals, true to form she offers an explanation that only implicates her in the very thing of which she is trying to exonerate herself: "I want to eliminate the medical and social systems that support transsexualism and the reasons why in a gender-defined society, persons find it necessary to change their bodies. Nowhere do I say, 'transsexuals should be eradicated on moral grounds,' which has overtone of ethnic cleansing. It's like saying I want to eliminate women in prostitution because I want to eliminate the system of prostitution."[7] In the face of Raymond's clearly articulated extinction phobia, however, the notion that advocating elimination of the "system" of transsexuality (or prostitution) is somehow different from seeking the elimination of transsexuality or transsexual people (or prostitution and prostitutes) seems tendentious at best.[8] Predation TERF extinction phobia becomes right-wing annihilationism, then, when and as it casts trans people—trans women in particular—as innately existential threats to (cis) women. Locating the source of women's oppression not in structures of power, inequality, or exploitation, Raymond and other predation TERFs identify the "fact" of maleness—whether understood most commonly as the presence of a penis or, when pressed, can extend to anything from XY chromosomes, a history of male experience, or the endurance of male divisiveness, energy, and entitlement—as the fount of domination. In so doing, they become right-wing annihilationists, advocating reactionary political solutions such as trans exclusion or—in some radical feminist excesses—actual extermination campaigns to eliminate trans people entirely.

Extinction phobia is also at the heart of much Zionist rationalization of the state of Israel. To connect predation TERF extinction phobia with Zionist extinction phobia, however, we must first take a detour through second-wave US feminism. It is at precisely the moment that predation TERF analysis is being articulated that there are "intensive disputes among U.S. feminists in the late 1970s and early 1980s about the differentiated lived experiences of racism, Zionism, and anti-Semitism" (Feldman 2015: 21).

II. Zionism in Twentieth-Century US Feminist and Lesbian Separatist Movements

The years 1967 and 1982—respectively, the beginning of the "official" Israeli occupation of Palestinian lands and Israel's brutal, second invasion of Lebanon—split the US Left in the late 1960s and the US feminist movement in the later 1970s and early 1980s (Feldman 2015; Fischbach 2020). Israel's 1967 war with Egypt, Jordan, and Syria mobilized American Jews to the cause of Zionism like never before. Subsequently known as the Six-Day War, it was presented to the world as a preemptive battle waged by an endangered Israeli David against a Goliath of Arab armies massing to destroy the Jewish state. Jubilant at Israel's quick military victory, "American Jews felt that Israel had just dodged the bullet of genocide" (Fischbach 2020: 60). American Jews' loyalty to Israel increased markedly at this moment, as did their understanding of the state as a necessary haven to protect Jewish people from another Holocaust (Balint 2010; Feldman 2015; Fischbach 2020). Even as both Israeli and US leaders, both at the time and since, acknowledged that Israel was under no credible existential threat by Arab armies in 1967, this war consolidated the now-common understanding of Israel as essential to protect Jews from eradication. Concomitantly, anti-Semitism was inflated into an innate principle of either human nature or world history, understood as both historically and globally ever-present, and always potentially genocidal in intent (Feldman 2015; Fischbach 2020; Zertal 2005).

By contrast, the US feminist movement did not become concerned with Judaism, anti-Semitism, Israel, or Zionism until a bit later. Some claim the turning point was the 1975 United Nations Women's Conference in Denmark (Milstein 2016), where controversy erupted over a proposed resolution declaring women to be "natural allies in the struggle against any form of oppression," including Zionism alongside racism, colonialism, and apartheid. The conflict over this resolution, which came to be known as the "Zionism is Racism" resolution, stretched throughout the UN Decade for Women (1975–85) and erupted at each of the three UN Women's Conferences held that decade. Others view 1982 as the turning point: the year of Israel's (second) war on Lebanon—which included the now-infamous massacres of hundreds of Palestinians in the Sabra and Shatila refugee camps (al-Hout 2004)—as well as a spate of public writings on Zionism and anti-Semitism in feminist periodicals, some of which predated this war (Cantarow 1988; Feldman 2015; Fischbach 2020; Bourne 1987).

For many American Jews, it came as a shock when US New Left movements named Israel a colonial power and defended Palestinians as victims of the same sorts of imperial domination and racial oppression as the Vietnamese abroad and African Americans at home (Feldman 2015; Fischbach 2020). Some American Jews claimed this critique was anti-Semitic insofar as it questioned

Israel's right to exist, Jews' status as an oppressed people, and Zionism's character as a national liberation movement. To question these things, for some, "constituted nothing less than an existential threat to Judaism" (Fischbach 2020: 61). Many Jewish-identified feminists also took this same position, even in the wake of the Lebanon invasion, "an event that signaled broadly across the Israeli and US Left the paucity of the existential vulnerability narrative to legitimate military violence" (Feldman 2015: 195). As Jenny Bourne (1987: 5) puts it,

> It was the invasion of Lebanon in 1982 and especially the massacres of innocent Palestinian refugees at Sabra and Shatila that finally threw Israel and everything it stood for into stark relief. How could a country set up as a refuge for the persecuted itself turn persecutor? How could a state whose leaders had faced extermination be a party to the extermination of other people? Where did securing one's borders end and aggressive colonization begin? Everything about Israel was now put in question, from its permanent war-footing to the racism of its Law of Return, from its support of South Africa to its dealings with the Chilean fascist junta.[9]

Needing to make sense of Israel's excesses in the face of an unquestioned Zionism ideologically established by the looming threat of a second Holocaust, American feminists turned to Jewish identity to shore up their commitment to Israel, transforming the question of Zionism into the question of anti-Semitism and insisting that both were fundamentally existential questions regarding Jewish survival.

The most forthright example of this is *Ms.* magazine editor Letty Pogrebin's (1982) article, "Anti-Semitism in the Women's Movement," published just before the Lebanon invasion. Pogrebin writes, "Like many Jews, I have come to consider anti-Zionism tantamount to anti-Semitism because the political reality is that its bottom line is an end to the Jews" (65). She explains,

> *To me, Zionism is simply an affirmative action plan on a national scale.* Just as legal remedies are justified in reparation for racism and sexism, the Law of Return to Israel is justified, if not by Jewish religious and ethnic claims, then by the intransigence of worldwide anti-Semitism.
>
> Because nations tend to be capricious about protecting Jewish rights, our survival has been tenuous throughout the ages. . . . Given virtually every country's record of treating us as surplus citizenry, the survival of Israel is vital to the survival of Jews. It's that simple. (65)

Pogrebin's is the most frequently cited article on this subject, but evidence suggests hers was not a minority position within the women's movement. Bourne

(1987: 10) provides an elaborate exposition of the many ways Jewish feminists dodged or equivocated on Zionism, noting that "what gained ascendancy" in the women's movement "from 1982 onwards was the charge that anti-Zionism equaled anti-Semitism." Similarly, Ellen Cantarow (1988) observes, "My own experience as an outspoken critic of Israeli policy was that among feminists there was snail's-horn sensitivity about matters Jewish. The constant assumption was that criticizing Israel meant being anti-Semitic."

Anti-Semitism became conflated with anti-Zionism as a result of Jewish feminists' turn to Jewish identity, which they understood as analogous to, if not identical with, race and racialization. So, for example, Pogrebin (1982: 46) laments "how often I had noticed Jews omitted from the feminist litany of 'the oppressed.' And I began to wonder why the Movement's healing embrace can encompass the black woman, the Chicana, the white ethnic woman, the disabled woman, and every other female whose existence is complicated by an extra element of 'outness,' but the Jewish woman is not honored in her specificity?" (cf. Taylor and Oppenheimer 1982: 6). Similarly, in an interview about her then-new book, *Nice Jewish Girls: A Lesbian Anthology*, Evelyn Torton Beck (1982a: 9) notes, "I didn't really become very Jewish-identified until I was deeply immersed in lesbian feminism and working on racism, trying to integrate women of color into all my courses. . . . I became very aware of the fact that the one group that was not visible in terms of its own cultural heritage were Jews." Moving beyond analogy and toward identification, many feminists observed Jewish women identifying themselves as "Third World" women (Smith 1984: 75; WAI 1982: 20). Judith Stein, in a discussion among Black and Jewish women published in *Conditions*, notes, "I don't feel like I'm white people. . . . And sometimes I talk about feeling dark in situations even though I am fair-skinned and light-eyed. And that to me is that I'm not like other white people" (Smith, Stein, and Golding 1981: 38).[10] And well before the Lebanon invasion, in 1977, Liza Cowan and Penny House (1977a: 20) argued that "no matter how any Jew feels about being Jewish, she can never be an ex-Jew. Judaism is more than a religion: it is a race and a culture. . . . The oppression of Jews is not based on an adherence to religious dogma but on racial heritage." In sum, a significant number of Jewish-identified feminist women committed themselves to Jewish identity via analogizing or identifying their experiences with the racial oppression of Black people and people of color in the United States.[11] This connection made it possible for Jewish women to understand (and present) themselves as victims of racial oppression as Jews in the United States. It also facilitated the conflation of anti-Zionism with anti-Semitism, since critics of Israel could be understood as animated by racial animus or an interest in eliminating the only safe place where Jewish people could be free from racial oppression and genocide. Eliminating Israel, in other words, became equivalent to annihilation of the Jews, Judaism, and/or Jewish-identified American women.

Notably, Jewish lesbians[12] took up this tactic as well but applied it slightly differently: rather than (or, sometimes, in addition to) asserting that Jewishness was "like" Blackness or race, they also asserted that being Jewish was like being lesbian, seeing an analogy between anti-Semitism and lesbian/woman hatred. The remarkable consequence, for these women, was an analogizing of Zionism with lesbian separatism. This connection is downplayed or overlooked by scholars who assert a more straightforward division in the women's movement between heterosexual Zionist feminists and anti-Zionist lesbian feminists (Lober 2019); what seems more accurate is that a contingent of specifically lesbian feminist separatists understood their lesbianism as analogous to their Judaism, leading them to construe Zionism as parallel to lesbian separatism, both being intentionally homogenous community-building efforts necessary to insulate themselves from harm, threat, and, ultimately, annihilation.[13] For example, in 1977, an article by Jewish lesbian Janet Meyers appeared in the short-lived lesbian/feminist/separatist periodical *Dyke: A Quarterly*, commissioned as part of its "ethnic lesbians issue." Lamenting the existence of Israel as a "tragic necessity," Meyers (1977: 14) argues,

> Nevertheless, as a Jewish lesbian, I think I understand the psychological and political motivation for such a choice [to create the state of Israel]. Jews and lesbians share the experience of having the centrality of their lives denied every day. Before Israel one did not have the sensation, as a Jew, that one's own ethnic world is the norm, the center, the hub. With few exceptions throughout the world this experience of centrality is available [to] every other group no matter how terribly oppressed they might be in other ways. Lesbians have no doubts about the exceptional nature of our lives and we have always been characterized as peripheral, fringe, *queer*. Especially after the Holocaust, Jews understood that it was necessary for them to regroup, to heal, but most importantly to learn what it is to experience ourselves as the norm, the center, as no longer a minority but a prevailing atmosphere. (cf. Pogrebin 1982: 46; Beck 1982b: xv)

For Meyers, the shared Jewish and lesbian experience of marginality, of living or being outside the bounds of normativity ("*queer*"), explains the impulse to separatist space. Meyers also sees connections between Left criticisms of Zionism and the feminist movement's critiques of lesbian separatism:

> Somehow Jewish nationalism is seen, especially by the Left, as the worst, most "sinful" kind of nationalism. It inspires a special kind of wrath in lots of people who barely ever mention Black nationalism in West Africa or Latin American Nationalism or even Arab Nationalism. Separatists are the pariahs of the women's movement, often without any notice being taken of the many definitions women

have of what separatism means. It seems that the notion of demons, monsters and devils, bonding together for the subversive purposes of fun, self-affirmation or survival is too terrible for the world to bear. (14)

Defying New Left analysis by setting Jewish nationalism beside the nationalist and anti-colonial movements of global South peoples, Meyers manages to present Zionists as doubly victimized: by an anti-Semitic world that would deny a liberatory expression of Jewish nationalism (13–14) and by US leftists who fail to recognize Zionism as a liberation movement akin to other anti-colonial nationalisms.

These connections become even more explicit later on, after Israel's war on Lebanon. For example, at the opening of the second Jewish Feminist Conference,[14] held in 1982 in San Francisco and attended by more than seven hundred women (both Jewish and non-Jewish), Teya Schaeffer and Meryl Lieberman McNew (1982) delivered a speech entitled "Statement to Gentiles," which clearly invokes the existential fears mobilizing American Jewish Zionism at the time (McNew is lesbian; Schaffer is not). They argued that, "since the days of exile from Israel and Judea, we [Jews] have experienced all the persecutions that humanity has ever invented, that nowhere has there been a place of security for us," and warned their audience to "never allow a discussion of zionism to forget that the creation of the modern state of Israel in 1948 was a direct consequence of the Holocaust" (7). This is a straightforward rehearsal of the narrative of eternal and universal anti-Semitism to justify Israel and Zionism (cf. Beck 1982a: 9; Meyers 1977: 13–14). Meanwhile, in their report on the conference for *off our backs*, Jewish lesbians Melanie Kaye and Irena Klepfisz (1982: 3) note, "In the course of the conference, some of us realized that just as we had learned to confront homophobes by calling ourselves *dykes* and to defy male 'radicals'' scorn of feminism as 'bourgeois' by proudly calling ourselves feminists, that now it is important to clearly name ourselves *Zionists*; that it is time to claim this particular yellow star." Identifying themselves as members of the "Jewish lesbian/feminist collective" Di Vilde Chayes (Yiddish for "The Wild Beasts"), the authors here conflate *dyke* with *Zionist* as terms that repurpose stigma into expressions of liberatory defiance; moreover, that stigma is explicitly associated with Jewish genocide insofar as both terms are described as "yellow stars." Thus the perceived existential threat that anti-Semitism always portends is here analogized with homophobia, implying the annihilatory character of both and implicitly suggesting the need for a lesbian separatist space, or a kind of "Israel" for lesbians.[15]

Not everyone found the conference so empowering. Lesbian separatist attendees, outraged by a perceived marginalization of separatism at the conference, came together at the end of the three-day event to strategize and organize. One result of this meeting was a nine-point statement of unity, quickly drafted and agreed to by all participants. In the statement, separatism is cast as a minoritized and embattled position that received little support at the conference (point 7) but is nonetheless essential for Jewish lesbians' safety and a "right" of both lesbians and Jews as oppressed people:

> 3. We believe as a political principle that any oppressed group can separate themselves from their oppressors. And as lesbians, we claim that right.

The statement then goes on to explicitly analogize Zionism with lesbian separatism:

> 5. The lesbian and feminist communities say many of the same things about separatists as non-Jews say about Jews. We encourage Jewish womyn here today to think about it; you might find a lot of similarities between lesbian separatism and zionism.

It then reprimands conference participants for failing to support separatism, in that, as mostly Jewish people, they should understand the reasons and rationale for separatism:

> 6. Jewish people have understood for centuries the need for separatism as Jews. The lack of separatist support at this conference is appalling.

And criticism of separatism—whether Jewish (Zionist) or lesbian—is warded off in the final plank:

> 9. It is offensive to Jewish lesbian separatists to make any comparison between separatism and nazism or racism. Don't. ("Lesbian Separatist Statement" [1982] 1988: 93–94).

Of course, allegations of racism were frequently leveled at lesbian separatists, whose solution to male power was to withdraw from men entirely and create all-women's communities. Ability to do so was considered an upper-class privilege and a simultaneous symptom and disavowal of whiteness: because white men are the oppressors, white women separating from them may indeed be a confrontation with their own, primary oppression. But because they do not suffer from racism, they do not need the comradery, community, or solidarity of men who are also racialized and oppressed, as many women of color felt they did (Combahee River Collective [1977] 2017). Some lesbian separatists dismissed this criticism as "divisive" and an attempt to distract women from the primary problem of male domination (Lucia-Hoagland and Penelope 1988). Regardless, this statement's final plank, a preemptive banning of this particular criticism of separatism, suggests not simply the critique's frequency but also, perhaps, some sense on the part of the authors that there may be some validity to a different set of parallels to be made between Zionism, lesbianism, separatism, and racism other than those being asserted by Jewish lesbian separatists.

In the months immediately following both the Jewish Feminist Conference and Pogrebin's *Ms.* article, Israel proceeded with its murderous attack on Lebanon, and an intense exchange of statements took place between Women Against Imperialism (WAI), a San Francisco–based organization of "anti-imperialist women," many of whom were Jewish, and the Jewish lesbian feminist collective Di Vilde Chayes (DVC). WAI's (1982: 20) statement, entitled "Taking Our Stand against Zionism and White Supremacy," was occasioned by their being "very disturbed at the growing tendency to use the issue of anti-semitism to justify Zionism and the colonization of the Palestinian people." Acknowledging the existence of anti-Semitism and the enormity of the Holocaust, WAI nevertheless asserted that the wrong conclusions were being drawn from this history: "For Jews and for all of us who know that genocide is not just a word, it is critical to recognize that it is colonized peoples not Jews who face genocide in the US today" (20). DVC took umbrage at this statement, responding with an equally pointed "Open Letter to the Women's Movement." They begin from the same starting point of Jewish insecurity in the face of ever-present anti-Semitism, arguing that "since 1948, Israel has served as a place of refuge and safety for Jews all over the world" (21). And, while they concede that Israel and its government are not perfect regimes, they nevertheless unequivocally affirm that

> Israel has a right to exist. *Zionism is one strategy against anti-Semitism and for Jewish survival. Anti-Zionism is Anti-Semitism.* Criticism of Israeli policy is not in and of itself anti-Semitic, nor is it anti-Zionist. But *anti-Zionism demands the dissolution of the state of Israel.* This would mean the destruction of Jews within Israel (European, African and Middle Eastern Jews);[16] it would also mean the destruction of a refuge for Jews suffering persecution in other countries. Ultimately, the dissolution of Israel would give license to increased anti-Semitism throughout the world and would endanger all Jews wherever we might live. *Any anti-Zionist position is, therefore, anti-Semitic.* (21)

Finally, as if their position were not clear enough, DVC conclude by stating that "Anti-Semitism must be a concern of our movement. To state that it is not as serious as other oppressions is to imply that Jews have no right to complain until we are being marched to the gas chamber" (21). Feminist failure to foreground or prioritize anti-Semitism, in other words, colludes with the potential genocide of Jewish women/lesbians.

Separatism, therefore, is a matter of survival—and this whether it is Jewish separatism or lesbian separatism. It is unsurprising, then, that the most vocally Zionist lesbians in the women's movement were also separatists. What makes this rehearsal of feminist and lesbian Zionism relevant for this article is its perhaps unexpected proximity to TERFism. To return to Meyers's essay, for example, it is worth noting not only the explicit connections she draws between lesbian separatism and Zionism but also the placement of this essay in *Dyke: A Quarterly*, a lesbian separatist periodical founded and edited by Jewish lesbian separatists Liza Cowan and Penny House. In this very same issue is an astonishing article that is not at all about "ethnic lesbians" but rather trans women, who are definitely not being cataloged as either ethnic or lesbian. Entitled "Can Men Be Women? Some Lesbians Think So! Transsexuals in the Women's Movement," this piece consists of a long introduction by Cowan and House, which prefaces an interview with psychologist Edna Lerner about the etiology, diagnosis, and treatment of transsexuality, and concludes with a conversation about that interview among Cowan, House, Meyers, and Alix Dobkin (Cowan's then-partner), all Jewish lesbian separatists.

Why might an article considering "Transsexuals in the Women's Movement" be included in a lesbian separatist periodical issue celebrating "Ethnic Lesbians"? Cowan and House (1977b: 30) declare its impetus in the very first paragraph: "When we heard that Olivia Records had hired a transsexual to be their recording engineer, and we began to hear of more and more male transsexuals [*sic*] invading the women's movement, our reaction was repugnance." Citing the predation TERF belief that removal of the penis does not "make" a (cis) woman, Cowan and House assert that not only are transsexuals disgusting, but they are threatening to overtake the women's movement. Cowan and House thus take it on themselves to educate *Dyke* readers about this new, menacing phenomenon. They claim to not want to broach the subject, noting that "some women have told us that they are already sick of reading and thinking about transsexuals. We, too, wish that we could stop thinking about it. It is painful in the same way that it is painful to think about women in prison, battered wives, genetic control and rape, but we recognize that it is vital for the community at large to deal with these issues" (30). Casting the existence of trans women as one of among many violations of (cis) women's rights and bodily integrity, including incarceration and domestic violence, Cowan and House insist that feminists not turn away from these considerations, no matter how upsetting they may be, because (cis) women's oppression cannot and should not be ignored. Moreover, it is no longer feasible to defer this conversation, since, "now that male transsexuals [*sic*] are trespassing in Lesbian communities, we must deal with them before a trickle becomes an avalanche" (30). Covering this subject in *Dyke*, then, even if a diversion from the issue's theme, is necessary not simply to ward off the horror trans women pose by their very existence but also to prevent the looming specter of their takeover of the women's movement.[17]

It is but a short step from here to the characterization of trans women as predators and existential threats to (cis) women/lesbians, a step that indeed gets taken over the course of the article. Moreover, this analysis is not actually tangential to the subject of "ethnic lesbians" after all, at least insofar as Jewish lesbians (as construed by Cowan, House, and Meyers) are concerned, because the consequence of this predation TERF investigation is the necessity of women's/lesbian separatism. Lerner does not go so far as to characterize trans women as dangerous or threatening, staying true to type as a psychologist in this historical moment in her account of transsexuals as "crazy," "psychotic," "narcissistic," or unable to accept the fact that they are actually homosexual men.[18] In their postinterview discussion, however, Meyers, Dobkin, Cowan, and House together construct an argument for lesbian/women's separatism, declaring that trans women are not women but rather predators created by the patriarchal medical establishment to eradicate (cis) women. From the outset, Cowan insists on the importance of being able to distinguish between "what is male and what is female" (34), the basis of her separatist philosophy (Cowan 1978). Meyers then ups the ante, noting that "most Lesbians come to the women's movement because they understand that there is something intrinsically *other* about being a woman and that is necessary for women to get together in order to understand what that means" (34). From here emerges the rationale for a separatism that is free of trans women. Cowan offers,

> What galls me so much is that we are just beginning to understand what it means to be a woman, really just beginning to be able to understand that there is something different that we are not fully conscious of yet about what it means to be a woman, and these *men* say that *they* are women, meaning that they know what it means to be a woman, and they are it. And now they want to participate in defining and creating women's culture. (34)

To this remark, Meyers responds, "I think there is probably something to the point that this is preparatory to dispensing with women entirely." Trans women are thus not simply interlopers in the women's movement, but their existence threatens to render (cis) women superfluous. Where Cowan, House, Dobkin, and Meyers go with this argument—the necessity of women's/lesbian separatism—is related as much to their Zionism as to their transphobia, insofar as Zionism offers a ready-made template and example of an ostensibly liberatory separatism created to provide protection from existential threat.

III. Right-Wing Annihilationism and Contemporary Predation TERFism

Keith Feldman (2015) has argued that Palestine functions as the "constitutive absence" in the American postwar period that enabled both its imperial culture and defined its race relations, whether within the Jewish and socialist left, the Black Power movement, or the feminist movement. I think this "shadow over Palestine" may well be recognized in Zionist lesbian separatists' engagement with the figure of the trans person—the trans woman in particular—who, like the Palestinian for Zionists, is the unthinkable, existential threat to the survival and integrity of a community, a culture, and indeed an entire people. First, and most evidently, predation TERFism was popular among a subset of lesbian separatists who also happened to be Jewish Zionists. I don't think this is coincidental; both lesbian separatism and Zionism have the same exclusionary impulse toward an ostensibly liberatory self-segregation that results in the radical, potentially annihilatory exclusion of "others" owing to a fear of their innate violence and predation. Second, while the formative predation TERFism of Raymond and others lacks any sort of international focus, much less a theorization of empire or colonization, there is a distinct echo of Zionist themes in Raymond's and Daly's casting of "the transsexual empire" and American gynecology as equivalent to the medical experimentation conducted in Nazi death camps. Elsewhere I have described this theme as "Holocaust Exceptionalism" (Schotten 2018), a Eurocentric worldview that obfuscates the history of racism and colonization by singling out the genocide of Jews in twentieth-century Europe as historically, morally, or politically unprecedented and unparalleled (Mamdani 2005). Regardless of the relative (de)merits of Raymond's and Daly's comparing patriarchy with Nazism, what is significant is not simply that they do so but also the way that they do so, which is by relying on the same mistaken interpretation of Arendt's now-famous phrase "banality of evil" to interpret the comparison. Both take Arendt to be saying that the "evil" of the Nazi Holocaust was trivialized at the Eichmann trial and mobilize this misinterpretation to claim that the predation and degradation of (cis) women is similarly trivialized in the United States, a trivialization they seek to end. Of course, Arendt offers this phrase to describe not the Holocaust at all but, rather, the unremarkable person of Adolf Eichmann himself, who is not a vicious monster, raving lunatic, or brainwashed fanatic but an ordinary (if perhaps especially diligent) worker and party officer. But Daly's and Raymond's misinterpretation makes clear the real reason they offer a comparison between "gynocide" or the "transsexual empire" and Nazism, namely, to exploit an implicitly exceptionalist claim to unique Jewish victimization via the Holocaust, an exceptionalism they seek to apply to their feminist analyses of the exceptional victimization of (cis) women.[19] As we have seen, this effectively casts trans women as (complicit with) Nazis and as subjecting cis women—cis lesbian feminists in particular—to a genocidal extinction scheme, thus bolstering the view that trans women must be eliminated if cis women are to be safe. While Raymond and Daly are neither Jewish nor demonstrably Zionist, their use of this Zionist rhetorical gesture is significant and would not have been possible at all were it not for the post-1967 Zionist ideology of ever-present Jewish victimization and its uptake in US identity politics at the time. As we have seen, Raymond even acknowledges her use of this tactic and its overuse, already in 1979.

As familiar and seemingly plausible as Zionist extinction phobia and Holocaust Exceptionalism may seem to be, it is important to remember that both are historically recent ideologies, deployed purposefully by Israeli and US elites to advance the causes of Israeli occupation and American empire (Finkelstein 2003; Kaplan 2018; Novick 1999). This version of Zionism, which casts Israel as forever threatened by a genocidal anti-Semitism, not only provides a rationale for Israel's creation—which resulted in the ethnic cleansing of 700,000–800,000 indigenous Palestinians and a current refugee population of over 7 million, whom Israel refuses to allow to return—but also justifies any abuse, massacre, torture, incarceration, or home demolition as fundamentally an act of self-defense. The transfer of threat from Germany and Europe to Palestine and the Arab World that occurred in this post-1967 Zionist emergence makes it possible to "Nazify" (Zertal 2005) Arabs and Palestinians as the new existential threat to Israeli existence, which also and simultaneously becomes Jewish existence insofar as Israel is claimed as a "Jewish state" created to protect Jews from genocide (conveniently eliding the distinction between "Jewish" and "Israeli" and sidestepping the fact that almost 25 percent of Israel's population is not Jewish). Despite, then, being massively more powerful—in 1948, 1967, and still so to this day—than the Palestinians whom they have displaced and turned into refugees and besieged, occupied people, in this ideological version of reality, Israel is the victim, the embattled and beleaguered party living in fear of extermination by an all-powerful and demonized enemy, Palestinians and/or Arabs, whose rage and despair at Israel's colonization, occupation, and apartheid regime become expressions of their fundamentally irrational, "savage," and violent nature. This is most commonly and familiarly rendered as a narrative about Palestinian "terrorism," which is understood not as legitimate political violence waged in response to colonial and military occupation but, rather, as the willful destruction of Jews by mindless savages who do not respect the rules of warfare, the nature of democracy, or the value of life (Schotten 2018). [20]

Similarly, in the case of predation TERFism, cis feminists cast themselves as the beleaguered victims of trans women, whose infiltration of (cis) women's spaces, communities, and movements constitutes both rape as well as an existential threat. The pivot that transforms their extinction phobia into right-wing annihilationism is an essentializing and dehumanizing abjection of trans women as innately predatory, thereby justifying their deliberate exclusion from feminism and even, as we have seen, their outright elimination. As Carol Riddell (2006: 152) notes, in one of the first trans feminist critiques of *The Transsexual Empire*,

> Nowhere in her book does Ms. Raymond give any accounts of trans-sexual life experience. . . . None of them emerges as a real person with a biography. No sensitive or caring collective account of the life experience of trans-sexuals, either pre-operative or post-operative, is presented. Instead, the most damning quotations possible are put together. Sometimes totally irrelevant information is presented as if it made a point. . . . I consider that to be dishonest.

In other words, trans women are either completely absent from predation TERF analyses or show up only in the most ugly and caricatured forms as epiphenomena of an all-encompassing patriarchal power that seeks nothing less than the elimination of cis women tout court.

Arabs and Palestinians were similarly absented in Zionist feminist and lesbian separatist analysis (Feldman 2015: 195). Returning to Meyers's (1977) article for a moment, recall her complaint that both Zionists and lesbian separatists are vilified by the Left. She concludes this complaint with the remark that "it seems that the notion of demons, monsters and devils, bonding together for the subversive purposes of fun, self-affirmation or survival is too terrible for the world to bear" (14). Dismissing the notion that (cis) women or Jewish people might be doing harm via their respective separatisms, Meyers implies that Zionism and lesbian separatism are benign projects of collective "fun" and "self-affirmation." Yet one is tempted to ask, with Edward Said ([1979] 1992), how this collective endeavor might be viewed "from the standpoint of its victims." Is lesbian separatism, in the case of predation TERFism, simply a harmless exercise in "fun" and "self-affirmation"? In the case of Jewish separatism, is the creation of the state of Israel simply a "withdrawal of energy" from an oppressor (as lesbian separatism was often described)? Or were these separatist communities both, albeit in different ways, communities constituted via the exclusion and abjection of a dehumanized other, justified by incredible allegations of potential extinction on the part of those doing the excluding? To be clear, not all lesbian separatisms were trans exclusionary. By contrast, the founding of the state of Israel was an act of colonial conquest, plain and simple. This fact is illegible in Zionist feminism and denaturalized in Jewish lesbian separatisms that equate Zionism and lesbian separatism.[21] Moreover, Meyers's seamless merger of "fun" and "self-affirmation" with "survival" as the shared purposes of Jewish and lesbian separatisms blends very different political projects, rendering separatism as a means of community building indistinguishable from separatism as a means of dispossession, ethnic cleansing, segregation, militarism, and apartheid. The comparison renders Zionism benign and lesbian separatism an aggressive ideological project with potentially annihi-latory aims. In both cases, the anxiety voiced earlier about separatism being lik-ened to "racism" or "Nazism" is unwittingly realized, insofar as the necessity of clear and strict boundaries is essential, not simply for "fun" and "self-affirmation" but also for "survival," an existential stake that makes this "fun" deadly serious.

These connections—like predation TERFism itself—have unfortunately not gone away. They have not gone away insofar as predation TERFs remain predation TERFs: Raymond and Jeffreys are as convinced of the correctness of their views as ever. The recently deceased Alix Dobkin contributed a chapter to the latest predation TERF anthology, *Female Erasure* (Barrett 2016) and is quoted in her *New York Times* obituary as saying, "It's OK to be a Jew, it's OK to be a lesbian—as long as you don't mention it. And what we also have in common is that we were never supposed to survive."[22] Meanwhile, Bev Jo (2008), militant West Coast lesbian separatist and predation TERFer, continues to publish her views on her blog and even in academic journals.

Yet even as the progenitors of predation TERFism inevitably age and pass away, they leave behind a legacy that far exceeds that of the twentieth-century women's movement, with significant and dire consequences for the twenty-first. Of course, 1970s predation TERFism did not have the backing of any state or military apparatus, whereas Zionism is a deliberate propaganda project deployed to advance the interests of the Israeli state and US empire. This seems to be changing, however, at least insofar as funding is concerned: the current TERF resurgence, figureheaded by Lierre Keith's Women's Liberation Front (WoLF), is funded by the Alliance Defending Freedom, itself funded by the National Christian Foundation, and working in tandem with a network of Catholic and Evangelical foundations, think tanks, and legal organizations including the Family Research Council, the Family Policy Alliance, and Focus on the Family (Greenesmith 2020b). While these organizations and their agenda would seem to have nothing to do with either Judaism or Zionism, other noteworthy members of this funding network include the Heritage Foundation, the Bradley Founda-tion, and the Sarah Scaife Foundation, all of which, historically, have been cru-cial players in the US neoconservative movement, the US Islamophobia network, and right-wing, pro-Israel movements more broadly (Ali et al. 2011; Bulkin and Nevel 2012; Duss et al. 2015; Heilbrunn 2008; IJAN 2015). Meanwhile, donor-advised funds like Fidelity Charitable Gift Fund and Donors Trust, which serve to anonymize donations made by known billionaires like the Koch and DeVos families, have directed money to a wide variety of Right-wing groups, organi-zations, and foundations, including not just TERF and SWERF organizations like the Alliance Defending Freedom and the Family Research Council, but also neoconservatives, the Islamophobia Network, and Zionist organizations like the David Horowitz Freedom Center and Frank Gaffney's Center for Security Policy.[23]

In short, the alternative genealogy of predation TERFism offered here suggests that this overlap of Right-wing funders and organizations is more than just coincidence. While the white Christian nationalist funding of contemporary predation TERFism is not obviously in service to US empire (or, at least, those connections have not yet been clearly established), the presence of Zionist, neo-conservative, and Islamophobia Network funders and organizations supporting contemporary TERFism raises the question of if, in fact, it somehow is in the service of foreign relations interests—not only US empire but also the Israeli colonization of Palestine. These connections, however, have yet to be fully articulated, due to not only the lack of transparency involved in these vast dark money systems but also the siloization of our movements into "international" vs. "domestic" concerns and an enduring reticence on our part to name or investigate Jewish-identified right-wing elites, organizations, and institutions (Gelman 2021) for fear of being labeled anti-Semitic. Thus, for example, there is a reasonable amount of Christian Zionism tracking, but little to no monitoring of the Jewish Zionism that is responsible for enormous harm to our movements, including Black liberation, women's liberation, queer liberation, Arab and Arab American liberation, and the list goes on (Drop the ADL Working Group 2020). Moreover, with few exceptions (e.g., Orly and Brenneman 2021), Christian Zionism is criticized or condemned for its anti-Semitism, but not at all for its Zionism—that is, for its total disregard for Palestinian people, who barely register as existing, much less worthy of freedom and liberation. The unfortunate ironies here are, first, that it is precisely a tactic of Jewish Zionist propagandists to label any and all criticism of Israel or Jewish elites anti-Semitic; and second, when the primary failing of Christian Zionism is consistently considered to be anti-Semitism, we unwittingly collude with the Zionist erasure of Palestine and Palestinians and the real harms of Zionism unfolding every day. That our movements falter here, at precisely these junctures, shows just how powerful the Jewish Zionist lobby is in controlling the discourse of liberation and forestalling an actual reckoning with just who, exactly, is being excluded from what.

It is crucial that these different parts of the Left recognize the historical, ideological, and material continuities between and among seemingly very different sectors of the Right so that we can build solidaristic movements able to account for the ways that all of our freedom is necessarily bound up together (Davis 2016) and so we do not perpetuate the shadow existence of Palestine and Palestinians in our work for trans liberation. None of us is free until all of us are free, and this includes Palestinians as much as it does transgender women as much as it does the transgender kids currently being targeted by newly ascendent TERFisms around the world.

C. Heike Schotten is professor of political science at the University of Massachusetts Boston, where she teaches political theory, feminist theory, and queer theory. She is a member of the organizing collective of the US Campaign for Academic and Cultural Boycott of Israel (USACBI) and the author of *Queer Terror: Life, Death, and Desire in the Settler Colony* (2018), *Nietzsche's Revolution: Décadence, Politics, and Sexuality* (2009), and many articles and book chapters in Nietzsche studies, critical political theory, feminist theory, and queer theory.

Acknowledgments

I am grateful for the comments and critical feedback provided by the following people, whose knowledge and insight both enriched my understanding and improved the final product: Ken Barney, Susanna Bohme, Sara Driscoll, Emmaia Gelman, Jude Glaubman, Lucas Goren, Sasha Gorsky, Heron Greenesmith, Megan J. Peterson, William Clare Roberts, Eleanor Roffman, Gayle Rubin, the USACBI organizing collective, two anonymous *TSQ* reviewers, and special issue editors Serena Bassi and Greta LaFleur.

Notes

1.   It is both the continuity and seeming intractability of these views that justifies their (re)examination here; unfortunately, it also reinforces their political hegemony. Such rehearsal also shores up the misinterpretation of 1970s US feminism as significantly defined by transphobia rather than—or also—liberatory, trans-led and trans-identified, feminist activism (Enke 2018; Stryker 2017). Thus let me be clear that, while TERFism originates with a small subset of 1970s feminists, it was never widespread within US feminisms, not even the white women's movement from which it originates; nor was it a hegemonic ideology within US feminisms, lesbian feminisms, or lesbian separatisms, about which more below (Heaney 2016; Stryker 2017; Williams 2016). With this article I intend to contribute to neither the continued hegemony of TERFism nor the too-common disparagement of 1970s feminism as uniformly transphobic; rather, I hope to provide a different entry point into the origins of TERFism within 1970s radical feminism to better combat the former and appreciate the latter.

2.   Thus extinction phobias are not versions of what Wendy Brown (1995) calls "wounded attachments" in her critique of so-called identity politics. In this famous essay, Brown fails to distinguish between oppressor and oppressed, thereby naturalizing oppression as the inevitable deserts of oppressed people whose critiques of power are somehow failed or moralistic (Schotten 2020). Extinction phobias, by contrast, are necessarily the beleaguered cry of the oppressor and, as such, neither a diagnosis nor criticism of "identity politics."

3.   I do not offer a comprehensive inventory of either radical feminisms or TERFisms here. However, to isolate the extinction phobia driving what I call predation TERFism, it is

necessary to distinguish it from the more socialist-inclined TERFism with which it is often elided.

4.   It is unclear what the difference is between a "direct comparison" and a "demonstration of value," not simply because Raymond seems obviously to be doing the former.

5.   Raymond ([1979] 1994: 152) offers another disclaimer here, stating that she does not seek "to exploit the very real difference between a conditioned 'voluntary' medical procedure performed on adult transsexuals and the deliberate sadism performed on unwilling bodies and minds in the camps." Yet, in a perhaps compulsive exercise in self-betrayal, Raymond names precisely what she has done and, in doing so, exposes the inanity of the claim.

6.   Including not just the rape claim but also the cumbersome disparagement "male-to-constructed-female" as well as the claim that "Dionysian boundary violation" is the mythical origin and explanation of trans women's existence. Daly (1978: 1) acknowledges in *Gyn/Ecology* that the work of "Jan Raymond" has "been so intertwined with my own for so long that it has often been impossible to tell whose ideas are whose"; meanwhile, Raymond ([1979] 1994: ix) dedicates *The Transsexual Empire* to Daly, noting, "It is difficult for me to separate my words and ideas from her own."

7.   It is no accident that prostitution surfaces here; Raymond is cofounder and former board member of the Coalition Against Trafficking in Women (CATW), which bills itself as an antitrafficking organization but has, as its driving purpose, the elimination of the sex trade. Singling out sex work as uniquely harmful to cis women and girls (and side-stepping the fact that trafficking is a problem for workers globally), CATW and other "abolitionist" feminist organizations are a by-product of the feminist porn wars (Levine and Meiners 2020: 129), use the same radical feminist analysis that generates predation TERFism, and rely on the same donors that fund contemporary TERFism (not to mention contemporary Zionism—more on this in the conclusion).

8.   Thus "abolitionist" feminist antitrafficking organizations are often described by the parallel acronym SWERF (sex worker–exclusionary radical feminism).

9.   The Law of Return, passed in 1950, stipulates that any Jewish person has the right to emigrate and become an Israeli citizen. Israel denies this same right to Palestinians, however, who were made refugees as a result of the ethnic cleansing and ensuing war involved in Israel's creation. For an account of Israel's creation as a "procedural democracy" at the expense of the removal of the indigenous population—as simultaneously a liberal and settler colonial regime—see Robinson 2013.

10.   In response to Stein's confession, Elli Johnson, a Black lesbian, says, "She [Johnson's former Jewish lover] used to talk about that too, about being dark, and that used to make me angry. I'd say, 'What do you mean, dark? You know you're not dark, you're white. I'm dark" (Smith, Stein, and Golding 1981: 38). Stein responds by transforming Jewishness into a racial category, arguing that Johnson's attraction to her former lover was an attraction to her difference from "regular Christian white people" (38).

11.   On the "ethnic turn" in white second-wave feminism more broadly, see Jacobson (2006: chap. 6), who argues it was part of a broader cultural turn toward ethnicity on the part of white people in the US postwar period, an ethnic revivalism that evaded white privilege and reconsolidated American nationalism. Indeed, at the time, many feminists argued that the newfound focus on anti-Semitism in the women's movement was a response to the rise of women of color feminism, an imitation of it, and/or a desire on the part of Jewish women to "participate in the politics of the oppressed" (Rosenfelt et al. 1983: 12; cf. Smith 1984: 78–79).

12. Pogrebin (1982: 69) and Morris (2017: 429) argue that the turn to Jewish-identified feminism was spearheaded by lesbians.

13. Sometimes this connection was made by heterosexual women as well; for example, Phyllis Chesler notes, "I am saddened and angered by feminists who would never call a separatist coffee house or women's center sexist, but who are quick to call the Law of Return racist" (quoted in Pogrebin 1982: 65).

14. For discussion of the first Jewish Feminist conference (1973), see Lober 2019.

15. It is worth noting that both women later became critical of Israeli occupation and broke publicly with aspects of Zionism. It remains unclear to this author, however, to what degree either has maintained the view that anti-Semitism is an existential threat that justifies Zionism. For a consideration of the limitations of Adrienne Rich's later critique of Israeli occupation after she had previously deemed criticism of Israel anti-Semitic, see Cable 2022.

16. Evident here is a different strategy to analogize Jewishness with race and/or people of color, namely, by arguing that Israeli Jews are not all white but instead a diverse mix of people from all over the world, including Africa and the Middle East (cf. Taylor 1982).

17. Cowan and House's argument is consonant with Raymond's, and they refer readers to her *Chrysalis* (1977) article (which they mistakenly cite as "The Transsexual Hoax"). This article appears to have received broad circulation in the women's movement, as evidenced by not only this *Dyke* piece (New York City) but also an article in Minneapolis's *Lesbian Insider/Insighter/Inciter* (Kezia and Thrace 1980) and a short transphobic piece by Gloria Steinem (1977) in *Ms.* that references the transsexual interview research of "Jan Raymond." On Raymond's influence in the women's movement, see Stone 2018.

18. It is uncanny just how well this psychologist's testimony conforms to the form, style, and content Sandy Stone ([1987] 2006) incisively analyzes in her canonical essay on this subject, a direct response to Janice Raymond, predation TERFism, and the predation TERF attacks on her person as the Olivia Records sound engineer in question.

19. It is worth noting that Arendt ([1963] 1994) explicitly rejects any sort of Jewish exceptionalism throughout *Eichmann in Jerusalem*, which is where the expression "banality of evil" occurs (albeit only once, at the very end of the book).

20. Directly tied to this is the long-standing trope that Palestinian mothers' greatest wish is for their sons grow up to become suicide bombers (Shibli 2017) or Benjamin Netanyahu's more recently infamous declaration, during Israel's 2014 massacre of Gaza, that Palestinians deliberately seek to produce "telegenically dead babies" to garner the world's sympathy and support for their cause (Buttu 2014).

21. It also raises important questions about, for example, the ways in which notions of "women's land" are inevitably caught up in and reproductive of settler colonial tropes and imperatives of dispossession (Morgensen 2011). See Weier 2021 for the disconcerting connections between predation TERF lesbian separatism and settler colonial ideologies at work in the Michigan Womyn's Music Festival.

22. Michigan Women's Music Festival historian Bonnie Morris (2017: 463–64) notes that Dobkin made this statement before the third song of every performance, and "singing, after that statement, in Yiddish, Alix wove two threatened identities together, a fist in Hitler's eye." Morris herself, meanwhile, a convener of the Jewish tent at Michfest for many years, likens the festival to a romanticized notion of Israel (434–39), complains that its legacy has been reduced to the controversy over trans inclusion, and compares *TERF*

to *PEP* (progressive except for Palestine) as a term that functions essentially as a slur rather than a description of a political position: "Some Jewish lesbians lament the dubious change from being called dyke and kike to TERF and PEP" (Morris 2015: 14).

23.   See www.unmaskingfidelity.org.

References

al-Hout, Bayan Nuwayhed. 2004. *Sabra and Shatila: September 1982*. London: Pluto.

Ali, Wajahat, Eli Clifton, Matthew Duss, Lee Fang, Scott Keyes, and Faiz Shakir. 2011. *Fear, Inc.: The Roots of the Islamophobia Network in America*. Washington, DC: Center for American Progress.

Alice, Gordon, Debbie, and Mary. (1973) 1988. "Problems of Our Movement." In Lucia-Hoagland and Penelope 1988: 379–94.

Arendt, Hannah. (1963) 1994. *Eichmann in Jerusalem: A Report on the Banality of Evil*. New York: Penguin.

Balint, Benjamin. 2010. *Running Commentary: The Contentious Magazine That Transformed the Jewish Left into the Neoconservative Right*. New York: Public Affairs.

Barrett, Ruth, ed. 2016. *Female Erasure: What You Need to Know about Gender Politics' War on Women, the Female Sex, and Human Rights*. Pacific Palisades, CA: Tidal Time.

Beck, Evelyn Torton. 1982a. "A Nice Jewish Girl: Evie Beck." Interview by Fran Moira. *off our backs*, August–September, 8–11.

Beck, Evelyn Torton. 1982b. "Why Is This Book Different from All Other Books?" In *Nice Jewish Girls: A Lesbian Anthology*, edited by Evelyn Torton Beck, xxi–xxxvi. Watertown, MA: Persephone.

Bev Jo. 2008. "Lesbian Community: From Sisterhood to Segregation." *Journal of Lesbian Studies* 9, nos. 1–2: 135–43.

Bourne, Jenny. 1987. "Homelands of the Mind: Jewish Feminism and Identity Politics." *Race and Class* 29, vol. 1: 1–24.

Brown, Wendy. 1995. "Wounded Attachments." In *States of Injury: Power and Freedom in Late Modernity*, 52–76. Princeton, NJ: Princeton University Press.

Bulkin, Elly, and Donna Nevel. 2012. "Follow the Money: From Islamophobia to Israel Right or Wrong," *AlterNet*, October 3. https://www.alternet.org/2012/10/follow-money -islamophobia-israel-right-or-wrong/.

Buttu, Diana. 2014. "Blaming the Victims." *Journal of Palestine Studies* 44, no. 1: 91–96.

Cable, Umayyah. 2022. "Compulsory Zionism and Palestinian Existence: A Genealogy." *Journal of Palestine Studies*. Published online April 19, 2022. https://doi.org/10.1080/0377919X.2022 .2040324.

Cantarow, Ellen. 1988. "Zionism, Anti-Semitism, and Jewish Identity in the Women's Movement." *Middle East Report* 154. https://merip.org/1988/09/zionism-anti-semitism-and-jewish -identity-in-the-womens-movement/.

Chapman, Kathleen, and Michael Du Plessis. 1997. "'Don't Call Me *Girl*': Lesbian Theory, Feminist Theory, and Transsexual Identities." In *Cross-Purposes: Lesbians, Feminists, and the Limits of Alliance*, edited by Dana Heller, 169–85. Bloomington: Indiana University Press.

Combahee River Collective. (1977) 2017. "The Combahee River Collective Statement." In *How We Get Free: Black Feminism and the Combahee River Collective*, edited by Keeanga-Hamahtta Taylor, 15–28. Chicago: Haymarket.

Cowan, Liza. 1978. "Separatist Symposium." In Lucia-Hoagland and Penelope 1988: 220–34.

Cowan, Liza, and Penny House. 1977a. "Anti-Semitism in the Lesbian Movement." *Dyke: A Quarterly*, no. 5: 20–22.

Cowan, Liza, and Penny House, eds. 1977b. "Can Men Be Women? Some Lesbians Think So! Transsexuals in the Women's Movement." *Dyke: A Quarterly*, no. 5: 29–35.

Daly, Mary. 1978. *Gyn/Ecology: The Metaethics of Radical Feminism*. Boston, MA: Beacon.

Davis, Angela. 2016. *Freedom Is a Constant Struggle*. Chicago: Haymarket.

Drop the ADL Working Group. 2020. "The ADL Is Not an Ally." August. https://droptheadl.org/the-adl-is-not-an-ally/.

Duss, Matthew, Yasmine Taeb, Ken Gude, and Ken Sofer. 2015. *Fear, Inc. 2.0: The Islamophobia Network's Efforts to Manufacture Hate in America*. Washington, DC: Center for American Progress.

Earles, Jennifer. 2018. "The 'Penis Police': Lesbian and Feminist Spaces, Trans Women, and the Maintenance of the Sex/Gender/Sexuality System." *Journal of Lesbian Studies* 23, no. 2: 243–56.

Engle, Vanessa, dir. 2006. *Lefties: "Angry Wimmin."* BBC documentary series.

Enke, Finn. 2018. "Collective Memory and the Transfeminist 1970s: Toward a Less Plausible History." *TSQ* 5, no. 1: 9–29.

Feldman, Keith. 2015. *A Shadow over Palestine: The Imperial Life of Race in America*. Minneapolis: University of Minnesota Press.

Finkelstein, Norman. 2003. *The Holocaust Industry: Reflections on the Exploitation of Jewish Suffering*. 2nd ed. New York: Verso.

Fischbach, Michael R. 2020. *The Movement and the Middle East: How the Arab-Israeli Conflict Divided the American Left*. Stanford, CA: Stanford University Press.

Gelman, Emmaia. 2021. "The Anti-democratic Origins of the Jewish Establishment." *Jewish Currents*, March 12. https://jewishcurrents.org/the-anti-democratic-origins-of-the-jewish-establishment.

Gorgons. 1978. "Separatist Symposium: Response by the Gorgons." In Lucia-Hoagland and Penelope 1988: 394–98.

Greenesmith, Heron. 2020a. "Gender Ideology Yesterday, Today, and Tomorrow." Political Research Associates, March 26. https://www.politicalresearch.org/2020/03/26/gender-ideology-yesterday-today-and-tomorrow.

Greenesmith, Heron. 2020b. "A Room of Their Own: How Anti-trans Feminists Are Complicit in Christian Right Anti-trans Advocacy." Political Research Associates, July 14. https://www.politicalresearch.org/2020/07/14/room-their-own.

Gutter Dyke Collective. (1973) 1988. "Over the Walls: Separatism." In Lucia-Hoagland and Penelope 1988: 27–31.

Hanisch, Carol, et al. 2013. "Forbidden Discourse: The Silencing of Feminist Criticism of 'Gender.'" https://meetinggroundonline.org/wp-content/uploads/2013/10/GENDER-Statement-InterActive-930.pdf (accessed June 18, 2020).

Heaney, Emma. 2016. "Women-Identified Women: Trans Women in 1970s Lesbian Feminist Organizing." *TSQ* 3, nos. 1–2: 137–45.

Heilbrunn, Jacob. 2008. *They Knew They Were Right: The Rise of the Neocons*. New York: Anchor.

hooks, bell. 1984. *Feminist Theory: From Margin to Center*. Boston: South End.

IJAN (International Jewish Anti-Zionist Network). 2015. "The Business of Backlash: The Attack on the Palestinian Movement and Other Movements for Justice." March. http://www.ijan.org/resources/business-of-backlash/.

Jacobson, Matthew Frye. 2006. *Roots Too: White Ethnic Revival in Post–Civil Rights America*. Cambridge, MA: Harvard University Press.

Jeffreys, Sheila. 2003. *Unpacking Queer Politics: A Lesbian Feminist Perspective*. Cambridge: Polity.

Jeffreys, Sheila. 2014. *Gender Hurts: A Feminist Analysis of the Politics of Transgenderism*. New York: Routledge.

Kaplan, Amy. 2018. *Our American Israel: The Story of an Entangled Alliance*. Cambridge, MA: Harvard University Press.

Kaye, Melanie, and Irena Klepfisz. 1982. "Jewish Feminist Conference: Thoughts and Impressions." *off our backs*, August–September, 2–3.

Kelly, Siobhan. 2016. "Feminist Transphobia, Feminist Rhetoric: From Trans-Exclusive Radical Feminism to HB2 (@theTable: Transcending Transphobia)." *Feminist Studies in Religion* (blog), August 30. https://www.fsrinc.org/feminist-transphobia-rhetoric/.

Kezia and Thrace. 1980. "Political Aspects of Transsexualism for the Lesbian Community." *Lesbian Insider/Insighter/Inciter* 1: 1, 6.

"Lesbian Separatist Statement from the Closing Session of the Jewish Feminist Conference, Held in San Francisco, May, 1982." (1982) 1988. In Lucia-Hoagland and Penelope 1988: 92–94.

Levine, Judith, and Erica Meiners. 2020. *The Feminist and the Sex Offender: Confronting Sexual Harm, Ending State Violence*. Brooklyn, NY: Verso.

Lober, Brooke. 2019. "Narrow *Bridges*: Jewish Lesbian Feminism, Identity Politics, and the 'Hard Ground' of Alliance." *Journal of Lesbian Studies* 23, no. 1: 83–101.

Lucia-Hoagland, Sarah, and Julia Penelope. 1988. *For Lesbians Only: A Separatist Anthology*. London: Onlywomen.

Mamdani, Mahmood. 2005. *Good Muslim, Bad Muslim: America, the Cold War, and the Roots of Terror*. New York: Doubleday.

Martínez, Juliana, and María Juliana Rojas. 2021. *Manufacturing Moral Panic: Weaponizing Children to Undermine Gender Justice and Human Rights*. The Elevate Children Funders Group and Global Philanthropy Project, March. https://globalphilanthropyproject.org/wp-content/uploads/2021/04/Manufacturing-Moral-Panic-Report.pdf.

Marty, with Help from the Dykes of S.E.P.S. 1983a. "Popular Separatist-Baiting Quotes and Some Separatist Responses." In Lucia-Hoagland and Penelope 1988: 343–45.

Marty, with Help from the Dykes of S.E.P.S. 1983b. "Relating to Dyke Separatists: Hints for the Non-separatist Lesbian." In Lucia-Hoagland and Penelope 1988: 95–97.

Meyers, Janet. 1977. "Diaspora Takes a Queer Turn: A Jewish Lesbian Considers Her Past." *Dyke: A Quarterly*, no. 5: 12–14.

Milstein, Hannah. 2016. "The United Nations Women's Decade and Jewish Feminist Identity." *Ex Post Facto* 25: 199–222.

Morgensen, Scott. 2011. *Spaces between Us: Queer Settler Colonialism and Indigenous Decolonization*. Minneapolis: University of Minnesota Press.

Morris, Bonnie. 2015. "The Hijacking of Lesbian History." *Gay and Lesbian Review Worldwide* 22, no. 4: 13–15.

Morris, Bonnie. 2017. *The Disappearing L: Erasure of Lesbian Spaces and Culture*. Albany: State University of New York Press.

Novick, Peter. 1999. *The Holocaust in American Life*. New York: Houghton Mifflin.

Orly, Aidan, and Jonathan Brenneman. 2021. "Progressive Movements Cannot Afford to Ignore the Role of Christian Zionism in the Dispossession of Palestinians." Political Research Associates, May 25. https://www.politicalresearch.org/2021/05/25/progressive-movements-cannot-afford-ignore-role-christian-zionism-dispossession.

Pogrebin, Letty Cottin. 1982. "Anti-Semitism in the Women's Movement." *Ms.*, June, 45–49, 62–72.

Raymond, Janice. 1977. "Transsexualism: The Ultimate Homage to Sex-Role Power." *Chrysalis* 3: 11–23.

Raymond, Janice. (1979) 1994. *The Transsexual Empire: The Making of the She-Male*. New York: Teachers College.

Raymond, Janice. 2014. "Dispelling Fictions and Disrupting Hashtags." Interview by Julian Vigo. *Counterpunch*, August 25. https://www.counterpunch.org/2014/08/25/dispelling-fictions -and-disrupting-hashtags/.

Riddell, Carol. 2006. "Divided Sisterhood: A Critical Review of Janice Raymond's *The Transsexual Empire*." In *The Transgender Studies Reader*, edited by Susan Stryker and Stephen Whittle, 144–58. New York: Routledge.

Robinson, Shira. 2013. *Citizen Strangers: Palestinians and the Birth of Israel's Liberal Settler State*. Stanford, CA: Stanford University Press.

Rosenfelt, Deborah, et al. 1983. "Letters Forum: Anti-Semitism." *Ms.*, February, 12–13.

Rubin, Gayle. 1984. "Thinking Sex: Notes for a Radical Theory of the Politics of Sexuality." In *Pleasure and Danger: Exploring Female Sexuality*, edited by Carole Vance, 267–319. Boston: Routledge and Kegan Paul.

Said, Edward. (1979) 1992. "Zionism from the Standpoint of Its Victims." In *The Question of Palestine*, 56–114. New York: Vintage.

Schaffer, Teya, and Meryl Lieberman McNew. 1982. "Statement to Gentiles." *off our backs*, August–September, 7.

Schotten, C. Heike. 2016. "Reading Nietzsche in the Wake of the 2008–09 War on Gaza." In *The Digital Dionysus: Nietzsche and the Network-Centric Condition*, edited by Dan Mellamphy and Nandita Biswas Mellamphy, 108–31. Brooklyn, NY: Punctum.

Schotten, C. Heike. 2018. *Queer Terror: Life, Death, and Desire in the Settler Colony*. New York: Columbia University Press.

Schotten, C. Heike. 2020. "Wounded Attachments? Slave Morality, the Left, and the Future of Revolutionary Desire." In *Nietzsche and Critical Social Theory: Affirmation, Animosity, and Ambiguity*, edited by Michael Roberts, 31–59. Leiden: Brill.

Schotten, C. Heike. Forthcoming. "Masters, Slaves, 'Terrorists': On Elitism and Existential Threats." In *Nietzsche and Politicized Identities*, edited by Allison Merrick and Rebecca Bamford. Albany: State University of New York Press.

Shibli, Adania. 2017. "The Making of Bad Palestinian Mothers during the Second Intifada." In *Bad Girls of the Arab World*, edited by Nadia Yaqub and Rula Quawas, 92–111. Austin: University of Texas Press.

Smith, Barbara. 1984. "Between a Rock and a Hard Place: Relationships between Black and Jewish Women." In *Yours in Struggle: Three Feminist Perspectives on Anti-Semitism and Racism*, by Elly Bulkin, Minnie Bruce Pratt, and Barbara Smith, 65–88. Brooklyn, NY: Long Haul.

Smith, Beverly, Judith Stein, and Priscilla Golding, eds. 1981. "'The Possibility of Life between Us': A Dialogue between Black and Jewish Women." *Conditions* 7: 25–46.

Stahl, Lynne. 2021. "The Latest Form of Transphobia: Saying Lesbians Are Going Extinct." *Washington Post*, March 19. https://www.washingtonpost.com/outlook/the-latest-form -of-transphobia-saying-lesbians-are-going-extinct/2021/03/18/072a95fc-8786-11eb-82bc -e58213caa38e_story.html.

Steinem, Gloria. 1977. "If the Shoe Doesn't Fit, Change the Foot." *Ms.*, February, 76, 85–86.

Stone, Sandy. (1987) 2006. "The *Empire* Strikes Back: A Posttranssexual Manifesto." In *The Transgender Studies Reader*, edited by Susan Stryker and Stephen Whittle, 221–35. New York: Routledge.

Stone, Sandy. 2018. "Sandy Stone on Living among Lesbian Separatists as a Trans Woman in the 70s." Interview by Zackary Drucker. *Vice*, December 19. www.vice.com/en/article /zmd5k5/sandy-stone-biography-transgender-history.

Stryker, Susan. 2017. *Transgender History: The Roots of Today's Revolution*. 2nd ed. New York: Seal.

Taylor, Lauren. 1982. "Race, Class, and Jewish Identity." *off our backs*, August–September, 6.

Taylor, Lauren, and Amy Oppenheimer. 1982. "Anti-Semitism in the Women's Movement." *off our backs*, August–September, 6.

WAI (Women Against Imperialism). 1982. "Taking Our Stand against Zionism and White Supremacy." *off our backs*, July, 20.

Weier, Jacklyn. 2021. "Settler Rural Imaginaries of MichFest: Connecting Settler Legacies and Cis Fear." *ACME: An International Journal for Critical Geographies* 20, no. 2: 171–88.

Williams, Cristan. 2016. "Radical Inclusion: Recounting the Trans Inclusive History of Radical Feminism." *TSQ* 3, nos. 1–2: 254–58.

Zertal, Idith. 2005. *Israel's Holocaust and the Politics of Nationhood*. Translated by Chaya Galai. New York: Cambridge University Press.

Is "Gender Ideology" Western Colonialism?

Anti-gender Rhetoric and the Misappropriation of Postcolonial Language

JENNY ANDRINE MADSEN EVANG

Abstract How should we interrogate and oppose the current anti-gender misappropriation of postcolonial thought and struggles? Recently, we have seen a resurgence of organized anti-gender sentiments across Europe and the globe. A specific anti-gender rhetoric of victimization defines so-called Western genderists as a common enemy and colonizing force against "the people." By focusing on some key European anti-gender actors, this article analyzes the strategic significance of the specific anti-gender assertion that gender is a neocolonial imposition. Beyond examining how the European anti-gender takeover of postcolonial framing is hypocritical — as anti-gender thinkers are themselves invested in the cisheterosexist myth that is perhaps the most colonial of all — the article argues that the misappropriation reveals something central about the racialized imaginary underpinning their rhetoric. They reproduce a racialized hierarchy of biological plasticity that positions white Europeans as both the ultimate saviors and the most vulnerable victims in the face of "genderism." By unpacking the politics through which European anti-gender actors use the "non-Western" world as a rhetorical ruse to further Western supremacy, the article also shows the danger of the impulse to suspend postcolonial feminist critique in an effort to distance oneself from the anti-gender misappropriation of such theory and to unite around a common liberal front. Instead, it proposes that postcolonial thought is more vital than ever if we are to counter current anti-gender movements, their Islamophobia, and their transphobia.
Keywords anti-gender movements, postcolonial theory, racialized plasticity, heteronationalism, Europe

I n 2019 the so-called gender critical feminist Posie Parker appeared in an interview with Jean-François Gariépy, a right-wing nationalist known for his call to institute a "white ethno-state." Uniting the two was their professed opposition to "gender ideology," which they proclaim is a dangerous system of belief destroying sexual dimorphism and women's protection in the name of trans* rights (Wang 2019a). This perhaps initially surprising cooperation between

TERFs—trans-exclusionary radical feminists—and right-wing conservatives as well as alt-right nationalists is no isolated phenomenon (Tudor 2021); referred to respectively as an "unholy alliance," "strange bedfellows," or a "deadly duo" (Wang 2019b; Brydum 2017; Nay and Steinbock 2021: 146), this association has a long historical trajectory. Indeed, the specter of "gender" has increasingly come to function as a "symbolic glue" (Grzebalska, Kováts, and Pető 2017) that allows a wide array of contradictory impulses to be united against an imagined enemy; anti-gender sentiments are where Richard Dawkins and Pope Francis can shake hands (Greenesmith 2021).

In the wake of her controversial interview with Gariépy, Parker denounced "white supremacy and the racism that fuels it" as having "no place in a civilised society," while immediately claiming that "as a free speech advocate [she] think[s] dialogue, even with those with the most odious prejudices, is essential. . . . These days so many people are called Nazis and far right that the prophetic warning that we will no longer recognise the real ones is beginning to come true" (as quoted in Wang 2019a). This rhetorical double move has become an emblematic gesture that unites TERFs and the alt-right; with one hand, Parker denounces white supremacy, racism, and misogyny, presenting herself as the guardian of "civilized society," while with the other, she legitimizes dialogue under the guise of "free speech" and calls into question the naming of Gariépy as "far right." Opposing "gender ideology" thus affords the right-wing anti-gender discourse a veneer of civilized respectability, while also allowing TERFs and alt-right activists to represent their struggle as a heroic endeavor of the marginalized against the tide of so-called cancel culture and woke orthodoxy (Siddiqui 2021). The relationship between "respectable" TERFS and alt-right anti-gender movements is one that "launders extremism," whereby TERFs avoid fully "endorsing, but [benefit] from, the activities of extremist anti-trans actors" (Gill-Peterson 2021).

The illusion of the feminist protection of vulnerable women that TERF rhetoric affords its anti-gender accomplices has more recently been joined by another façade of victimization; the claim that gender is a (neo)colonial Western imposition silently forcing itself onto the ignorant global masses (Korolczuk and Graff 2018; Hemmings 2020). In a startling rhetorical turn, certain strands of the anti-gender movement are uniting the gender critical vocabulary derived from TERFs with a seemingly postcolonial breakdown of LGBT rights, gender mainstreaming, and Western feminism, all while retaining a conservative nostalgia for cisheteronormative Western Christian legacy. This strategic catering to anti-colonial sentiments allows the anti-gender movement to once again cast itself as being on the side of the vulnerable, oppressed people of the world while speaking truth to (Western) power and its colonizing force. This emerging anti-gender narrative poses a pressing conundrum for queer and feminist postcolonial criticism that has a long history of interrogating gender as a colonial construct;

how are we to deal with the fact that Eurocentric gender, neoliberal feminism, and Western rights discourse—those structures that we ourselves have been invested in critically interrogating and opposing—are now being tactically called out by anti-gender activists in the name of restoring some mythic notion of a "natural" (pre)colonial gender binary?[1]

This article attempts to wade through this contradictory landscape by unpacking the racialized and gendered politics of this disturbing trend. By closely reading central claims by two key European anti-gender thinkers—the German sociologist Gabriele Kuby and the Belgian journalist Marguerite Peeters—in combination with statements from anti-gender actors in different European countries, I hope to highlight the complexity of the declaration that so-called gender ideology is a coherent, neocolonial imposition. It would be easy to dismiss the claim as a conspiracy theory that awkwardly bulks together everything from Sigmund Freud to poststructuralism to the United Nations (UN) by pointing out the ways in which the coherency of "gender ideology" itself is a fiction. While that is clearly true, I think it is worth moving beyond this assertion to analyze more granularly the European misappropriation of postcolonial language to show that the rhetoric reveals something central about the racialized imaginary of gender underlying European anti-gender theory. Only by holding onto postcolonial critique does it become obvious that anti-gender actors' hostile and superficial takeover of postcolonial rhetoric is duplicitous—indeed, it is "more than hypocritical" of anti-gender rhetoric to "suggest that the modern binary heteronormative sex/gender system that was imported through colonialism . . . is an 'authentic' non-Western one" (Tudor 2021: 245).[2] By naturalizing the colonial structure of cisheteropatriarchy as inherent to the global South while also lamenting the dismantling of Western tradition, European anti-gender thinkers use the "non-Western world" as a rhetorical ruse in their quest to restore Europe to a mythic past before "Western values" were tainted by the "gender lobby"—a cultural heyday that itself corresponds to the peak of early colonial expansion and Eurocentric modernity. This European anti-gender "imperialist nostalgia"—whereby the West is both the historical beacon of civilization and the current center of an undemocratic force brainwashing victimized masses—itself relies on a colonial rhetoric that asserts cisheteropatriarchy as simultaneously the natural, local state of affairs everywhere, and as a structure that can be successfully cultivated only by white, European tradition (Rosaldo 1989). "Non-Western people," frequently painted through the homogenizing collapse of culture, geography, religion, and nation, thus come to carry a double rhetorical burden; they are interchangeably painted as common victims that can resist the ludicrousness of "gender ideology" and as uncivilized others that are unable to obtain the forgiving (Christian) tools necessary to foster proper, healthy heterosexuality, thus themselves presenting a danger comparable to that of "gender ideology" to the "cultural backbone" of Europe (Kuby 2015: 8). I argue that this constitutive duality is central to the ways in which the anti-gender discourse echoes a much longer history of racialized plasticity; indeed, anti-gender actors reinforce a hierarchy between civilized, plastic white bodies capable of cultivating proper sex/gender and uncivilized, racialized bodies unable to live up to the same level of accumulated plasticity, only ever embodying lesser, "savage" copies of the refined ways of Western sex/gender (Schuller 2018). While anti-gender thinkers preach the universality and naturalness of biological sex and sexuality, it is their anxieties bound to the bio-political discourse of plasticity that allow them to frame white Europeans as the most impressionable and sophisticated—the most human—and therefore the ultimate victims of, as well as the final guardians against, the "social engi-neering" of a new human that trans* feminists and queer theory scholars are said to be imposing.

All this is to say that the anti-gender misappropriation of postcolonial vocabulary reinforces, rather than undermines, Europe as an ongoing colonial project (Glissant 1989) invested in a particular anthropological and biological vision of the sexed human. My aim in drawing on examples from across Euro-pean currents is not to imply the false homogeneity of a European anti-gender movement; indeed, many approaches have highlighted how diverse and complex the different (national) iterations are (Nash and Browne 2020; Kuhar and Pater-notte 2017). Rather, in centering the specificities and commonalities of Euro-pean misappropriations of postcolonial theory, I aim to bring into focus how they are variously invested in a mythic imaginary of Europe as the coherent center of civilized sex/gender. In order to analyze—and resist—the ways that European anti-gender discourse is strategically co-opting postcolonial vocab-ulary while simultaneously ramping up Islamophobic anti-immigration rhet-oric on the path to reentrench Western supremacy, it is more vital than ever to thoroughly revisit postcolonial critiques of the racialized articulations of gen-der and sexual exceptionalism.

"White Women Are Saving Brown Women from Decadent Western 'Gender Ideologues'"; or, How the Anti-gender Movement Echoes Femonationalism

In her groundbreaking essay "Can the Subaltern Speak?," Gayatri Spivak ([1988] 2015: 92) proposes the formulation "white men are saving brown women from brown men" to (psycho)analyze the colonizer's imperial fantasy. In the aftermath of this distilled phrasing, which captures the crux of a now well-known savior dynamic, the centrality of white feminist rhetoric to the continued imperial functioning of the West has been well established (Farris 2017; Lugones 2016; Mohanty 1988). Key to this dynamic is the representation of women of color as in need of rescue from patriarchal and repressive men coupled with a rearticulation of Western gender norms as the universal telos of gender equality, sexual democracy, and egalitarianism. This framing reinforces a linear axis of civilization whereby Europe functions as the center of universal reason, equality, and justice while imagined racialized elsewheres are framed as lagging behind, unable to catch up to Western progress and forever in need of guidance.[3]

Universal human rights present one central pillar in the contemporary landscape of neo-Orientalist femo- and homonationalisms—as Jasbir Puar (2007: 139) famously argues, the human rights industrial complex functions to separate the world into "women and gay friendly" countries versus regressive and homophobic ones along a racialized geopolitical vector. This cognitive mapping is especially overdetermined when it comes to "terrorist look-alike" populations that are figured as entrenched threats to women and sexual minorities—a rhetoric that conveniently fuels nationalist and racist anti-immigration policies while reinforcing the fantasy of the West as a safe haven for queer people and women. In the final instance, this framing rehearses a familiar clash-of-civilizations discourse cloaked in rainbow colors.

Is it really this underlying coloniality of the Western discourse on gender and sexuality that certain anti-gender actors are somehow onto? As early as 1997, the Catholic journalist Dale O'Leary argued in her influential book *The Gender Agenda* that Western gender policies reiterate neocolonialism. This argument has picked up steam in current European anti-gender circles; Gabriele Kuby (2015: 5, 12), an important German anti-gender thinker with a large following, calls on people to stand with her "against the tide" of a gender totalitarianism cloaked in "freedom, tolerance, justice, equality, anti-discrimination and diversity—ideological backdrops that prove to be amputated, distorted terms." In a similar vein, Marguerite Peeters claims,

> In the West, the homosexual movement is prevalent while in developing countries there are feminist programmes which aim to promote a mentality which opposes the filial, maternal and conjugal identity of women. They teach them that the differences between a man and a woman are social constructs, and denigrate the family . . . as [a] social constraint which oppose[s] equality and freedom of citizens. The underlying message is that in an advanced society these "old fashion" traditions must be discouraged with every means. (quoted in Battista 2017)

Both writers frame "gender ideology" as a decadent, Western-bred ideology, simultaneously destroying the cultural skeleton of Christian Europe while being exported to "unknowing" cultures outside the West. Pointing to the hypocrisy of the universal purchase of the language of freedom, human rights, and diversity, they want to build a counterhegemonic movement in the name of the defenseless masses of the world. Central to their take is their laudatory framing of "non-Western societies" as "more traditional" when it comes to gender, sexuality, and the family, since "gender ideology" has not yet gone as far there as in the West. Thus their argument relies on essentializing the very same conceptualization of "cultural difference" that structures femonationalist arguments in the first place, namely, that racialized, imagined elsewheres are stuck in a more traditional gender pattern, unable to keep up with the rampant development of the West; the difference between the two is just that, while femonationalists celebrate this rampant development as the epitome of Western progress, the anti-gender writers lament it as marking the death of tradition, family, and humanity writ large, longing instead for what they see as the (pre)colonial, natural gender order.

It becomes clear that, even if anti-gender rhetoric is right to regard gender as a colonial construct, they have missed the key component. In fact, the complementary gender roles they are preaching as a natural state, now threatened by the socially engineered human, turn out to be the most colonial of all; as Maria Lugones (2016: 15) argues, "Biological dimorphism [and] heterosexual patriarchy" are the central structuring principles of the coloniality of gender. There is a startling "irony of critiquing feminists for their imposition of 'gender ideology' by those who seek to re-entrench those naturalised categories of sex and gender that are the hallmark of colonial endeavour" (Hemmings 2020: 31). The coloniality of the anti-gender conceptualization goes further than the naturalization and universalization of binary gender; as I explore later in this article, the anti-gender movement reestablishes an internal hierarchy within the victimized group itself that distinguishes between the civilized and cultured traditional Western gender and the imitative, uncivilized traditions in the "non-Western" world that it superficially and ambivalently romanticizes in service of restoring the former.

Profiting off the strategic rhetoric of gender as Western colonialism displacing the natural order of sexual difference, the European anti-gender crowd claims a common vulnerability with the non-Western world, all the while reframing themselves as the most courageous guardians of humanity's survival. Peeters (2011), for example, argues that, while "non-western cultures, foreign to western 'laïcité' wouldn't freely choose [the] proposals" that "gender ideology" is said to be imposing, they are in need of the West to "give them a voice" in order to be able to resist them. Only then can the "non-western cultures . . . help the West recover its soul" (Peeters 2011). In a similar vein, Kuby (2015: 278) preaches for heterosexual, Christian Europe to become a "new—global—saviour" for the "rootless, dependent . . . masses" of the global South. This paradoxical boomerang effect is important to both their savior fantasies; the non-Western cultures can—through their lack of impressionability in encounters with "gender ideology"—inspire a challenge to the alleged "silent gender revolution," but only once Christian Europe manages to stand up and give this challenge a voice and a face can it develop into proper counterhegemonic resistance. This anti-gender savior fantasy is especially overdetermined in relation to Eastern Europe—indeed, anti-gender actors manage to give a positive spin to the often-rehearsed Western European narrative that frames the region as in need of catching up to Western Europe's sexual and gender equality by arguing instead that Eastern Europe is the last European beacon of natural gender and thus a natural global leader (Korolczuk and Graff 2018). The problematic lumping together of Eastern Europe and the non-Western world under the common trope of Western European colonization has indeed become a hallmark of anti-gender rhetoric in Europe; the conjoining allows anti-gender actors to frame Eastern Europe in a victimized position by erasing its investments in coloniality and anti-Blackness, while at the same time upholding cherished hierarchies so that Eastern Europe is painted as the exemplary "good victim" representing the necessary anti-gender vanguard that might inspire the less civilized masses to follow in its footsteps. In all cases, it is clear that European anti-gender rhetoric frames non-Western populations as infantilized, rootless, and dependent, in need of being given a voice—ironically, all key traits of the femonationalist white savior fantasy that anti-gender thinkers claim to be combating in opposing "gender ideology." In most cases, the rhetorical use of *non-Western cultures* merely helps European anti-gender thinkers proclaim the need for reviving the West as the natural global governing power, while superficially asserting to be standing up against Western colonization.

Anti-gender Actors' Ambivalent West and the Mythic Heyday

Despite cloaking itself in a postcolonial costume, it comes as no surprise that the competing anti-gender savior fantasy is accompanied by a—sometimes thinly veiled—racist and xenophobic nationalist fantasy. Indeed, it is no coincidence that much of the vocabulary used to describe "gender ideology" sounds like an echo to anyone familiar with European anti-immigration rhetoric: "Ebola from Brussels,"[4] "gender terrorists," "more dangerous than nuclear weapons," and "destroyers of civilization" are only a few of the catchphrases. This echo should not be understood as a mere analogy, in which the discourse of the threat of "gender ideologues" simply borrows from an earlier vocabulary of xenophobic anti-immigration rhetoric—indeed, "gender conservatism is not just racism's younger sibling" (Graff, Kapur, and Walters 2019: 550). Rather, the two fears are inextricable insofar as the stabilization of gender and sexuality is dependent on a racialized construction of the civilized culture—and human subject—that the anti-gender movement wants to revitalize. As much as they claim to "build consensus, in a bottom-up, participatory manner, involving non-western cultures, on what is genuinely universal" (Peeters 2012), it is clear that the "universal" to which they are attached is one deeply rooted in what Alexander Weheliye (2014: 21) describes as "the colonial and racialist histories of the modern incantations of the human." We see this even more clearly in Kuby's (2015: 22) claim that the alleged gendering of society "is astonishing because it destroys the conditions that brought forth European high culture—a model of success for the entire world." Yet again, a boomerang argument appears: the alleged involvement of "non-western cultures" in restoring "what is genuinely universal" allows anti-gender actors to frame themselves as speaking in the name of "the human species"; all the while the culture they actually want to get back to is "European high culture" by reproducing the "overrepresentation of [Western bourgeois] Man" as the universal human (Wynter 2003: 267).

The final "product" of "gender ideology" is often identified by anti-gender actors as the trans* child, represented as emblematic of a new,[5] socially engineered human, devoid of history, and external to the pillars of Western biology, politics, and culture. While the genealogies that anti-gender thinkers present for the specter of "gender ideology" vary—some start with Margaret Sanger, others trace it back to Alfred Kinsey, the United Nations, or even Marxism writ large—there seems to be a general consensus that the "gender proposal is the logical fruit" of a remarkably destructive process that has led "true" Western values astray (Peeters 2011). While Kuby (2015: 51), for example, claims that "gender ideology" was "prepared by the intellectual trailblazers from the French Revolution to the postmodern gender ideology of one Judith Butler," she is quick to emphasize that we need to recover the "benevolent spirits of reason, conscience, and brotherhood"—a clear echo of the Enlightenment heritage from the French Revolution's "liberté, égalité, fraternité."

Recognizing this central ambivalence in regard to so-called Western values—whereby they are cast out as "postmodern authoritarianism" only to be embraced as the "true spirit" of societies to come—is essential to understanding the strategic significance of the anti-gender misappropriation of postcolonial language. This ambivalence sheds light on the fact that the superficial takeover frames the "gender ideology" colonizer not simply as the "West as such but [rather as] the West whose healthy (Christian) core had already been destroyed by neo-Marxism and feminism in the 1960s" (Korolczuk and Graff 2018: 812). Very often, the anti-gender misappropriation takes on a decidedly Islamophobic hue; for all their catering to anticolonial sentiments, anti-gender thinkers often claim that "gender ideology," with its historical roots in anti-European "neo-Marxism and feminism," goes hand in hand with the threat of (Muslim) immigration. A blatant example of this can be found in former Cardinal Sarah's proclamation against the two unexpected threats of our times:

> On the one hand, the idolatry of Western freedom; on the other, Islamic funda-
> mentalism: atheistic secularism versus religious fanaticism. To use a slogan, we
> find ourselves between *"gender ideology and ISIS."* . . . From these two radicali-
> zations arise the two major threats to the family: its subjectivist disintegration in
> the secularized West [and] the pseudo-family of ideologized Islam which legiti-
> mizes polygamy [and] female subservience. (Sarah 2015)

Sarah aggressively draws up a dual picture of the true enemy—the biopolitical
survival of the family is threatened on the one hand by excessive secularization
and sexual freedom, and on the other by "ideologized Islam's pseudo-family,"
which marks the degraded and uncivilized counterpart to Christianity's proper
tradition. This discursive construction of "terrorist look-alikes" as possessing an
excessive, uncultivated, and dangerous sexuality yet again plays into the same
fundamental racialized mapping of progress that colonial gender undergirded
(Puar 2007). This rhetoric is mirrored by Norwegian right-wing politician Per-
Willy Amundsen (2021) when he writes that

> I will never celebrate pride. First of all, there are only two sexes: man and woman,
> not three—that is in contradiction with all biological science. Even worse, they are
> allowed access to our kids to influence them with their radical ideology. This has to
> be stopped. If FRI [the national LGBT organization] really cared about gay rights,
> they would get involved in what is happening in Muslim countries, rather than
> construct fake problems here in Norway. But it is probably easier to speak about
> "diversity" as long as it doesn't cost anything. (Amundsen 2021; translation by
> author)

Here Amundsen draws on the well-known trope of trans∗ and queer people
"preying on our kids" while at the same time reinforcing the homonationalist notion that Europe, and in particular Norway, is a safe h(e)aven for queer
people—perhaps a bit too much so. In his response to Amundsen, Thee-Yezen
Al-Obaide, the leader of SALAM, the organization for queer Muslims in Norway,
aptly diagnoses Amundsen's rhetoric as "transphobia wrapped in Islamophobia"
(as quoted in Berg 2021). Amundsen mirrors a central tenet of TERF rhetoric
by claiming to be the voice of science, biology, and reason in order to distinguish his own resistance to "gender ideology" from the repressive, regressive one
of Muslims. In this way, his argumentation, which basically claims that trans∗
people don't exist[6] and certainly shouldn't be recognized legally, attempts to
come off as benign, while Muslim opposition to "gender ideology" is painted as
destructive and anti-modern.

This double gesture, which allows Amundsen to have his cake and eat it
too, is a central trope in different European iterations of anti-gender rhetoric. In

France, for example, such discourse claims that, "while 'gender ideology' goes too far on the one hand, the patriarchal control of Islam threatens to pull us back into an excessive past. Here of course, 'Frenchness' is always already neither Muslim, nor queer (and certainly not both)" (Hemmings 2020: 30). Therefore the French anti-gender movement sees itself as the defender of true Western civilization, both from Western "gender ideology" and from uncivilized "primitives" who are nevertheless themselves victims of "gender ideology." A similar dynamic plays out in Britain: "Reading Muslims as dangerous heteroactivists and Christians as benign points to how racialization and religion create specific forms of heteroactivism. . . . Even where 'Muslim parents' are supported by Christian heteroactivists, they remain other to the nation, and not central to its defence" (Nash and Browne 2020: 145).[7] In the British example, it is clear that white anti-gender actors represent themselves as moderate, reasonable, and caring—often claiming that their resistance to the "politicization" of the classroom has nothing to do with transphobia and homophobia.

Certain strands of anti-gender rhetoric claim that the true intent of "gender ideology" is to undermine "Western values" altogether by allegedly opening the door to non-Western mass immigration;[8] this line of thinking asserts that left-wing trans* feminists, UN diplomats, and queer theorists—all key actors behind "gender ideology"—are actively inviting all types of "diversity" that might conflict with the tradition of "European high culture"—including racial and cultural as well as gender and sexual minorities. Amundsen's invocation of "gender ideology" preaching multiculturalism echoes this conspiracy; in his imaginary, it is as if "gender ideology" is actually paving the way for Sarah's "second demonic culture"—Islamic fundamentalism—to ruin the last mores of Western civilization. In Poland anti-gender actors have claimed that "the real purpose of global elites is to enable mass migration from Africa to Central and Eastern Europe," which will destroy Polish culture and families (Korolczuk and Graff 2018: 811). Some anti-gender thinkers, following this line of argumentation to its logical end point, perform an astounding rhetorical backflip; in a somewhat humorous mirroring of the well-known Marxist notion that capitalism sows the seeds of its own destruction, they argue that "gender ideology" indeed has done just that. "Gender ideology" will thus be riveted by its own ideological blinders: "the crisis ensuing from the uncontrolled mass immigration to Europe since autumn of 2015, mainly of young Muslim men, . . . will reveal the gender agenda to be the delusion of a decadent society and put us back on the solid ground of human reality— man and woman, father, mother, and children. . . . The victory of evil only sets the stage for the triumph of good" (Kuby 2015: 280). The ludicrousness of "gender ideology" will finally be disclosed when non-Western immigration reaches a critical level, though at that point, it might already be too late to save the ruins of European culture and reason.

In the last instance, the majority of European anti-gender rhetoric that benefits from a seemingly postcolonial framing seems to be preaching different iterations of a common trope; the non-Western cultures can have their "less civilized" knock-off copies of Christian traditions as long as they stay where they are. Whether framed as victims in need of a European savior to guide them or as dangerous primitives to be kept at bay, non-Western others function as key figures for the anti-gender aspiration of national and cultural Western homogeneity. As Elżbieta Korolczuk and Agnieszka Graff (2018: 812) put it in the Polish context, the "two narratives—the one that identifies the peoples of Africa as victims of a global conspiracy and the one placing Poles in this role, a nation to be replaced by Africans—may appear to be mutually exclusive. In fact, however, they converge in their valorization of ethnic and national homogeneity and local rootedness, as well as in their vilification of Western elites." In other words, if non-Western people can "help the West recover its soul" (Peeters 2011), they have to do it from afar.

In their important article, Korolczuk and Graff (2018: 810) go on to entertain the idea that the anti-gender misappropriation of postcolonial theory might show "a problem inherent within postcolonialism itself [which] makes the seemingly hostile takeover unavoidable: namely, the tendency to essentialize cultures and to validate authenticity and the local at the expense of the foreign and universal." In their reading, postcolonial theory itself is in danger of essentializing and romanticizing "the local and authentic" through some vulgar notion of cultural relativism. While I agree with Korolczuk and Graff that we need to continuously interrogate our own theoretical approaches, I would argue that their suggestion that postcolonial theory itself essentializes local cultures seems to somewhat miss the mark; indeed, a key qualm in postcolonial critique is with the very notion of comparing "homophobic cultures" with "progressive" ones—or cultural comparison writ large—as the premise of geopolitical claims of static, local difference (Puar 2007). While it is certainly true—as Korolczuk and Graff argue—that anti-gender actors essentialize the local and authentic in their misappropriation of postcolonial language, postcolonial theory has a long tradition of interrogating the underlying epistemological stakes of the very notions of locality and authenticity; if anything, this emphasizes the superficiality of the anti-gender strategic misappropriation of postcolonial language, rather than revealing a pitfall in postcolonial critique itself.

It is also crucial to remember that the anti-gender romantization of the local wants to reject "gender ideology" as a universalizing discourse only to "build consensus . . . on what is genuinely universal" (Peeters 2012)—thus, in contradiction to critiques of Western universalisms rooted in postcolonial theory, this strand of anti-gender discourse wants to throw out one universalism only to replace it with a more "proper," authentic one. In light of this, I diverge from Korolczuk and Graff's (2018: 816) claim that "today it is clear that a wholesale rejection of universalism plays into the hands of right-wing populists. We do not offer a solution to this dilemma, but our analysis suggests the need to rethink feminist critiques of universalism in a world where the hegemony of liberal democracy can no longer be taken for granted." Though not stated explicitly, an implication of Korolczuk and Graff's arguments seems to be that we might no longer have the same room for postcolonial critiques of universalisms and sexual rights as human rights; maybe we might even need to sideline them to protect the basic, universal values "we all agree on" against anti-gender movements. I argue, however, that those very critiques that might be seen as potential stumbling blocks for a coherent resistance to anti-gender movements are essential if we are to fully unpack—and counter—the anti-gender nostalgia for the imagined Western Christian heyday and the accompanying colonial imaginary of gender. Only then can we deconstruct the ways that European anti-gender actors are deeply intertwined with the ramping up of a colonial and Islamophobic discourse of immigrants and "unchristian" people—particularly Muslims—threatening the democratic, religious, and symbolic pillars of the West, even if they paint themselves as waging a postcolonial attack on the contemporary West gone overboard.

Drawing on analyses of colonial gender, it becomes clear that anti-gender rhetoric is itself steeped in a racialized and gendered dynamic of reason that is tethered to saving the Western project of modernity/coloniality (Mignolo 2011). For this reason, I think it is a mistake to claim that "gender conservatism is, above all, an *antimodern* discourse" (Graff, Kapur, Walters 2019: 546; emphasis added). While it is certainly true that anti-gender discourse, particularly in Europe, is built around a collective nostalgia for a mythic heyday, it is precisely the imaginary of Western modernity that they are hungry for.[9] Framing anti-gender rhetoric as an anti-modern regression might allow a Western Enlightenment heritage to get away unscathed and to be represented as a sufficient language alone in which to counter anti-gender rhetoric as something simply peripheral to the "true project" of modernity. Certain tendencies seem to point to the fact that, in desperately wanting to grasp for some universal good, the willingness to dispense with critiques of exclusionary and xenophobic universalities might grow in some circles. As an International Planned Parenthood Federation representative argued in a debate in the European Union parliament, "We cannot afford internal debates now, we have to contend with the Right" (quoted in Kováts 2019).[10] Defining the specter of "the Right" as an external, homogenous entity that must be combatted by a united leftist front risks precluding any thorough engagement of the EU's—or any other entity's—own investments in continued inequality. If we protectively take recourse to some commonsense conception of joint, liberal pillars of gender equality and Western feminism in order to contend with the "real enemy," who will be left behind?

Anti-gender Thinkers and the Racialized Hierarchy of Plasticity; or, They Are Teaching "How to Bring Your Kids up Trans"[11] in Primary School!

As mentioned, anti-gender paranoia is particularly overdetermined when it comes to the fear mongering around the figure of the white child being led astray from the natural order of proper heterosexuality, sexual differentiation, and science. The metaphor of the child in danger of being perverted by "gender ideology" often goes hand in hand with white extinction fears. The chair of Poland's far-right anti-immigration ruling party, Law and Justice (PiS), Jaroslaw Kaczynki, for example, who previously said that Muslims bring "parasites and protozoa" to Poland, exclaimed that the threat of "gender ideology" is a "direct attack on the family and children—the sexualization of children, that entire LBGT movement, gender. This is imported, but they today actually threaten our identity, our nation, its continuation and therefore the Polish state" (Gera 2019). We find an aggressive, visual example of this biopolitical panic in a poster featured (and later withdrawn) by French protesters affiliated with Manif Pour Tous (Protest For All), featuring an anti-Black caricature of the former Guinean French minister of justice, Christiane Taubira (see Massillon 2013 for poster). Taubira is known for having introduced same-sex marriage legalization in France in 2013 before she resigned in protest of a bill that would strip alleged terrorists of their French citizenship. In the poster she is pictured cutting down trees with a chainsaw with the following play on words: "Wherever Taubira passes, the family tree passes away" (Où passe Taubira, la filiation trépasse); also pictured is a small cartoon drawing of a "typical nuclear family" holding hands with the inscription "Everyone is born of a man and a woman" (Tous nés d'un homme et d'une femme).[12] Other posters released at the same time featured racist caricatures of Chinese children, meant to invoke the specter of authoritarianism, communism, and the threat to free speech, and yet another depicts Taubira spanking a naked child with the new civil code. The figuration of Taubira as a "torturer of children" conjures the moral panic that anti-gender thinkers associate with the figure of the (usually white) child in danger of being replaced, a danger sometimes figured through the explicit racialization of the child as Chinese (Massillon 2013).

A popular joke poking fun at a central paradox of TERF and anti-gender alarm about the possible perversion of the child goes something like this: if sexual difference is natural, biological, or God given, why would it be put in jeopardy simply by reading a fairytale in which the prince ends up with the prince, or from having a trans* teacher teach sex ed in primary school? Do anti-gender thinkers really think that nature is that fragile? As Eva von Redecker (2016: 5) puts it, "Most anti-gender positions refer to a supposedly natural or divine order to counteract constructivism, yet the very fear that gender might be messed with highlights that they have learned something from feminism—they just do not like it." Redecker's point seems to be that the fear of "gender" destroying sex presupposes a notion of the (sexed) body as malleable, which, according to her, comes from feminist theory. While I agree that a humorous paradox structures anti-gender thinkers' moral panic, I don't think it is sufficient to trace the genealogy of the plasticity of biological gender back to feminism's radical theorizations. Instead, building on Kyla Schuller's work, I contend that the seemingly contradictory framing of sex as biological and therefore natural and universal *and* in need of refinement, protection, and stabilization shows how anti-gender theorists are embedded in a longer genealogy of racialized plasticity that was—and to a certain extent still is—central to colonial discourses of civilization and the scientific production of sex/gender writ large.

The premise of Kuby's (2015: 9) book "is that the beautiful gift of sexuality requires *cultivation* if it is to allow people to have successful relationships and a successful life." While sexuality is a natural, beautiful gift from God/nature, it nevertheless is in need of proper cultivation to flourish; in the absence of this, it might "miss its aim" (xvi). Somewhat surprisingly, perhaps, we see that anti-gender rhetoric echoes the nineteenth-century understanding of sex and sexuality "as the accumulative result of matter made 'malleable' over generations by the technologies of civilization, and as open to 'transformation' and technological production as any other capacity of whiteness" (Schuller 2018: 24), not as something that was simply biologically predetermined and fixed. Sexual dimorphism and proper gender roles—the highest treasures of the anti-gender movement—historically functioned to illustrate the capacity of whiteness for progress, evolution, and national/personal self-discipline over and against the un/gendered, racialized person.

This notion of racialized plasticity sheds new light on the implicitly racialized biological discourse that allows anti-gender actors to reintroduce a civilized/uncivilized binary that feeds the aforementioned xenophobic internal hierarchy of white Europeans versus non-Westerners, even as both are framed as common victims of "gender ideology." As Robert Spaemann emphasizes in the introduction to Kuby's (2015: xvi) influential book, "Wherever there is life, species aim at fulfilling their nature in *their own specific ways*." Indeed, the ways in which cisheterosexual "nature" can be fulfilled are constructed as culturally specific; the discourse of "recovering authentic" sex—contrasted with the scapegoat of the "socially engineered trans* person"—seamlessly sutures universal "human nature" to a notion of cultivated Western tradition as the vanguard of the "human species." When anti-gender thinkers thus present themselves as defending "humanity" against extinction, the "genre of man" they are universalizing as under siege is rooted in a racialized hierarchization of who is more or less human that springs from the gendered colonial heritage of Western Enlightenment (Wynter 2003).

This hierarchy of the human is tethered to a notion of impressibility as "a key measure for racially and sexually differentiating the refined, sensitive, and civilized subject who was embedded in time and capable of progress, and in need of protection, from the coarse, rigid, and savage elements of the population suspended in the eternal state of flesh and lingering on as unwanted remnants of prehistory" (Schuller 2018: 8). We see this racialized hierarchy of plasticity play out as an implicit foundation in anti-gender rhetoric. As Peeters (2012) emphasizes, "The gender agenda divorces the human from . . . his or her body and *anthropological structure*. . . . Gender is a purely intellectual construct, hardly to be grasped by nonwestern cultures" (emphasis added). Key to Peeters's conceptualization is the fact that natural sex as a bodily truth is in fact contingent on the "anthropological" context of the subject—thus the natural sex that is under attack from "gender ideology" is not simply an unchangeable static truth but also an outcome of accumulated cultural and religious cultivation, or lack thereof. In Peeters's assertion, non-Western cultures have an altogether different traditional history and structure, one that has not prepared them to even grasp, yet alone be impressed or changed by, the vulgar sophistication of Western "gender ideology." Thus, non-Western cultures are seen as resistant to "gender ideology" not because of their advanced grasp of the cultivation of "authentic sex" but because of their "coarse and rigid" prehistorical ways and nonplastic biology. This leads us back to the internal differentiation of "gender ideology" victims as either leaders or followers: while the anti-gender movement, particularly its iteration in parts of Eastern Europe, is framed as resistant to "gender ideology" because of its well-developed capacities for reason, sentimentality, and proper gender roles, the non-Western world is framed as resistant because of its lack of capacity to evolve, its biologically entrenched psychic structure wanting in refinement, impressionability, and sophistication.

Underlying the white child's sex is centuries of accumulative civilization that imbues it with advanced impressionability—this is what allows it to be represented as at once the beacon of the West's future and the ultimate victim of gender ideology. This overdetermined anxiety is well exemplified by the TERF discourse vilifying the misguided trans* child and teenager through the specter of the so-called epidemic of "rapid onset gender dysphoria"; or as Kuby (2015: 106) claims, "gender ideology'" targeting the "ambiguity of children's gender identity is no liberation, but an ideological abuse of dependent children." This construction of the "inherent susceptibility of the 'advanced' body" of the white child, capable of great cultivation as well as vulnerable to corruption, in turn "helps produce other [racialized bodies] as projects to be saved or persons to be expelled" (Schuller 2018: 20). The victimization of racialized "others" has a decidedly different hue than that of the innocent, susceptible white child that needs to be protected from the alleged "ideological abuse" turning them trans*. In fact, while the protection of children from becoming trans* and losing their righteous path is framed as the very stakes of humanity's future survival, the precarious interpolation of the non-Western person into the victimized serves primarily as a mark of white empathy, emotion, and expansive love for the "other." As Peeters (2012) puts it, "Westerners who love Africans as brothers are eager to learn from them. . . . It is not only nor primarily because we are citizens that we are equal, but because we are human persons. . . . *Love* makes us equal" (emphasis mine). Of course, it is all but too easy to see that the (unrequested) "love of Africans" that Peeters imposes in the name of "humanity" is drawing on a long tradition of colonial imposition cloaked in humanitarianism. Thus, while the strategic call for "loving" the imagined coarse non-Western person signals the anti-gender actors' capacity for sympathy, it is always accompanied by the underlying specter of that "racial other" turning into an existential threat if they get too close. At the same time, the white child is pictured as the fountain of future life and national prosperity, which will suture the family, nation, and the West back together if not derailed by dangerous outsiders.

Conclusion: Do We Need to Become "What They Fear We Are"?

Mary Anne Case (2019: 642), in her analysis of anti-gender rhetoric, calls on us to become "what they fear we are," by which she means "a united front working productively together to achieve a seamless garment of liberty and equality for all regardless of sex or gender." It is precisely this tempting rhetorical appeal to suspend our differences so as to gather around the humanist ideals of "liberty and equality" that this article has sought to oppose by analyzing the racialized politics of anti-gender misappropriations of postcolonial theory. It is essential to resist interpretations that abide by a rhetoric of mutual exclusion between (good) sexual citizenship and (bad) anti-gender theory that would simultaneously stabilize the impunity of the former and the regressive and external placement of the latter. Such dichotomous framings would likely entail the sidelining or over-looking of the implications of postcolonial critique of Eurocentric constructions of sexual citizenship. In the worst case, such framings might even lead to the impli-cit scapegoating of postcolonial theory—perhaps seen as a hindrance to reaffirm-ing the virtue of Western progressive gender and sexual norms—for opening the door to its anti-gender appropriations. As Gill-Peterson (2021) argues, "The prob-lem with recuperation [of collective liberal values] as remedy [to anti-gender actors] is that it doubles down on the fantasy that conspiracy theory, disinformation, and authoritarianism are simple errors of fact or reality, rather than complex positions central to the very structure of Enlightenment's heritage." In fact, many European anti-gender actors, borrowing rhetoric from TERFs, tend to present themselves as the benign voices of reason, simply standing up against the ideological tide of gender indoctrination.[13] The way that "gender paranoia" gets cloaked in reason and logic so as to launder itself through the liberal grinder is symptomatic of the Enlightenment construction of reason writ large—we might be reminded of Theodor W. Adorno and Max Horkheimer's (2002: 28) claim that the Enlightenment, in its pursuit of reason, becomes ever more steeped in unreason, so that the "curse of irresistible progress is irresistible regression." In any case, framing anti-gender actors as outdated, irrational, or extremist "blasts from the past" that might be countered by further embracing liberal humanist ideals not only lets the wannabe respectable, conservative anti-gender forces off the hook; it also leaves us without any tools for deconstructing or countering the heritage of coloniality that accompanies a recourse to Western progress narratives, rationality, or science—both in its homonationalist and anti-gender iterations.

I have shown that engaging postcolonial critique enables us to precisely gauge the ways in which European anti-gender rhetoric theorizes the body on multiple intertwined levels: those of the properly sexed body, the correctly racialized body, the national body, and, finally, "Fortress Europe," which together combine to construct the human body in whose name the actors speak. The strategic framing of (Eastern) Europeans as leaders and non-Western populations as followers in resisting Western "gender colonization" appeals to both a well-known geopolitical mapping of civilization along racialized vectors of (excessive/lacking) progress and the historical scientific construction of biology rooted in racialized plasticity. Yet again, this harkens back to the appeal to reason; the "achievement of rationality—a key component of civilization—is made possible only through the sex difference allegedly lacking in the racialized. Binary sex is both cause and effect of reason" (Schuller 2018: 15).

Paradoxically, the malleability that white, civilized subjects are imbued with can backfire; it is what makes white women and children particularly susceptible to being perverted and exploited by "gender ideologues" and "racialized others." The structural and biological conditions of the human thus decide who can be strategically and temporarily interpolated into a collective victimhood, and who decidedly and unequivocally is always already at the center. While I have limited myself to studying specific European anti-gender misappropriations of postcolonial rhetoric, it would be interesting to further analyze the dynamics of anti-gender misappropriations of postcolonial theory as seen from the perspective of how it plays out in various countries in the global South. This could shed new light on the trend from a perspective that moves beyond the European misuse of the non-Western world as a strategic, rhetorical ruse, as I discussed in this article. Hopefully, my analysis can function as a steppingstone in the attempts to deconstruct—and consequently resist—the new Right, not by searching for some stable foundation in liberal feminism we can all protect but, instead, by supporting the struggle to build a transfeminist, anti-racist counterhegemonic alternative.

Jenny Andrine Madsen Evang is a PhD candidate in modern thought and literature at Stanford University, where she is also pursuing PhD minors in gender and sexuality studies and comparative studies of race and ethnicity. Her research explores the relations among anti-gender movements, the rhetoric of gender equality, and homonationalisms by drawing on queer and trans theory, postcolonial studies, and critical race theory.

Acknowledgments

With the warmest thanks to the two anonymous peer reviewers, the guest editors of the special issue, and Míša Stekl for their invaluable comments on this manuscript.

Notes

1. This parenthesis in *(pre)colonial* is foreshadowing the crux of the argument in this article, namely, that the anti-gender thinkers are using the ruse of celebrating allegedly precolonial and traditional gender to advocate for what they are actually nostalgic for—a specific Western and colonial gendered order that could, after all, never be perfected in so-called non-Western contexts according to them. This structuring paradox rehearses the yearning that Renato Rosaldo (1989: 108) describes as "imperialist nostalgia"; the anti-gender agents seemingly "mourn the passing of what they themselves have transformed." The myth of some precolonial, natural binary gender untainted by the West—itself a product of colonial imagination—gives a guise of innocence to the colonial gendered epistemology that the anti-gender actors continuously enact.
2. The choice of the word *imported* is perhaps a bit unfortunate in this quotation, as it seems to suggest that the colonies simply invited the gender binary as a norm to be adopted—nevertheless, the main point, that the gender binary was a central feature and tactic of colonial oppression, stands.
3. As Sara Farris (2017: 11) importantly argues, "gender equality [is used as] a tool to depict male Others as sexual threats and female Others as sexual victims and as the property of western 'saviors.'" This "establishe[s] Europe as a mythical identity in opposition to the gendered, racial, religious, and cultural Other" who is metaphorically—and literally—up for grabs, to be (ab)used in order to reaffirm the purity and progressiveness of Western supremacy (Nay and Steinbock 2021: 148).
4. As Korolczuk and Graff (2018: 811) explain, "In the context of the [Polish] right-wing rally, the word 'Ebola' epitomized fear of the abject and the racial other."

5. See Jules Gill-Peterson's (2018) *Histories of the Transgender Child* for an in-depth decon-struction of the rhetoric of newness that haunts the trans* child.

6. See Eva Hayward's 2017 article "Don't Exist" for an exploration of this ontological rhetoric.

7. Nash and Browne (2020: 26) use the term *heteroactivism* to refer to "the organised resis-tances to sexual and gender politics that defines the sexual and gender politics of the 21st century" instead of the more commonly used *anti-gender movement*. They use this term to emphasize the complexity and differences among heteroactivist networks, and to avoid the naturalness and oversimplification of a geopolitical mapping of "progress" that would locate anti-gender politics in specific geographical, political, and religious places. While I have continued to use the term *anti-gender movement* in this article, I am nevertheless building on the insight of the nuances and heterogeneity of hetero-activist approaches that Nash and Browne bring to the fore.

8. As I argue elsewhere, despite what some anti-gender thinkers would have us believe, the antagonism between Islam and European societies is hardly absent from so-called gender ideology itself, in its "blind celebration" of multiculturalism; rather, this same antagonism often remains a central homonationalist tenet undergirding Islamophobic anti-immigration rhetoric in the name of protecting vulnerable sexual minorities (Evang, forthcoming).

9. See also Paternotte's (2020) discussion on the misleading use of the term *backlash* to describe the contemporary anti-gender movement.

10. While Eszter Kováts (2019) argues that it is essential to allow internal debates in the "progressive camp" rather than dispensing with them to embrace the lowest common denominator, she seems to refer to something decidedly different from what I have in mind. Echoing a TERF trope, she writes, "Whatever we may think of non-binary gender identities, one thing is certain: there is no consensus about them in the progressive camp, let alone in society. And when progressives call the fact that humans exist—except few exceptions, the intersexuals—as male or female, a right-wing ideology, as often happens, it should come as no surprise to them that a gap opens up between their agendas and the people within the societies they seek to represent" (2019). The internal differences she wants to debate seem to be around whether non-binary identities exist and should be accepted. She even suggests that pointing out the transphobic nature of biologizing discourse, that is, the claim that humans exist only as either male or female, is shooting ourselves in the foot, as it distances us from the people we allegedly "truly" want to represent. We might ask, with Gill-Peterson (2021), who is being sacrificed in the name of the people at "the altar of liberalism?" The answer seems pretty clear.

11. See Eve Kosofsky Sedgwick's canonical "How to Bring Your Kids up Gay" and Gill-Peterson's (2018) chapter alluding to Sedgwick, "How to Bring Your Kids up Trans," in her book *Histories of the Transgender Child*, for reference.

12. Looking at the caricature, one might also note that it seems to present her with somewhat androgynous traits—she looks aggressive and masculinized—reflecting the history of the anti-Black un/gendering of female flesh that Hortense Spillers (1987) theorizes.

13. A striking example of claiming this Enlightenment genealogy comes from the Twitter TERF @sationhund, who compares "gender critical" feminists being silenced if they don't accept that "sex is a spectrum" to Galileo Galilei being forced to "say that the sun went round the earth when he knew it did not" (see LMD 2021).

References

Adorno, Theodor W., and Max Horkheimer. 2002. *Dialectic of Enlightenment*. Translated by Edmund Jephcott. Stanford, CA: Stanford University Press.

Amundsen, Per-Willy. 2021. "Jeg feirer ikke Pride." Facebook, June 29. https://www.facebook.com /permalink.php?story_fbid=1154304328383041&id=176208612859289.

Battista, Stefano Di. 2017. "The New Language of Power Speaks in the Name of Gender." *Family and Media*, May 16. https://familyandmedia.eu/en/family-and-media-studies/the-new -language-of-power-speaks-in-the-name-of-gender-here-we-find-out-how-the-lobbies -have-set-the-agenda-of-many-countries-through-the-major-un-conferences/.

Berg, Tora Lind. 2021. "Langer ut mot Per-Willy Amundsen:—Han Bruker Skeive Muslimers Kropper som Slegge I Sin Kamp mot Islam" ("Argument against Per-Willy Amundsen— He Is Appropriating Muslim Bodies as a Weapon in His Fight against Islam"). *iTromsø*, July 2. https://itromso.no/nyheter/2021/07/02/Langer-ut-mot-Per-Willy-Amundsen---Han -bruker-skeive-muslimers-kropper-som-slegge-i-sin-kamp-mot-islam-24218905.ece.

Bracke, Sarah, and David Paternotte. 2016. "Unpacking the Sin of Gender." *Religion and Gender* 6, no. 2: 143–54. https://doi.org/10.18352/rg.10167.

Brydum, Sunnivie. 2017. "Right Wing Christians and Radical Feminists Form an Odd (Trans-phobic) Couple." *Religion Dispatches*, January 19. https://religiondispatches.org/right -wing-christians-and-radical-feminists-form-an-odd-transphobic-couple/.

Case, Mary Anne. 2019. "Trans Formations in the Vatican's War on 'Gender Ideology.'" *Signs* 44, no. 3: 639–64. https://doi.org/10.1086/701498.

Evang, Jenny Andrine Madsen. Forthcoming. "Anti-gender Politics in Queer Times: 'Gender-ismus' and Norwegian Homonationalism." *Lambda Nordica*.

Farris, Sara R. 2017. *In the Name of Women's Rights: The Rise of Femonationalism*. Durham, NC: Duke University Press.

Gera, Vanessa. 2019. "Party Leader Calls LGBT Rights an Imported Threat to Poland." *ABC News Network*, April 25. https://abcnews.go.com/International/wireStory/polish-leader-lgbt -rights-import-threatens-nation-62617985.

Gill-Peterson, Jules. 2018. *Histories of the Transgender Child*. Minneapolis: University of Minne-sota Press.

Gill-Peterson, Jules. 2021. "From Gender Critical to QAnon: Anti-trans Politics and the Laun-dering of Conspiracy." *New Inquiry*, September 13. https://thenewinquiry.com/from -gender-critical-to-qanon-anti-trans-politics-and-the-laundering-of-conspiracy/.

Glissant, Édouard. 1989. *Caribbean Discourse: Selected Essays*. Charlottesville: University Press of Virginia.

Graff, Agnieszka, Ratna Kapur, and Suzanna Danuta Walters. 2019. "Introduction: Gender and the Rise of the Global Right." *Signs* 44, no. 3: 541–60. https://doi.org/10.1086/701152.

Greenesmith, Heron. 2021. "Atheist Richard Dawkins Swings to Anti-trans Right in Grasp at Broader Intellectual Relevance." *Religion Dispatches*, November 30. https://religion dispatches.org/atheist-richard-dawkins-swings-to-anti-trans-right-in-grasp-at-broader -intellectual-relevance/.

Grzebalska, Weronika, Eszter Kováts, and Andrea Petö. 2017. "Gender as Symbolic Glue: How 'Gender' Became an Umbrella Term for the Rejection of the (Neo)Liberal Order." *Political Critique*, January 13. https://politicalcritique.org/long-read/2017/gender-as-symbolic-glue -how-gender-became-an-umbrella-term-for-the-rejection-of-the-neoliberal-order/.

Hayward, Eva S. 2017. "Don't Exist." *TSQ* 4, no. 2: 191–94. https://doi.org/10.1215/23289252 -3814985.

Hemmings, Clare. 2020. "Unnatural Feelings: The Affective Life of 'Anti-gender' Mobilisations." *Radical Philosophy*, no. 209: 27–39. https://radicalphilosophy.com/commentary/unnatural -feelings.

Korolczuk, Elżbieta, and Agnieszka Graff. 2018. "Gender as 'Ebola from Brussels': The Anti-colonial Frame and the Rise of Illiberal Populism." *Signs* 43, no. 4: 797–821. https://doi .org/10.1086/696691.

Kováts, Eszter. 2019. "New Courage Instead of New Taboos: Overcoming Dilemmas of Gender Politics in the EU." *Heinrich-Böll-Stiftung*, April 29. https://eu.boell.org/en/2019/04/29 /new-courage-instead-new-taboos-overcoming-dilemmas-gender-politics-eu.

Kuby, Gabriele. 2015. *The Global Sexual Revolution: Destruction of Freedom in the Name of Freedom*. Translated by James P. Kirchner. Kettering, OH: LifeSite.

Kuhar, Roman, and David Paternotte. 2017. Introduction to *Anti-gender Campaigns in Europe: Mobilizing against Equality*, edited by Roman Kuhar and David Paternotte, 1–23. London: Rowman and Littlefield International.

LMD (@sationhund). 2021. "Galileo was forced to say that the sun went round the earth when he knew it did not." Twitter, September 26, 5:03 p.m. https://twitter.com/Sationhund/status /1442233278862295041.

Lugones, Maria. 2016. "The Coloniality of Gender." In *The Palgrave Handbook of Gender and Development*, 13–33. London: Palgrave Macmillan UK. https://doi.org/10.1007/978-1-137 -38273-3_2.

Massillon, Julien. 2013. "Les affiches aux relents racistes de la 'manif pour tous'" ("The Racist Overtones of 'Manif pour Tous' Posters"). *KOMITID*, March 11. https://komitid.fr/2013 /03/11/les-affiches-aux-relents-racistes-de-la-manif-pour-tous/.

Mignolo, Walter D. 2011. *The Darker Side of Western Modernity: Global Futures, Decolonial Options*. Durham, NC: Duke University Press.

Mohanty, Chandra. 1988. "Under Western Eyes: Feminist Scholarship and Colonial Discourses." *Feminist Review* 30, no. 1: 61–88.

Nash, Catherine Jean, and Kath Browne. 2020. *Heteroactivism: Resisting Lesbian, Gay, Bisexual, and Trans Rights and Equalities*. London: Zed.

Nay, Yv E., and Eliza Steinbock. 2021. "Critical Trans Studies in and beyond Europe." *TSQ* 8, no. 2: 145–57. https://doi.org/10.1215/23289252-8890509.

O'Leary, Dale. 1997. *The Gender Agenda*. Lafayette, LA: Vital Issues.

Paternotte, David. 2020. "Backlash: A Misleading Narrative." London School of Economics blog, March 30. https://blogs.lse.ac.uk/gender/2020/03/30/backlash-a-misleading-narrative/.

Peeters, Marguerite A. 2011. "Interview with Marguerite A. Peeters on the Gender Theory." Interview by F. R. Zenit. *Pontificio Consiglio per i Laici*, September 28. http://www.laici .va/content/laici/en/sezioni/donna/notizie/interview-with-marguerite-a--peeters-on -the-gender-theory.html.

Peeters, Marguerite. 2012. "Towards Preserving the Universality of Human Rights." *EWTN Global Catholic Television Network*, March 9. https://ewtn.com/catholicism/library/towards -preserving-the-universality-of-human-rights-2672.

Peeters, Marguerite. 2016. "Protecting Christian Values in Central and Eastern Europe and Beyond." *Religious Information Service of Ukraine*, June 10. https://risu.ua/en/protecting-christian -values-in-central-and-eastern-europe-and-beyond_n79933.

Puar, Jasbir K. 2007. *Terrorist Assemblages: Homonationalism in Queer Times*. Durham, NC: Duke University Press.

Redecker, Eva von. 2016. "Anti-Genderismus and Right-Wing Hegemony." *Radical Philosophy*, no. 198. https://www.radicalphilosophyarchive.com/issue-files/rp198_commentary_redecker_anti_genderismus.pdf.

Rosaldo, Renato. 1989. "Imperialist Nostalgia." *Representations*, no. 26: 107–22. https://doi.org/10.2307/2928525.

Sarah, Robert, 2015. "ISIS and Gender Ideology Are Like 'Apocalyptic Beasts.'" *National Catholic Register*, October 12. https://www.ncregister.com/blog/cardinal-sarah-isis-and-gender-ideology-are-like-apocalyptic-beasts.

Sedgwick, Eve K. 1998. "How to Bring Your Kids Up Gay." In *The Children's Culture Reader*, 231–40. New York: NYU Press.

Schuller, Kyla. 2018. *The Biopolitics of Feeling: Race, Sex, and Science in the Nineteenth Century.* Durham, NC: Duke University Press.

Siddiqui, Sophia. 2021."Feminism, Biological Fundamentalism, and the Attack on Trans Rights." *Institute of Race Relations*, June 3. https://irr.org.uk/article/feminism-biological-fundamentalism-attack-on-trans-rights/.

Spillers, Hortense J. 1987. "Mama's Baby, Papa's Maybe: An American Grammar Book." *Diacritics* 17, no. 2: 65–81.

Spivak, Gayatri Chakravorty. (1988) 2015. "Can the Subaltern Speak?" In *Colonial Discourse and Post-colonial Theory*, edited by Patrick Williams and Laura Chrisman, 66–111. https://doi.org/10.4324/9781315656496-13.

Tudor, Alyosxa. 2021. "Decolonizing Trans/Gender Studies?" *TSQ* 8, no. 2: 238–56. https://doi.org/10.1215/23289252-8890523.

Wang, Esther. 2019a. "Of Course TERFs Have Found Common Cause with White Nationalists." *Jezebel*, October 17. https://jezebel.com/of-course-terfs-have-found-common-cause-with-white-nati-1839129243.

Wang, Esther. 2019b. "The Unholy Alliance of Trans-exclusionary Radical Feminists and the Right Wing." *Jezebel*, May 9. https://jezebel.com/the-unholy-alliance-of-trans-exclusionary-radical-femin-1834120309.

Weheliye, Alexander. 2014. *Habeas Viscus: Racializing Assemblages, Biopolitics, and Black Feminist Theories of the Human.* Durham, NC: Duke University Press.

Wynter, Sylvia. 2003. "Unsettling the Coloniality of Being/Power/Truth/Freedom: Towards the Human, after Man, Its Overrepresentation—An Argument." *CR: The New Centennial Review* 3, no. 3: 257–337.

TERF or Transfeminist Avant la Lettre?

Monique Wittig's Complex Legacy in Trans Studies

BLASE A. PROVITOLA

Abstract French lesbian author and theorist Monique Wittig's early contestations of woman as the subject of feminism have played an important role in gender studies in both anglophone and francophone spaces. Since the mid-1990s, French lesbian studies scholars and queer theorists alike have looked to her to anchor their contestations of normative sexuality within a French tradition and counter some of the universalizing aspects of Anglocentric queer theory. As a result, polarizing debates have sprung up over interpretations of Wittigian political lesbianism, typically focusing on divergent readings of her theorization of sex and gender between radical lesbians on the one hand and queer theorists on the other. However, far less attention has been paid to the implications of such debates for transgender studies. Since she has been claimed by trans-exclusionary radical feminists as well as by queer and materialist transfeminists in France, her legacy serves as a rich site through which to understand how the ideological conflicts between those groups relate to feminist history. Taking as a point of departure the appropriation of her name by the anti-trans group Résistance Lesbienne (Lesbian Resistance) that took over the 2021 Paris Pride March, this article fleshes out the implications of her work concerning the place of transgender people, and especially transgender women, in feminist spaces. Ultimately, it is her complexity that makes her a crucial figure for transgender studies insofar as she elucidates French "gender-critical" feminism and its transfeminist critics.
Keywords Monique Wittig, transfeminism, radical lesbianism, queer theory, materialist feminism

> Make an effort to remember. Or, failing that, invent.
> —Monique Wittig, *Les Guérillères*

At the Paris Gay Pride parade on June 26, 2021, a group calling itself Résistance Lesbienne (Lesbian Resistance) temporarily took the lead of the march, sporting banners reading "Lesbians don't have penises" and "Lesbians need feminism, not mutilating transitions." This group of self-identified "radical lesbian feminists," inspired by the Get The L Out movement that appeared at London Pride in 2018, attributes lesbian erasure and oppression to the very existence of transgender people. In an online manifesto, Résistance Lesbienne

TSQ: Transgender Studies Quarterly ★ Volume 9, Number 3 ★ August 2022 **387**
DOI 10.1215/23289252-9836050 © 2022 Duke University Press

(2021b) presents consensual lesbian sex between cis and trans women as "rape culture against lesbians," and it defines medical transition undertaken by transmasculine people as a form of false consciousness presented in "queer milieus" as "the only solution to a discontent fundamentally created by men's misogyny and lesbophobia."[1] During the march, this rhetorical violence translated into concrete threats against trans women: when a prominent activist for migrant, trans, and sex workers' rights—herself a trans woman—intervened to tear down one of their banners, she was led away by police, who reportedly threatened to revoke her residency permit.[2] Queer and Trans People of Color Autonomes Paris (2021) was one of several activist collectives to denounce the ideological affinities between the Far Right and this self-proclaimed group of radical feminists, opposing their attempts to "co-opt feminism and lesbianism in service of their own fascist aims, to the detriment of those who are most minoritized within and representative of our communities."

In France trans-exclusionary radical feminists' (TERFs) rhetoric of sexual difference sometimes overlaps with that of the Catholic Right. Catholic conservatives, who have been particularly vocal since debates about same-sex civil partnerships in the late 1990s, hit a fever pitch in the 2010s when the Manif Pour Tous (Protest For All) movement formed in opposition to same-sex marriage (known as *mariage pour tous* or marriage for all), as well as education reforms that would incorporate basic notions of gender equality into curricula nationwide. Scholars have analyzed the influence of psychoanalytic and structuralist theory on the nation's sanctioned conception of sexual difference (Robcis 2013), and they have detailed the conservatives' defense of sexual complementarity and their attack on gender studies, often caricatured in mainstream media outlets as a dangerous American imposition (Fassin 1999; Perreau 2016). Some have argued that French feminists have paradoxically naturalized the category of woman as the subject of feminism (Scott 1996), with others suggesting that queer feminism offers an alternative and more progressive vision of gender politics (Guénif Souilamas and Macé 2004; Bourcier 2006). However, less attention has been devoted to French transfeminist[3] activists' and scholars' responses to transphobic discourses of sexual difference in feminist subcultures—responses that sometimes seek political forebears in the very same figures that tend to be claimed by TERFs.

In France both TERFs and transfeminist thinkers looking to ground their arguments in a French theoretical tradition have evoked lesbian feminist Monique Wittig. Résistance Lesbienne released a statement on social media prominently featuring a quote from Wittig's feminist classic *Les Guérillères*: "Make an effort to remember. Or, failing that, invent" (1971: 89).[4] Taken out of context, that citation might appear ironic given that the Paris-based feminist and transgender organization OUTrans cites Wittig as an inspiration thanks to her early critique of the political subject of woman as the basis of feminism.[5] As a transgender Wittig scholar, I have been tempted to defend her legacy against what I have judged to be transphobic appropriations—if not outright misreadings—of her work, in order to show the opportunities that her thought offers for trans liberation. This is partially what I sought to do at the "Drafting Wittig" conference hosted by Yale University in October 2019, which marked the fiftieth anniversary of *Les Guér-illères'* publication. As the only openly transgender speaker at the conference, I was eager to present Wittig as a proto-transfeminist theorist in the face of a few attendees who I knew supported the exclusion of trans people from certain feminist and lesbian spaces in Paris. After my panel, however, one attendee—a prominent French writer and admirer of Wittig's work—responded by asserting that trans women "appropriate" women's experiences to an audience who, myself included, voiced no protest.

This article is in part an attempt to break my silence in the face of the transmisogyny voiced that day. My failure to speak up was not because I doubted that I could mobilize Wittig to defend trans people, but because I knew that Wittig, like many other materialist feminists, was sometimes instrumentalized by TERFs, especially in their attacks against trans women. Some part of me felt that if she could be turned against trans people, then it must mean that her thought lends itself to trans-exclusionary interpretations. In this article, I have taken what began as a desire to neatly defend her as a transfeminist, turning it into a reflection on what it means for a figure to have inspired both the most virulently transphobic radical feminists and the most vocally trans-inclusive queer feminists. Thus, rather than performing a close reading of Wittig's oeuvre to reduce it to a single meaning, I take the polysemy of her theoretical and literary work as symptomatic of some of the ongoing tensions between materialist feminism and queer theory. At a time when the need to drown out TERFs has sometimes understandably led to a simplistic opposition between transphobic materialist feminism and purportedly trans-inclusive queer theory, I take a closer look at a figure who has been claimed by both schools of thought to argue that it is often unproductive to either defend past figures as trans friendly or cast them out as transphobic; rather, it is often messiness and ambivalence that allow for an informed and nuanced application of past figures' thought to contemporary political contexts. For me, revisiting Wittig in her many guises has, in a roundabout way, become a conduit through which to understand the complex and shifting landscape of contemporary transfeminisms.

By giving a glimpse into the controversies sparked by Wittig's ideas, this article shows that debates predating the rise of transfeminism have influenced the development of both queer and materialist transfeminisms in France, including their responses to materialist feminist transphobia. Each section's title represents an intellectual movement that Wittig has influenced: materialist feminism and radical lesbianism, queer transfeminism, and materialist transfeminism. The first section shows how the marginalization of Wittig's theorization of sex/gender in France in the 1970s and 1980s laid the groundwork for materialist feminists' subsequent rejection of so-called gender theory and the transgender people with which it is mistakenly associated. I examine that "gender-critical" backlash in the second section, in which I outline the emergence of a Wittigian queer transfeminism that materialist feminists charge with depoliticizing feminism altogether. In the third and final section, I delve into recent controversies about "woman-only" spaces, which have been the site of confrontations not only between materialist TERFs and queer transfeminists but also between queer transfeminists and an emerging group of materialist transfeminists that differently harness Wittigian lesbianism to combat transphobia and transmisogyny. While the brevity of this article means that I cannot do justice to the complex and multifaceted nature of each movement I discuss, I hope the reader will nonetheless come away with a sense of the nuanced and exciting work that Wittig continues to inspire.

Materialist Feminism and Radical Lesbianism

Trans-exclusionary radical feminism is a transnational movement insofar as groups with common aims and ideological references have sprung up across Europe and North America. This section's overview of radical feminism in France lends important context to contemporary conflicts between TERFs and transfeminists and helps explain why Wittig, as I shall demonstrate in later sections, has remained an important reference in French transfeminism today. Revisiting this history also counteracts the US academy's limited conception of so-called French feminism, a term that has come to be synonymous with psychoanalytically influenced theorists of language and femininity (namely, Hélène Cixous, Luce Irigaray, and Julia Kristeva) despite the fact that they do not all identify as feminists and have for decades been critiqued as essentialists by radical feminists (Moses 1998; Delphy 2000; Costello 2016).

In France, what are often referred to as "second-wave" feminisms grew out of the leftist groups associated with May 1968.[6] In 1970, after the founding of the Mouvement de libération des femmes (Women's Liberation Movement, MLF), the movement quickly became divided between various reformist and radical tendencies. Radical feminism primarily took the form of what we today refer to as materialist feminism, which uses the tools of Marxism to theorize women's oppression from an anticapitalist perspective without subordinating women's struggles to class struggle. Though each strand of French materialist feminism has its own nuanced perspective, its main tenets—outlined in the theories of figures like Christine Delphy, Colette Guillaumin, Nicole-Claude Mathieu, and Wittig—include the views that the binary sexes are comparable to social classes,

that the social construction of the sexes is naturalized to justify the appropriation of the class of women by the class of men, and that feminism must be
revolutionary and anticapitalist (Mathieu 1991; Guillaumin 1992; Wittig 1992;
Delphy 1998). However, Wittig's place among the canon of materialist feminist
thinkers is often minimized, and today she is claimed primarily by radical lesbians associated with the lesbian archives in Paris (Archives Recherches Cultures
Lesbiennes) and the now-defunct Franco-Canadian journal *Amazones d'hier,*
lesbiennes d'aujourd'hui (*Amazons of Yesterday, Lesbians of Today*).

After cofounding the MLF, Wittig broke with it in part because she made
the structural critique of heterosexuality—and not just patriarchy—a central
part of her political philosophy. She then went on to form autonomous lesbian
groups such as the Paris-based Gouines Rouges (Red Dykes, 1971–73) and the
short-lived Front Lesbien International (International Lesbian Front) following
the International Feminist Conference in Frankfurt in 1974. She is known for her
literary experimentations with gender and language: scholars have explored the
epicene pronoun *on* in *The Opoponax*, the universalization of the traditionally
feminine third-person plural pronoun *elles* in *Les Guérillères*, and the fragmen-
tation of the first-person singular pronoun *je* (*j/e*) in *The Lesbian Body* (Ostrovsky
1991; Shaktini 2005; Bourque 2006; Davis 2010; Robin 2011). Yet her influential
conception of lesbianism beyond gender faced such tremendous backlash from
feminists in France that Wittig left for the United States in 1976: "They almost
managed to destroy me entirely and, yes, they drove me out of Paris" (Wittig
quoted in Eloit 2020: 135). This is why her activist and theoretical writings were
compiled and published in English for the first time in 1992 as *The Straight Mind*.

Even after her departure, disagreements about the category of sex within
feminism contributed to a growing schism between materialist feminists, who
viewed all women as part of a united, oppressed class, and radical lesbians, whose
political identity, heavily influenced by Wittig's writings, critiqued the system of
heterosexuality and the binary sexes on which it depends. Her pathbreaking essays
"The Straight Mind" and "One Is Not Born a Woman," originally published in
1980 in the materialist feminist journal *Questions féministes* (*Feminist Questions,*
QF), defined heterosexuality as a political and economic institution that per-
petuates itself by producing the so-called natural binary sexes. Heterosexuality is
rooted in the "obligatory social relationship between 'man' and 'woman,'" whose
"characteristic is ineluctability in culture, as well as in nature," dividing humanity
into two unequal and naturalized sexes (Wittig 1992: 27; 2013: 62).[7] Like Karl Marx's
view of the social classes, Wittig's vision of the social sexes seeks to eliminate
the category of sex as an organizing principle of society. The only way to resist
the category of woman is to politically become a lesbian, such that the sexual
categories produced by the "straight mind" are no longer operative: "It would

be incorrect to say that lesbians associate, make love, or live with women, for 'woman' has meaning only in heterosexual systems of thought and heterosexual economic systems. Lesbians are not women" (1992: 32; 2013: 67). Just as the revolutionary proletariat has the potential to revolt against the ruling classes and destroy the class system altogether, lesbians can work against heterosexual epistemology and create a more just social and economic world that does not depend on the hierarchical binary sexes.

In the same issue of *QF* in which "The Straight Mind" first appeared, Emmanuelle de Lesseps (1980: 66) published an essay taking issue with certain strands of political lesbianism for their presumption that heterosexuality is necessarily anti-feminist: "It is not heterosexuality that is the problem; it is oppression. One cannot conflate the two in a single concept."[8] Though her essay was meant to critique the condescending universalism of some American lesbian feminists, de Lesseps's reduction of heterosexuality to a sexual preference appeared to many as an attack on Wittig's definition of heterosexuality as a political system. In 1980, disagreements on the relationship between lesbianism and feminism contributed to the dissolution of *QF,* whose editorial board split between those who, like Wittig, conceived of lesbianism as "the only way to abolish the classes of sex" and those who, like de Lesseps and Delphy, conceived of lesbianism as a sexual orientation and remained "attached to the universal subject of woman" (Pavard, Rochefort, and Zancarini-Fournel 2020: 329). In 1981 the latter group would go on, much to the former group's dismay, to found, with the support of Simone de Beauvoir, what continues to be the most prominent materialist feminist journal in France: *Nouvelles questions féministes* (*New Feminist Questions, NQF*).

As a result, it is not until recently that feminist historians have traced the influence of Monique Wittig's antiessentialist political lesbianism on early contestations of the category of sex as the basis of feminism (Chetcuti and Michard 2003; Eloit 2019, 2020). Instead, Wittig continues to be classified as a sex-based separatist, even by materialist feminists who otherwise share many of her views. Indeed, if Delphy positively reviewed Wittig's *Across the Acheron* in *NQF* in 1985, it was in part because she read it as a metacommentary on Wittig's past shortcomings: "Manastabal's dialogue is a far cry from the separatist discourse we knew!" (155). Though Delphy insists that feminist conflicts with so-called lesbian separatist groups were often unrelated to Wittig's influence, she nonetheless affirmed that "One Is Not Born a Woman" contained "the seeds of the separatist position" (152). Delphy (1998), whose theory that social gender hierarchy produced the so-called natural sexes had influenced Wittig, viewed her critiques of heterosexuality as divisive among the class of women. For many, however, what was really at stake was whether the class of "woman" should constitute the subject of feminism, and whether lesbians in fact operate within or beyond the binary sex system (Brossard 2003).

Those conflicts led to her erasure from French feminist history beginning in the early 1980s (Möser 2013: 70–72). As the following remarks from a recent volume on the topic make clear, Wittig is often framed as a failed lesbian separatist, influential only insofar as she is a precursor to queer theory:

> Monique Wittig's position is thus in the minority and marginalized in 1980. If she marks a rupture for the small circle of Parisian militants who had been close to her since the start of the MLF, her position finds little echo beyond that. It does not give way at the time to a radical separation of lesbians from the feminist movement. Nevertheless, through the theoretical split that she proposes with woman as the political subject of feminism, Wittig foreshadows the queer evolutions of the following decade. (Pavard, Rochefort, and Zancarini-Fournel 2020: 330)[9]

If Wittig's association with sex-based separatism contributed to her marginalization within French materialist feminist historiography, Judith Butler's (1990) well-known interpretation of her work in *Gender Trouble* subsequently acted as a double-edged sword. On the one hand, it led to renewed interest in her work. On the other hand, Butler's interpretation—while more thoughtful and generous than those of many others—ultimately reinforced existing misperceptions of Wittigian lesbianism by calling it a form of "separatist prescriptivism" that is "surely no longer viable" (162). Many queer studies scholars have followed in Butler's footsteps.[10] This is why Brad Epps and Jonathan Katz (2007: 444), in their introduction to the special issue of *GLQ* memorializing Wittig after her untimely death in 2003, refuse to dismiss her as "an essentialist, a utopianist, a nondialectical separatist, and so on." At the same time, they also acknowledge that "there is no easy alliance between Wittig and queer theory" (433). However, many queer studies scholars in France have worked hard to establish such an alliance, in part in the name of trans inclusion. As the following section demonstrates, queer theorists inspired by Wittig's ambivalence to the category of woman would go on to play an important role in French debates on the place of transgender people in feminism, and they would be met with TERF backlash that in some ways resembles that which Wittig had faced at the hands of materialist feminists decades prior.

Queer Transfeminism

Wittig's ambivalence to the category of woman—and materialist feminist resistance to it—would go on to influence the development of transfeminism in France. If in their introduction to *TSQ*'s special double issue titled "Trans/Feminisms"

Susan Stryker and Talia M. Bettcher (2016: 11) state that, in English, transfeminism "usually connotes a 'third wave' feminist sensibility that focuses on the personal empowerment of women and girls, embraced in an expansive way that includes trans women and girls," they also recognize that its definition varies culturally and geographically. In that same issue, Karine Espineira and Sam Bourcier (2016) situate multiple genealogies of contemporary French transfeminism, including anglophone third wave feminisms, French contributions to queer theory in the late 1990s, and grassroots movements in Spain. One year earlier, prominent transfeminist sociologist Maud-Yeuse Thomas (2015: 62) wrote that it was only when intersex and trans issues began to be combined with "the interdisciplinary knowledge of *studies (postcolonial, subaltern, gender)*" that there appeared "a trans identity [une transidentité] linked to the political resistance of Monique Wittig." Influenced by anglophone interdisciplinary areas of study that have received little institutional recognition in France, queer studies scholars returned to Wittig as they sought to ground gender studies in French feminist history.

Founded in 1996, Le Zoo was the first officially "queer" academic group to exist in France. It organized a series of seminars in the Paris region dedicated to the translation of foundational queer theorists (such as Judith Butler and Teresa De Lauretis) as well as the seminal French authors who influenced them. Amid the male-dominated canon of poststructuralist and deconstructionist thinkers like Gilles Deleuze, Jacques Derrida, and Michel Foucault, Wittig stood out as a prominent lesbian thinker who anchored the politicization of sexual identity in a French materialist feminist tradition (Bourcier 1998: 132). Butler's interpretation of her work in *Gender Trouble*, while widely critiqued, nonetheless led to renewed interest in *The Straight Mind* in particular, which had never been published in its entirety in French. Some queer studies scholars in France began to reframe Wittig's challenge to sexual difference as a defense of various forms of gender subversion.

Sam Bourcier, who helped translate *The Straight Mind* into French, co-organized a 2001 seminar on Wittig's work following its publication.[11] Their preface presents Wittig as a maverick of gender nonconformity: "Only Wittig no longer prescribed identification as a woman, leaving the door open to bearded lesbians" (Wittig 2013: 33).[12] Wittig was, after all, no stranger to gender bending, having apparently been known as Théo to her close friends. As Bourcier has progressively critiqued anglophone queer theory in favor of a queer-inflected transfeminism, so too has Wittig been implicitly positioned as a transfeminist avant la lettre. Bourcier's (2017: 12) most recent book begins with their intention to draw out "the trans* side" of Wittig's theory, to reclaim her philosophy for "trans* people, queer people, and transfeminists," whose coalitional politics shares a commitment to combatting "cis-straight thought."

In a similar vein, Paul Preciado (2000: 27) dedicated his *Countersexual Manifesto* to Wittig, designating gender outlaws of all stripes ("the faggot, the fairy, the drag queen, the lesbian, the dyke, the bull dyke [*la camionneuse*], the tomboy, the butch, F2Ms and M2Fs, transgenders")[13] as examples of what Wittig would characterize as "ontological jokes" on the straight mind. The original French edition states that, in countersexual society, such bodies would even be called "*lesbian bodies* or 'wittigs' [*des corps lesbiens* ou '*wittigs*']" (39).[14] Preciado has repeatedly evoked the apocryphal anecdote according to which, during a talk at Vassar College, Wittig responded to a cheeky question from an audience member by stating that she did not have a vagina. Preciado (2002: 205–6) remains inspired by what Wittig subsequently denied having ever said: "By locating oneself outside of the regimes of straight sexuality, one can say that one does not have a vagina and thus does not have a body that can be called 'woman.'"[15] Aren't many trans people grappling with the same refusal to accept the cultural translation of their skin? If the *elles* of *Les Guérillères* was never a group of women but rather a group of people refusing the category of sex, and if *The Lesbian Body* parodied any attempt at narrowly defining the very object of its title, then aren't trans people the logical extension of her project, the ultimate "runaways" from the universalist regime of sexual difference? This line of thinking has informed queer theorists and activists who push Wittig's arguments to their logical transfeminist conclusion to defend trans people's presence in feminist spaces.

Some of the same materialist feminists who rejected Wittig's theorization of the sexes would also go on to wholesale reject queer theory—and trans people—in the name of protecting feminism. Nicole-Claude Mathieu (2014: 25) dismissed transsexuals as dupes of the patriarchy's naturalization of the sexes. In a 2013 interview Delphy infamously stated that, ever since the "question of transsexuality" has come to play a more central role in feminism, "we lose sight of the feminist struggle to rid of gender."[16] The supposed "individualism of the queer movement" has allowed people to "change sex, without questioning those categories," which, for her, "does not constitute a political fight." That same year, Delphy was the only French signatory of an international statement signed by dozens of radical feminists protesting the rise of "gender studies": "With a huge boost from the 'new' academic theory coming out of those programs, heavily influenced by postmodernism, 'gender identity' has overwhelmed—when not denying completely—the theory that biological women are oppressed and exploited as a class by men and by capitalists due to their reproductive capacity" (Hanisch et al. 2013). For an increasingly vocal minority of radical feminists, gender identity as a concept and transgender people as an embodiment of that concept pose a threat to a materialist feminist analysis of the oppression of the class of "biological women" (to use the statement's term) at the hands of the class of men.

Delphy has more recently endorsed TERF discourse targeting trans lesbians in particular. On August 1, 2017, she reposted a French translation of J. J. Barnes's (2017) article "Lesbianism Is under Attack, though Not by the Usual Suspects," specifying that this time it is a "liberal-friendly kind of bullying that condemns lesbians for not embracing sex with people who have penises on the grounds of discrimination."[17] The French translation, which includes more gendered nouns and adjectives, intentionally misgenders trans women by referring to them in the masculine. Given that Résistance Lesbienne (2021a) ventriloquizes the arguments of Barnes, it is unsurprising that Delphy republished their statement regarding the 2021 Pride Parade. If Delphy's materialism was initially based on a rejection of biologism, it is now the so-called biological woman who must be protected. According to Ilana Eloit (2019: 397), French feminists' hostility to queer theory echoes their resistance to Wittig's theorization of heterosexuality: "In a sense, gender theories repeated in English for a French audience what had forcefully been made unspeakable in French in the MLF: that heterosexuality is . . . an oppressive regime of power through which oppositional and naturalised gendered positions are stabilized." Delphy's anti-trans rhetoric in the 2010s echoes the anti-lesbian rhetoric of the early 1980s: those critical of the naturalized division of the sexes are charged with anti-feminism, and those who refuse the false neutrality of problematic so-called sexual preferences are accused of coercing women into having sex with (trans) women.

Transfeminist responses to Delphy in turn recall Wittig's resistance to materialist feminists, whom she saw as depoliticizing the issue of heterosexuality. In 1983, with the materialist feminist protection of heterosexual sexual difference fresh on her mind, Wittig wrote, "*Desire:* that cliché that every woman slips into to avoid looking at it too closely . . . What remains unclear is how there could ever be an exquisite essence of 'female heterosexual desire' . . . that would flutter about the landscape to embalm her far, far away from the political categories and classes of sexes that we should be destroying" (13).[18] Over thirty years later, bloggers also responded to Delphy by politicizing desire: "One can and must state that our desires are constructed, and that yes, for many, we are fatphobic, ableist, racist, transphobic etc in our desires. Does that mean that we should 'force ourselves' [i.e., to have sex with any particular person]? Absolutely not."[19] However, materialist feminists in the early 1980s and TERFs today take the above statements to mean that individuals should immediately alter their sexual behavior; lesbians (by definition cis) should sleep with trans women, and women (by definition cis) should stop sleeping with men (also presumed to be cis). What Wittig and Wittigian queer transfeminists are really asking, though, is that individuals look critically at the social structures that produce such "preferences" in the first place—a claim that should hardly be shocking to materialist feminists.

Perhaps even more surprisingly, some radical lesbians who have defended Wittig against charges of separatism have adopted a similarly transphobic agenda—largely in service of protecting Wittig's legacy from supposed queer misreadings of her work. As Louise Turcotte puts it in her otherwise astute introduction to the 2013 French edition of *The Straight Mind*, the notion of "*gender*" (cited in English in her text) gave way in the 1990s to "another trend, that of '*transgender*,' more often called '*queer theory*,'" whose insistence that gender can be changed "can only consolidate the categories of sex and gender" (in Wittig 2013: 21). Such summaries conflate queer theory with not only transgender studies but also transgender people themselves, ensuring Wittig's status as first and foremost a lesbian and materialist thinker. Given that Wittig came to blows with materialist feminists like Delphy over the question of sexual difference, it is highly ironic that both materialist feminists and radical lesbians have come to agree on one thing: transgender liberation, like the concept of gender itself, is a threat to feminism, and trans women's mere presence threatens women's spaces. It is to the latter idea that I will now turn as I explore why queer transfeminism has been critiqued not just by materialist TERFs but also by an emerging wave of materialist transfeminists who agree that queer theory's focus on individual identity threatens materialist feminism—and also believe that it depoliticizes trans issues.

Materialist Transfeminism

Trans access to feminist spaces has been an ongoing site of conflict between trans-inclusive feminists and TERFs, and France is no exception. The French term *mixité* typically refers to the social mixing of genders (though it sometimes refers to the mixing of other social groups). Some feminist spaces, such as Paris's international lesbian feminist film festival (Cineffable), have a "woman-only" policy, designated by the phrase *non-mixité entre femmes* (literally meaning nonmixing between women). Though such organizations do not explicitly adhere to a single definition of what it means to be a lesbian, a feminist, or even a woman, their gender policies are rooted in the materialist feminist view that the heterosociality of gender-mixed spaces oppresses women regardless of the individual intentions of those present. Every year, entitled cisgender men take a reactionary stance against this feminist principle on Cineffable's Facebook page. Some queer transfeminists have taken issue with "woman-only" spaces for a different reason: they demand that the festival adopt the policy, common at some queer events, to welcome all genders except for cis men, sometimes indicated by the phrase *non-mixité meufs gouines trans* (nonmixing [between] women, dykes, trans people).[20] As one blogger put it, "Patriarchy isn't just cis guys on top exploiting the women below them. Patriarchy is something where cis guys exploit *non*-cisguys."[21] In such debates about *non-mixité*, an emergent materialist transfeminism, partially inspired by Wittig, has challenged the idea that materialism is necessarily at odds with trans inclusion.

In November 2018 two self-identified transgender lesbian feminists, one of them writing under the tongue-in-cheek pen name Delphine Christy, defended Cineffable's woman-only policy against its queer critics. On their blog, tellingly titled *Questions trans et féministes* (QTF), they recognize the relevance of woman-only spaces as well as its Wittigian critics, while also implying that certain TERFs appropriate such critiques to their own ends:

> This turn of phrase [woman-only] is often critiqued, (rightly) considered misogynist by radical feminists who refuse, in the tradition of the *Radicalesbians* or Monique Wittig, the fact that women are asked to "identify" with their dehumanized status. Sometimes, this critique is in bad faith and those who bring it forward, calling themselves a part of the *gender-critical* movement, are actually only looking to point the finger at the presence of trans women in their milieus. More rarely, it is taken up by trans activists who consider themselves *materialist* or *radical*.[22]

In other words, for trans activists in the materialist feminist tradition, Wittig's definition of the category of woman is not in itself transmisogynist, but it has sometimes been instrumentalized to transmisogynist ends. However, for *QTF*, woman-only spaces like Cineffable remain "precious" because they, unlike queer spaces, resist the "degendering [*dégenrage*] that deprives them of any radicalness and revolutionary substance" and that results from analyzing women's oppression through the lens of the broader term *gender*.[23] Like Delphy and Mathieu, they are concerned by queer transfeminism's shift away from a focus on women, be they cis or trans, which may lead to unacknowledged transmisogyny in self-proclaimed "trans-friendly" queer spaces. As one blogger and self-identified trans woman concisely put it, there is still "the primacy of cisgender women over transmasculine people, who are themselves more highly regarded than transfeminine people" (*L'écho des sorcières* 2015: 25).[24]

While this cissexist and transmisogynist hierarchy is hardly foreign to queer spaces in the United States, anglophone transfeminisms have sometimes appeared better equipped to deal with it, owing to the focus on combating transmisogyny in foundational works such as Julia Serano's *Whipping Girl* and Emi Koyama's "Transfeminist Manifesto." In *Cahiers de la transidentité*'s 2015 issue titled "Transféminismes," one contributor stated that, unlike its "twin sister of Anglo-Saxon transfeminism," French transfeminism does not currently offer the same tools for fighting misogyny because it has thus far been less focused on "affirming the existence of trans women/lesbians and their legitimacy in feminist movements" than on "including in feminist movements people who are not women/lesbians (notably trans men, transmasculine people, transgender people, genderqueer people, non-binary trans people, etc.) and their issues (notably around gender, the man/woman binary, masculinities, etc.)" (Grüsig 2015: 32).[25] This form of transfeminism is qualified as *franchouillard*, a slang, pejorative adjective defined by the Larousse dictionary as "exhibiting the flaws traditionally attributed to the average French person (especially chauvinism, narrow-mindedness)," which suggests that there is something distinctly French about transfeminism's shift to focus on nonwomen.[26] Could it be that queer transfeminism's reliance on Wittig in part accounts for this so-called "narrow-mindedness"? After all, it seems more than coincidental that, as is clear in the work of Bourcier and Preciado, Wittig tends to be mobilized by transmasculine theorists seeking to move the subject of feminism beyond the binary sexes. Though this intends to make space for all non-cisgender people in feminist movements, it often does more to justify the presence of trans men than it does to justify the presence of trans women. As Jacob Hale wrote in "Are Lesbians Women?" (1996: 116–17), the space that Wittig creates for subjectivity beyond sexual difference "loosens the stranglehold, coming from both the dominant culture and also from some versions of cultural and radical feminism, of nonconsensual gender on those birth-designated females who have felt profound discomfort at being in, being placed by others within, or proclaiming themselves to be within, the category *woman*." However, when "birth-designated females" who refuse that designation look to Wittig to understand their role in feminist spaces, they sometimes unwittingly ignore how some of those same arguments can be used at the expense of trans women (and transfeminine people in general).

The need for new theoretical tools to combat transmisogyny motivated Noémie Grunenwald—the same person cited above as critiquing queer transfeminism's focus on nonwomen—to translate *Whipping Girl*. In her preface to the translation, she notes that up until that point it had been practically unheard of to see trans women's struggles viewed first and foremost as women's struggles: "This shift in approach changed everything. From then on it was possible to examine trans women's issues through a long history of feminist theorization, activism, disagreement, and solidarity. And strictly queer approaches were no longer the sole options available" (Grunenwald 2020: 10).[27] Transfeminists are reclaiming materialist feminist thought, including certain critiques of queer approaches; in this case, however, they are critical of the latter not because they are equated with trans identity but, rather, because they do not allow for a robust understanding of trans women's experiences.

Especially since the 2010s, voices like Grunenwald's, which had previously been scattered across blogs and zines, have coalesced into a political philosophy that I will broadly refer to as materialist transfeminism. In 2021 Grunenwald and

Pauline Clochec (2021) (a contributing writer to *QTF*) edited *Matérialismes trans* (*Trans Materialisms*), which grew out of a symposium on March 30, 2019, at the École Normale Supérieure of Lyon. This is the first volume in France to approach trans studies and activism through the lens of materialist feminism. Though the diversity of contributions is meant to encourage new lines of inquiry rather than present a unified political program, Clochec's introduction presents some of the overarching concerns and principles that led to the volume's creation: the need to overcome liberalism's grasp on trans personhood through the concept of "gender identity," a dissatisfaction with queer theory's individualistic and discursive approach to gender, and the refusal to throw the materialist baby out with the TERF bathwater.[28] For Clochec (2021: 37) the problem with Mathieu and Delphy is that they "present a cissexist criticism of transness [*transitude*], as well as a rejection of the participation of trans women in feminism, as the supposed corollary of an otherwise pertinent critique of queer theories."

In the fight to disentangle queer theory from transfeminism, Delphy, Guillaumin, Mathieu, and Wittig remain significant theoretical influences. Wittig is first and foremost presented as a materialist feminist whose strength lies precisely in the challenge that she presents to queer theory's focus on performativity, instead "[understanding] transness [*transitude*] in accordance with a conceptualization of gender in the singular, as a social system, and not of individual genders in the plural" (44). This avoids the psychologization of gender and shifts instead to understanding the medical, legal, and economic apparatuses that produce the hierarchical sexes (Delisle 2017; Batteux 2021). Indeed, the very use of the neologism *transitude* ("transness" or "transhood," as in womanhood), rather than the more common *transidentité*, emphasizes the collective and social experience of gender over its status as an individual identity.

Furthermore, analyzing gender transitions through the framework of the "classes" of the sexes renders trans men and women, as Emmanuel Beaubatie (2021) has shown, "sex renegades [*transfuges de sexe*]"[29] in very different ways: some trans men may experience relative social mobility, whereas trans women are nearly always "downgraded [*déclassées*]." Viewed from that perspective, trans women's issues are not reducible to trans issues but must be considered women's issues, even as that category continues to be deconstructed: "As women, they [trans women] must be able to contribute to struggles that advance the interests of their class" (Lefebvre 2021: 125).[30] While this approach may be too monolithic to take into account racial and economic factors that constitute the sexes (Gabriel 2021; Danjé 2021), it nevertheless contributes to an emerging body of queer, transgender, and Marxist scholarship seeking to challenge liberal conceptions of sex, gender, and the body (Liu 2015; Popa 2021; Gleeson and O'Rourke 2021).

Ultimately, after several years of reflection, I can only respond to my titular question about Wittig—TERF or transfeminist avant la lettre?—by refusing its terms. The goal of my contribution has not been establishing whether she was either of those things but, rather, reflecting on what we can and cannot do with the tools that she provides. Wittig's work continues to play a role in transfeminist thought precisely because of its multiple and sometimes contradictory interpretations, its ambiguities, its gaps, and its capacity to incite dialogue about what it would mean for bodies to exist differently in the world. It is only by embracing such ambivalence that feminists might look to the theoretical tools of materialism while avoiding the pitfalls of transmisogyny and trans exclusion. Instead of poring over Wittig's writings for evidence that she was either definitively a TERF or transfeminist, let us instead ask what her work can do. And if she is too complex of a figure to serve transfeminism merely through her memory, then perhaps, failing that, it is time to invent.

Blase A. Provitola is assistant professor of language and culture studies and women, gender, and sexuality at Trinity College. They have published on queer and lesbian activism and identity, postcolonial literature, intersectional feminisms in France, and transgender-inclusive pedagogy.

Notes

1. All translations are mine unless otherwise noted.
2. This was reported in a press release by the Inter-LGBT, the official organizers of the march, in conjunction with the organizations Acceptess-T, Nouveau Parti Anticapitaliste LGBTI, FièrEs, STRASS, and Act-Up Paris. For coverage of this incident and link to the full statement, see Lavigne 2021.
3. In this article I use the term *transfeminist* to broadly refer to the political and philosophical affiliation with trans-inclusive feminism.
4. "Fais un effort pour te souvenir. Ou, à défaut, invente" (Wittig 1969: 127).
5. Wittig is the only French reference in their list of feminist influences. See OUTrans 2013.
6. For critiques of the "waves" model of feminism in a French context, see Pavard 2018.
7. Unless otherwise noted, all quotes from *The Straight Mind* are listed from the 1992 English edition first, with the corresponding pages in the 2013 French edition listed afterward.
8. "Ce n'est pas l'hétérosexualité qui est un problème, c'est l'oppression. On ne peut confondre les deux dans un même concept."
9. "La position de Monique Wittig est donc minoritaire et marginalisée en 1980. Si elle marque une rupture pour le petit cercle des militantes parisiennes qui avaient été proches d'elle depuis les débuts du MLF, sa position a peu d'écho au-delà. Elle ne donne pas lieu sur le moment à une séparation radicale des lesbiennes du mouvement féministe. Néanmoins, par la rupture théorique qu'elle propose avec le sujet femme comme sujet politique du féminisme, Wittig annonce les évolutions queer de la décennie suivante."
10. To cite only a few examples, Christopher Robinson (1995: 176) classifies her as a lesbian separatist who "[promotes] the isolation of lesbians from the rest of society," and Leo

Bersani (1995: 41–45) wholesale dismisses her lesbian feminism in favor of a blatantly androcentric "homo-ness." For an excellent critique of Butler's misinterpretation of Wittig, see De Lauretis 2007.

11.   For conference proceedings, see Bourcier and Robichon 2002.

12.   "Il n'y a que Wittig pour ne plus prescrire l'identification à la femme et à laisser la porte ouverte aux lesbiennes barbues."

13.   "Le pédé, la folle, la drag queen, la lesbienne, la gouine, la camionneuse, le garçon manqué, la butch, les F2M et les M2F, les transgenres." The term *camionneuse*, which literally refers to a female trucker, is also a derogatory term wielded against and sometimes reclaimed by butch lesbians.

14.   In the more recent Spanish and English editions of this text (whose translations were approved by Preciado), *lesbian bodies* is translated as "postbodies [postcuerpos]." I wonder if this is because the target audience might be less familiar with Wittig, or whether Preciado no longer found in Wittig's lesbian body the same inspiration as he had previously.

15.   "En se situant hors des régimes de la sexualité *straight*, on peut dire que l'on n'a pas de vagin et donc pas de corps qui puisse être appelé 'femme.'"

16.   "On perd de vue la lutte féministe: pour la disparition du genre." The interview, originally published in *Politis*, is available on Delphy's (2013) blog.

17.   For the original article in the *Feminist Current*, see https://www.feministcurrent.com/2017/07/08/lesbianism-attack-though-not-usual-suspects/. The original French translation is available at https://tradfem.wordpress.com/2017/07/19/le-lesbianisme-est-la-cible-dattaques-mais-pas-de-la-part-de-ses-adversaires-habituels/.

18.   "*Désir*: cette tarte à la crème sur laquelle chacune ne manque pas de déraper en toute hâte pour échapper à son examen . . . Ce qui est peu clair c'est comment il peut y avoir une exquise essence 'désir hétérosexuel féminin' . . . qui viendrait flotter dans le paysage pour l'embaumer, loin, bien loin des catégories politiques et des classes de sexe qu'on est censées détruire."

19.   "On peut et on doit dire que nos désirs sont construits, et que oui, pour beaucoup, nous sommes grossophobes, validistes, racistes, transphobes etc dans nos désirs. Est-ce que cela signifie qu'il faut 'se forcer'? Absolument pas." See *Réflexions trans* 2017.

20.   The term *meuf* is back-slang for *femme* (woman).

21.   "Le patriarcat c'est pas un truc avec les mecs aux dessus [*sic*] qui exploitent les meufs en dessous. Le patriarcat c'est un truc avec les mecs *cis* qui exploitent les *non*-mecs cis." Though this blog no longer exists, this post was originally accessible at https://transgrrrls.wordpress.com/2018/11/04/un-peu-de-solidarite-trans/. For an account of Francophone feminism's consistent exclusion of trans men in an academic context, see Baril 2016.

22.   "Cette tournure [non-mixité entre femmes] est souvent critiquée, considérée (à raison) comme misogyne par les féministes radicales qui refusent, dans la lignée des *Radicalesbians* ou de Monique Wittig, qu'on demande aux femmes de 's'identifier' à leur statut déshumanisé. Parfois, cette critique est de mauvaise foi et celles qui l'avancent, se revendiquant de la mouvance *gender-critical*, ne cherchent en réalité qu'à pointer du doigt la présence de femmes trans dans leurs milieux. Plus rarement, elle est reprise par des militantes trans se revendiquant *matérialistes* ou *radicales*." See *Questions trans et féministes* 2018.

23.   "Ce dégenrage qui leur ôte toute leur radicalité et toute leur substance révolutionnaire." This reflects broader materialist feminist critiques of the disappearance of feminist studies in the name of gender studies.

24.   "La primauté des femmes cisgenres sur les personnes transmasculines, elles-mêmes mieux considérées que les personnes transféminines."

25.   "Il ne s'agit plus seulement de rappeler l'existence des femmes/lesbiennes trans et leur légitimité à participer aux mouvements féministes, mais d'inclure dans les mouvements féministes des personnes qui ne sont pas femmes/lesbiennes (notamment les hommes trans, les personnes transmasculines, les personnes transgenres, les personnes *genderqueer*, les personnes trans non-binaires, etc.) et leurs problématiques (notamment autour du genre, de la binarité homme/femme, des masculinités, etc.)."

26.   "Familier et péjoratif. Qui présente les défauts traditionnellement attribués au Français moyen (en particulier chauvinisme, étroitesse d'esprit)." See *Larousse*, s.v. "franchouillard," https://www.larousse.fr/dictionnaires/francais/franchouillard/35028 (accessed August 15, 2021).

27.   "Ce glissement d'approche changeait tout. Il était désormais possible d'aborder les problématiques vécues par les femmes trans à travers une longue histoire de théorisation, de militantisme, de désaccord et de solidarité féministes. Et les approches strictement queer n'étaient plus les seules et uniques options envisageables." Though publishing under the name Noémie Grunenwald at the time of writing in January 2022, this author previously published under the name Noomi B. Grüsig.

28.   This echoes critiques of queer theory from a materialist perspective in a US context, some of which have explicitly drawn on Wittig. See for example Hennessey 1993 and Hale 1996.

29.   In sociology, the term *transfuge de classe*, which can be translated as either "class renegade" or "class defector," connotes someone who has left their class of origin through downward or upward mobility (though it is nearly always used to connote the latter).

30.   "En tant que femmes, elles doivent pouvoir contribuer à des luttes qui font avancer leurs intérêts de classe."

References

Baril, Alexandre. 2016. "Francophone Trans/Feminisms: Absence, Silence, Emergence," translated by Catriona LeBlanc. *TSQ* 3, nos. 1–2: 40–47. https://doi.org/10.1215/23289252-3334175.

Barnes, J. J. 2017. "Le lesbianisme est la cible d'attaques, mais pas de la part de ses adversaires habituels," translated by TRADFEM. *Christine Delphy* (blog), August 1. https://christine delphy.wordpress.com/2017/08/01/le-lesbianisme-est-la-cible-dattaques-mais-pas-de-la -part-de-ses-adversaires-habituels/.

Batteux, Séverine. 2021. "Autonomie et autodétermination." In Clochec and Grunenwald 2021: 83–99.

Beaubatie, Emmanuel. 2021. *Transfuges de sexe: Passer les frontières du genre*. Paris: La Découverte.

Bersani, Leo. 1995. *Homos*. Cambridge, MA: Harvard University Press.

Bourcier, Sam [Marie-Hélène], ed. 1998. *Q comme queer: Les séminaires Q du Zoo (1996–1997)*. Lille: Gai Kitsch Camp.

Bourcier, Sam [Marie-Hélène]. 2006. *Queer zones: Politique des identités sexuelles et des savoirs*. Paris: Amsterdam.

Bourcier, Sam. 2017. *Homo inc.orporated: Le triangle et la licorne qui pète*. Paris: Éditions Cambourakis.

Bourcier, Sam [Marie-Hélène], and Suzette Robichon, eds. 2002. *Parce que les lesbiennes ne sont pas des femmes: Autour de l'œuvre politique, théorique et littéraire de Monique Wittig, actes du colloque des 16–17 juin 2001, Columbia University, Paris*. Paris: Éditions Gaies et Lesbiennes.

Bourque, Dominique. 2006. *Écrire l'inter-dit: La subversion formelle dans l'œuvre de Monique Wittig*. Paris: L'Harmattan.

Brossard, Louise. 2003. "Adrienne Rich et Monique Wittig: Un point de départ pour penser l'hétérosexualité et les rapports sociaux de sexe." In Chetcuti and Michard 2003: 23–32.

Butler, Judith. 1990. *Gender Trouble: Feminism and the Subversion of Identity*. New York: Routledge.

Chetcuti, Natacha, and Claire Michard, eds. 2003. *Lesbianisme et féminisme: Histoires politiques*. Paris: L'Harmattan.

Clochec, Pauline. 2021. "Introduction: Du spectre du matérialisme à la possibilité de matérialismes trans." In Clochec and Grunenwald 2021: 17–64.

Clochec, Pauline, and Noémie Grunenwald, eds. 2021. *Matérialismes trans*. Paris: Hystériques et AssociéEs.

Costello, Katherine. 2016. "Inventing 'French Feminism': A Critical History." PhD diss., Duke University. https://hdl.handle.net/10161/12235.

Danjé, Michaëla, ed. 2021. *AfroTrans: Perspectives, entretiens, poésie, fiction*. Paris: Cases Rebelles Éditions.

Davis, James Douglas. 2010. *Beautiful War: Uncommon Violence, Praxis, and Aesthetics in the Novels of Monique Wittig*. New York: Peter Lang.

De Lauretis, Teresa. 2007. "When Lesbians Were Not Women." In *Figures of Resistance: Essays in Feminist Theory*, edited by Patricia White, 72–82. Urbana: University of Illinois Press.

Delisle, Circé. 2017. "Autodétermination et autonomie." *Les AssiégéEs* 2: 8–15.

Delphy, Christine. 1985. "La passion selon Wittig." *Nouvelles questions féministes*, nos. 11–12: 149–56.

Delphy, Christine. 1998. *L'ennemi principal*. Paris: Syllepse.

Delphy, Christine. 2000. "The Invention of French Feminism: An Essential Move." In *Fifty Years of Yale French Studies: A Commemorative Anthology. Part 2: 1980–1998*, edited by Charles A. Porter and Alyson Waters, 166–97. Yale French Studies 97. New Haven, CT: Yale University Press.

Delphy, Christine. 2013. "Un entretien avec Christine Delphy—Politis." Interview by Ingrid Merckx. *Christine Delphy* (blog), November 14. https://christinedelphy.wordpress.com/2013/11 /14/un-entretien-avec-christine-delphy-politis.

Eloit, Ilana. 2019. "American Lesbians Are Not French Women: Heterosexual French Feminism and the Americanisation of Lesbianism in the 1970s." *Feminist Theory* 20, no. 4: 381–404. https://doi.org/10.1177/1464700119871852.

Eloit, Ilana. 2020. "Trouble dans le féminisme. Du 'nous, les femmes' au 'nous, les lesbiennes': Genèse du sujet politique lesbien en France (1970–1980)." *20 et 21: Revue d'histoire*, no. 148: 129–45.

Epps, Brad, and Jonathan Katz. 2007. "Monique Wittig's Materialist Utopia and Radical Critique." *GLQ* 13, no. 4: 423–54. https://doi.org/10.1215/10642684-2007-001.

Espineira, Karine, and Marie-Hélène/Sam Bourcier. 2016. "Transfeminism: Something Else, Somewhere Else." *TSQ* 3, nos. 1–2: 84–94. https://doi.org/10.1215/23289252-3334247.

Fassin, Éric. 1999. "The Purloined Gender: American Feminism in a French Mirror." *French Historical Studies* 22, no. 1: 113–38.

Gabriel, Joao. 2021. "Devenir l'homme noir, repenser les expériences transmasculines au prisme de la question raciale." In Clochec and Grunenwald 2021: 169–86.

Gleeson, Jules Joanne, and Elle O'Rourke, eds. 2021. *Transgender Marxism*. London: Pluto.

Grunenwald, Noémie. 2020. "Préface: Une invitation au décentrement." In *Manifeste d'une femme trans et autres textes*, by Julia Serano, translated by Noémie Grunenwald, 9–14. Sorcières. Paris: Cambourakis.

Grüsig, Noomi B. 2015. "Transféminisme à la française: Enjeux et embûches?" In "Transféminismes." Special issue, *Cahiers de la transidentité*, no. 5: 29–48.

Guénif Souilamas, Nacira, and Éric Macé. 2004. *Les féministes et le garçon arabe*. La Tour d'Aigues: Éditions de l'Aube.

Guillaumin, Colette. 1992. *Sexe, race et pratique du pouvoir: L'idée de nature*. Paris: Editions Indigo et Côté-Femmes.

Hale, Jacob. 1996. "Are Lesbians Women?" *Hypatia* 11, no. 2: 94–121.

Hanisch, Carol, Kathy Scarbrough, Ti-Grace Atkinson, and Kathie Sarachild. 2013. "Forbidden Discourse: The Silencing of Feminist Criticism of 'Gender.'" Open statement, August 12. https://meetinggroundonline.org/wp-content/uploads/2013/10/GENDER-Statement-Inter Active-930.pdf.

Hennessy, Rosemary. 1993. "Queer Theory: A Review of the *differences* Special Issue and Wittig's *The Straight Mind*." *Signs* 18, no. 4: 964–73.

Lavigne, Alice. 2021. "L'Inter-LGBT et les collectifs du pré-cortège 'Pôle des Luttes' dénoncent des agressions transphobes lors de la Marche des Fiertés." *Komitid*, July 13. https://www .komitid.fr/2021/07/13/linter-lgbt-et-les-collectifs-du-pre-cortege-pole-des-luttes-denoncent -des-agressions-transphobes-lors-de-la-marche-des-fiertes-de-paris/.

L'écho des sorcières. 2015. "L'écho des sorcières: Entretien," edited by Maud-Yeuse Thomas, Noomi B. Grüsig, and Karine Espineira. In "Transféminismes." Special issue, *Cahiers de la transidentité*, no. 5: 21–28.

Lefebvre, Constance. 2021. "Femmes trans et féminisme: Les obstacles à la prise de conscience féministe et le ciscentrisme dans les mouvements féministes." In Clochec and Gru-nenwald 2021: 103–26.

Lesseps, Emmanuelle de. 1980. "Hétérosexualité et féminisme." *Questions féministes*, no. 7: 55–69.

Liu, Petrus. 2015. *Queer Marxism in Two Chinas*. Durham, NC: Duke University Press.

Mathieu, Nicole-Claude. 1991. *L'anatomie politique: Catégorisations et idéologies du sexe*. Paris: Côté-Femmes.

Mathieu, Nicole-Claude. 2014. *L'anatomie politique 2: Usage, déréliction et résilience des femmes*. Le genre du monde. Paris: La Dispute.

Möser, Cornelia. 2013. *Féminismes en traductions: Théories voyageuses et traductions culturelles*. Paris: Éditions des Archives Contemporaines.

Moses, Claire Goldberg. 1998. "Made in America: 'French Feminism' in Academia." *Feminist Studies* 24, no. 2: 241–74.

Ostrovsky, Erika. 1991. *A Constant Journey: The Fiction of Monique Wittig*. Carbondale: Southern Illinois University Press.

OUTrans. 2013. "OUTrans: Le transféminisme." *Observatoire des transidentités* (blog), April 6. www.observatoire-des-transidentites.com/2013/04/06/page-8618633/.

Pavard, Bibia. 2018. "Faire naître et mourir les vagues: Comment s'écrit l'histoire des fémin-ismes." *Itinéraires*, no. 2017-2. https://doi.org/10.4000/itineraires.3787.

Pavard, Bibia, Florence Rochefort, and Michelle Zancarini-Fournel. 2020. *Ne nous libérez pas, on s'en charge: Une histoire des féminismes de 1789 à nos jours*. Paris: La Découverte.

Perreau, Bruno. 2016. *Queer Theory: The French Response*. Stanford, CA: Stanford University Press.

Popa, Bogdan. 2021. *De-centering Queer Theory: Communist Sexuality in the Flow during and after the Cold War*. Manchester: Manchester University Press.

Preciado, Paul [Beatriz]. 2000. *Manifeste contra-sexuel*. Translated by Sam [Marie-Hélène] Bourcier. Paris: Jacob Duvernet.

Preciado, Paul [Beatriz]. 2002. "Gare à la gouine garou! Ou comment se faire un corps queer à partir de la pensée straight?" In Bourcier and Robichon 2002: 179–214.

QTPOC Autonomes Paris. 2021. "Communiqué de presse de QTPOC Autonomes post Marche des Fiertés de l'inter-LGBT du 26 juin 2021." Facebook, June 30. https://www.facebook .com/QTPOCautonomes/posts/348130233329930.

Questions trans et féministes (blog). 2018. "À propos de Cineffable." https://questions.tf/a-propos -de-cineffable-en-defense-de-la-non-mixite-femmes/ (article removed; accessed October 8, 2019).

Réflexions trans (blog). 2017. "Les femmes trans sont-elles des violeurs? Une réponse à J. J. Barnes (et à Christine Delphy)." August 3. https://reflexionstrans.wordpress.com/2017/08/03 /premier-article-de-blog/.

Résistance Lesbienne. 2021a. "Communiqué de Résistance Lesbienne—Agression lesbophobe à la Marche des Fiertés le 26 juin à Paris 2021." *Christine Delphy* (blog), July 5. https://christine delphy.wordpress.com/2021/07/05/communique-agression-lesbophobe-a-la-marche-des -fiertes-paris-2021/.

Résistance Lesbienne. 2021b. "Texte de notre tract—Marche des Fiertés Paris 2021." July 2. https:// resistancelesbienne.fr/2021/07/02/notre-tract-marche-des-fiertes-paris-2021/ (accessed July 12, 2021).

Robcis, Camille. 2013. *The Law of Kinship: Anthropology, Psychoanalysis, and the Family in France.* Ithaca, NY: Cornell University Press.

Robin, Kate. 2011. "Au-delà du sexe: Le projet utopique de Monique Wittig." *Journal des anthro- pologues*, nos. 124–25: 71–97. https://doi.org/10.4000/jda.5279.

Robinson, Christopher. 1995. *Scandal in the Ink: Male and Female Homosexuality in Twentieth- Century French Literature.* New York: Cassell.

Scott, Joan Wallach. 1996. *Only Paradoxes to Offer: French Feminists and the Rights of Man.* Cambridge, MA: Harvard University Press.

Shaktini, Namascar, ed. 2005. *On Monique Wittig: Theoretical, Political, and Literary Essays.* Urbana: University of Illinois Press.

Stryker, Susan, and Talia M. Bettcher. 2016. "Introduction: Trans/Feminisms." *TSQ* 3, nos. 1–2: 5–14. https://doi.org/10.1215/23289252-3334127.

Thomas, Maud-Yeuse. 2015. "Transféminisme ou postféminisme?" In "Transféminismes." Special issue, *Cahiers de la transidentité*, no. 5: 55–64.

Wittig, Monique. 1969. *Les Guérillères.* Paris: Éditions de Minuit.

Wittig, Monique. 1971. *Les Guérillères.* Translated by David Le Vay. New York: Viking.

Wittig, Monique. 1983. "Les questions féministes ne sont pas des questions lesbiennes." *Amazones d'hier, lesbiennes d'aujourd'hui* 2, no. 1: 10–14.

Wittig, Monique. 1992. *The Straight Mind and Other Essays.* Boston: Beacon.

Wittig, Monique. 2013. *La pensée straight.* Paris: Amsterdam.

Insidious Concern

Trans Panic and the Limits of Care

MIKEY ELSTER

Abstract This article examines media that couches criticism of trans medicine, pediatrics, and activism in terms of "care" or "concern" for trans people and youth in particular. It identifies these as "insidious concerns," speech acts, utterances, and proclamations that would harm that which they claim to care for or about. It proceeds to argue that this type of discourse is endemic to a wider crisis of social reproduction exacerbated by neoliberal economic restructuring. Through historical contextualization, cultural analysis, and ethnography, this article highlights the racist, nationalist, and reactionary undercurrents motivating the current trans panic in the United States. It concludes that theoretical attention to social reproduction might offer new insights for trans studies that can act as counterdiscourse to "insidious concern."

Keywords anthropology, political economy, medical anthropology, trans pediatrics

I t's a Sunday morning in July, and I'm at a meeting for parents of trans people, as I have been once or twice a month every month during the summer of 2019. As we go around introducing ourselves, Olivia,[1] one of the moms in the group, reflects on how witnessing her child's transition has changed her view on gender, saying, "we really do need a more expansive view of gender," and after a beat adds tongue-in-cheek, "I don't want it to be *my* kid that does it, but there should be one!" The rest of the group responds with a knowing laughter. Olivia's joke is less about her child's gender expression than it is about one of the central ambivalences that comes with raising—or being—a trans kid. On the one hand, the parents at this meeting see the family as a unit of personal privacy and responsibility, normatively removed from the politics and criticism of the public sphere, where happiness exists independent of politics. On the other, raising a trans child or being a trans child quickly exposes that many actually existing families are not immune to becoming the locus of political battles.

Given these contradictions, my ethnographic research on what constitutes good care in transgender pediatrics in New York often gives me the feeling of

TSQ: Transgender Studies Quarterly ∗ Volume 9, Number 3 ∗ August 2022 **407**
DOI 10.1215/23289252-9836064 © 2022 Duke University Press

whiplash. At the same time that there are free or low-cost clinics for transgender pediatric services in cities like New York, there has been a surge of anti-trans legislation at the state level across the United States. And while my research is primarily on the provision of care by supportive parents and doctors, it has immediately struck me that a lot of anti-trans rhetoric is framed within the register of care. Consider, for instance, a discussion of trans suicide rates from the *Federalist*, a right-wing blog. Author Daniel Payne (2016) argues that the suicide rate for trans people cannot be attributed to discrimination, stigma, or rejection. Instead, it is because being transgender is a mental illness: "Individuals who believe they are a different sex than that of their biology are psychologically ill—self-evidently so" (2016). Yet, he concludes his article with "Transgender individuals are precious, irreplaceable children of God. They deserve better than the cultural zeitgeist that has decided a sky-high suicide rate is an acceptable externality of modern-day progressive sexual ideology" (2016). This is essentially a call for conversion therapy. Because "transgenderism is a deleterious psychological affliction" (2016), it must be treated as something to cure rather than affirmed for the sake of "progressive sexual ideology." To save trans people from suicide, this article implicitly says, we must stop any trans people from existing. Nonetheless, trans people are "precious, irreplaceable children of God." Even in state legislatures, anti-trans bills like Texas's Senate Bill 1311, which seeks to curb access to trans pediatric medicine, are being described by their authors as intending to "improve the mental health of Texans who may later come to regret their transition" (Munce 2021). Sources outside government are happy to chime in as well, reiterating the premise that an increase in trans youth is a problem that requires intervention, that is, reduction. Kathleen Stock (2021: chap. 1) claims she is "critical of gender identity theory—not of trans people, for whom I have friendly sympathy and respect"[2] while also writing that "there are no circumstances in which minors should be making fertility—and health—affecting decisions involving blockers, hormones, or surgery" (chap. 4, para. 16). While a misrepresentation of what trans pediatric treatment usually entails, this statement would also bar minors from obtaining hormonal birth control without their parents' knowledge. In the name of defending women, girls, children generally, and the trans people for whom she has "sympathy and respect," Stock argues for a position that is decidedly anti-feminist and detrimental to reproductive health and justice.

What are we to make of these statements? They are obviously transphobic, and while to name them as belonging to the phenomenon of transphobia is indisputable, doing so is also "a convenient (and not altogether innocent) placeholder for the intellectual work that remains to be done" (Bettcher 2014a: 251). How do statements couched in terms of care and concern for trans people that effectively call for limiting their access to health care hold together internally for their speakers, or for the publics in which they circulate? One solution is to adopt Lisa Stevenson's (2014: 3) definition of care as "the way someone comes to matter and the corresponding ethics of attending to the other who matters." This definition opens up space for considering how these expressions of care or concern are "directed at populations rather than individuals" (3), and how in these utterances trans people and/or children stand in for a conception of the population rooted in cis, heterosexual, and white assumptions.

I call this rhetorical move "insidious concern." While it couches critique in terms of benevolence, it simultaneously calls for the destruction of the object of concern. Of particular interest is how children are doubly situated as a symbol of population in need of saving, as well as actually existing children who stand to suffer from the prescribed interventions of insidious concern. As a tone within trans-exclusionary ideologies, it is indicative, I argue, of a convergence between trans-exclusionary thought and what Sophie Bjork-James (2020: 59) has called "white sexual politics," a defense of the normative family that "is offered as a way to defend a lost social order, all the while obscuring the changed economic reality that now offers precarity to the majority." Sharing the assumptions that "racial politics are deeply entwined with sex and gender, particularly in the defense of white racial privilege," I argue that insidious concerns are "often expressed not in explicitly racial terms but through norms about the family, romantic heterosexual love, and innocent children" (59).

In what follows I first trace a brief history of the sex panics that provide the moral scaffolding for contemporary right-wing and trans-exclusionary logic, often as coalescing around a defense of the white, heteronormative patriarchal family in which parental authority is the principal arena of moral and political education. Having traced this history, I then argue that insidious concern invokes "children," "mom and dad," or "families" as stand-ins for a normative reproductive order in need of protection rather than actually existing children, parents, or families. By positioning children in need of saving from themselves, insidious concern makes calls for restricting access to health care more palatable to cis audiences. I then examine how this rhetorical move creates a public, accommodated by both neoliberalism and a growing right wing, that reimagines citizenship and belonging on exclusionary terms. This public and its political entanglements threaten both access to public accommodations or services for trans people as well as deeper political engagement based on the ability to occupy space.

I conclude by theorizing the trans politics at stake in the context of a crisis of social reproduction. Looking to some ethnographically grounded examples of how people seeking trans care have navigated this moment, I argue that people can reappropriate gendered meaning in enactments of care that decenter "dominant imaginaries of how care labor does and should operate" (Malatino 2020: 7). Spurred by a need to access care under increasingly precarious conditions, new subjectivities can arise through a strategic, situated ambivalence in relation to medical institutions and disciplining practices.

Moral Panic: Race, Sexuality, and Gender

Insidious concern shares with other sex panics the assumption that sexual and gendered norms are fundamental parts of social reproduction, and therefore changes to them are potentially destabilizing when left morally or politically unregulated.[3] In this section I trace a brief history of some twentieth-century sex panics to illustrate the historical context that lends its moral assumptions to insidious concern. Jeff Maskovsky (2021) argues that the alt-right imagines the maintenance of racial, sexual, and gendered hierarchies as central to the project of producing a white race. Expanding on this argument, I offer that insidious concern pulls from not only this recent discourse but also a history of sex panics that has configured the moral and political regulation of sex and gender as central to reproducing social relations.

Early twentieth-century sex panics share with insidious concern a general sense that sex, sexuality, and/or gender are central to the maintenance of a nationalist order and that radical changes to either can disrupt that order. The modern nationalist sex panic has its roots in the early twentieth-century development of sexology, on the one hand, and changing global power dynamics on the other. In *The Hirschfeld Archives*, Heike Bauer (2017) demonstrates how both Magnus Hirschfeld's homosexual advocacy and his reception were embedded in anxiety over the recession of the German colonial empire. As Bauer explains, the outbreak of the Harden trial—in which a journalist accused a diplomat of engaging in a homosexual affair with a German military commander—occurred "partly in response to a perceived colonial weakening of Kaiser Wilhelm, the German emperor, in the early 1900s" (25). As Harden was tried for defamation, Hirschfeld defended homosexuality as part of the trial. As a result, some "challenged his status as a medical expert by instead depicting him as a political agitator" (25). Hirschfeld's political advocacy for homosexual rights, itself enabled by Germany's colonial efforts, was nonetheless received as part and parcel of the diminishing strength of Germany's colonial standing. The logic of this is, of course, couched in stereotypes surrounding feminine men in particular and femininity in general—that homosexual men were "weaker," and thus the decline of German national strength could be directly tied to an increase in homosexuality.

Sex panics took a solid hold of nationalist discourses in the United States by the middle of the century, fueled by a fear of the civil rights movement, sexual liberation, the women's movement, and communism. One of the more enduring legacies has its roots in the Cold War, in which homosexuality, gender noncon-formity, and the "destruction" of the nuclear family were directly tied to com-munist plots to undermine the United States. In 1958 Cleon Skousen, a former FBI agent, published *The Naked Communist*, a book that claims to explore the nature of communist ideology by uncovering its roots and listing the "45 goals" of communists. In 1963 Congressman Albert S. Herlong Jr. (1963) from Florida, then a member of the Democratic Party, submitted the "45 goals" to the congressio-nal record. They include number 26, to "present homosexuality, degeneracy, and promiscuity as 'normal, natural, healthy.'"[4] As of May 2021, Conservapedia—a wiki style encyclopedia with the stated goal of combatting liberal bias in sources like Wikipedia—contains a page on "the homosexual agenda" that claims part of the agenda is to "legalize various forms of alternative partnerships" such as "man and man . . . woman and box turtle, man and sex toy" (Conservapedia, "Homo-sexual Agenda"). And their page on "Feminism" directly references feminist goals as being "derived from Communism," citing communist goal number 26 (Con-servapedia, "Feminism").

At the same time, the sex panics of the mid-twentieth century were as much racializing projects as they were informed by global politics. Contempo-raneous to Herlong's reading of communist goals into the congressional record, sociologist Daniel Patrick Moynihan was assembling a report that would be published two years later in 1965. *The Negro Family: The Case for National Action*, or the Moynihan Report as it came to be known, blamed not communism or homosexuality for the structural inequalities that Black families face, but the model of the female head of household. While this legacy of blaming Black mothers "undoubtedly did not *begin*" with Moynihan, his "work helped to shape the idea that Black families were pathological, which he attributed to female-headed households" (Davis 2019: 78). This pathologization of the Black family, and of Black women in particular, was itself part of the same project of mobilizing concern in service of the normative model of white heterosexual social repro-duction, especially in that this concern played "on the theme of degeneracy," claiming that Black mothers "transmitted a pathological lifestyle to their chil-dren, perpetuating poverty and antisocial behavior from one generation to the next" (Roberts 1997: 16). A threat to the nuclear family is at the center of both Moynihan's report and anticommunist anxiety. As such, both resulted in calls for moral and sexual regulation and were mutually reinforcing. Skousen argued that communists aimed to destabilize American society by normalizing sexual degeneracy, and therefore sexuality required regulation. Meanwhile Moynihan pointed to single motherhood among Black households as an example of moral decline when one deviates from monogamous heterosexual norms.

The moral panic around AIDS employed similar tropes, demonizing homosexuals as socially destabilizing and dangerous. But unlike the rhetoric discussed above, it was also the point where the category of trans people, and by extension trans children, began to emerge as its own object of governance and concern (Valentine 2007). As Reese, a fictional character from Torrey Peters's 2021 novel *Detransition, Baby,* puts it,

> Back in the eighties the big institutions looking at AIDS noticed a population with wildly high rates of infection—a population that wasn't captured in the usual categories of "gay" or "Men Who Have Sex with Men." A certain kind of people slipped through the gaps, people who went by all sorts of names: transvestites, drag queens, sissies, cross-dressers, transgender, transexuals, fairies, and on and on. But institutions require categorical names in order to function—the guys at the CDC can't be writing a new grant or reworking studies every time a nancy starts calling herself a nelly. So they assigned a name to this population: the umbrella term "transgender." (307)

This conceptual division created a new section of the population for institutions to "care" about, allowing for the category of "transgender" to be positioned against homosexuality, as it sometimes is by some transphobes and gender critical feminists. This is not to say that trans subjectivity cannot be located or excavated elsewhere in the past, as scholars like Jules Gill-Peterson (2018) and C. Riley Snorton (2017) have done. Rather, the institutional conceptual division between gender and sexuality represents a moment when the category of transgender became an institutionally intelligible, legible subject, such that a "transgender child" could become an object of political debate. This allows for a "submerged logic in which no sexual provocation [is] necessary" because gender presentation itself can be "a panic-inducing provocation" (Gill-Peterson 2018: 5) that drives trans panic (Salamon 2018: 5).

The Insidiously Concerned

Insidious concern differs from former sex panics primarily through its bifocal view of children: because children often symbolically represent heteronormativity, the family, and whiteness, actually existing trans children are simultaneously configured as imperiled subjects requiring protection and dangerous actors in need of regulation. This is ultimately a biopolitical move, following Lisa Stevenson's (2014: 3) use of "the biopolitical" to mean "a form of care and governance that is primarily concerned with the maintenance of life itself, and is directed at populations rather than individuals." Life itself, imagined as always cisgender, calls for restricting access to health care for individuals as compulsory members of the cisgender population. This dual move allows a slippage between protection and regulation, care and abandonment, in three different ways. First, the assumption that any increase in the proportion of trans people is inherently problematic, rather than a reasonable result of expanded access to health care or a change in policy, carries with it the implicit notion that the number of trans people needs to be reduced, usually through restricting access to legal recognition or forms of care. Second, insidious concern neglects, ignores, or erases the narratives of people of color that would bring to light the imbrication of race, sex, and gender. This is part of the same trans necropolitics that Snorton and Jin Haritaworn (2013) have identified, in which trans of color life gains publicity only through death and often via incorporation into a narrative that glosses the specificity of trans of color experience. Finally, instead of couching grievances in explicitly racial terms, insidious concern invokes a morality of the family rooted in white normative assumptions. In any case, actually existing trans kids are abandoned while care is afforded only for a normative family structure. Taken together, these aspects highlight how concern is consolidated around whiteness, while it is insidious because of its reliance on tropes familiar to a wider cis audience.

In what follows I look at three texts I came across during fieldwork, either through my own passive media consumption or because they were mentioned by my interlocutors, that are representative of insidious concern. I argue that they draw their moral force from the same themes explored above, but what sets them apart is their circulation beyond extreme right-wing media. The specific context enabling their general circulation is described in the next section.

The Premise: There Are Too Many

Usually with some reference to the myth of rapid onset gender dysphoria (ROGD), insidious concerns posit that the increase in trans people, especially young trans people, is in and of itself evidence of a social problem. The implication is that the number of trans people today is misrepresentative, evidence of misled teens, and that something ought to be done to reduce it. Kathleen Stock frames the problem in the introduction to her 2021 book *Material Girls* by contrasting the estimated number of trans people in the United Kingdom in 2004 (around two thousand) to 2020 (around two hundred thousand or so). Abigail Shrier (2020: xxiv) is a little more up front, leaving nothing to subtext: "Some small portion of the population will always be transgender. But perhaps the current craze will not always lure in troubled young girls with no history of gender dysphoria, enlisting them in a lifetime of hormone dependency and disfiguring surgeries. If this is a social contagion, society—perhaps—can arrest it." Because insidious concerns configure children as in need of saving from themselves, detransition often functions as the constitutive outside of trans identity. The general thrust of this argument is, we know being trans is getting too popular because there are people who have detransitioned, so a call to reduce the number of trans people by limiting access to care is a moral position that protects would-be detransitioners from transgender influence.

As another example, Leslie Stahl's *60 Minutes* segment on trans health care, which aired in late May 2021, spends a disproportionate amount of time on detransition being the result of doctors too hastily handing out transition services to young adults (CBS News 2021). It jumps from a story about how more trans kids have access to affirmative forms of care to stories of detransition being the consequence of this expansion. At one point, Grace Lindski-Smith, one of the featured detransitioners, claims, "I can't believe I transitioned and detransitioned, including hormones and surgery in the course of less than one year. It's completely crazy." While doctors might be part of an outside threat to children, the overarching message is that restricting access to trans health care could save children from themselves (CBS News 2021).

The opposition between trans people and detransitioners is solely about framing and a commitment to cisnormativity (Serano 2017). Detransition is not the "other side" of trans health care, but framing it as such serves to position any potential transition as a threat. As such, insidious concern is presented as protecting children, when in fact its aim is to reduce their access to medical transition services. Moreover, depicting detransitioners as "duped" into transitioning runs the risk of smuggling in arguments against medical autonomy for young people in general, such as restricting access to hormonal birth control. More often than not, those who are most vocally concerned for detransitioners use them to argue for reduced patient participation in health decisions, a stance that curtails the autonomy of both trans and detrans patients alike.

Erasure
Insidious concern glosses over race or racism, as if stories of transition exist independently from race, class, or other intersecting social categories. In doing so it recenters whiteness by framing gender as the only operative category. As Talia Mae Bettcher (2014b: 391) has argued, in theorizing the axes of oppression that trans people face, "Since the vast majority of trans women killed are trans women of color, trans women who are poor, and trans women who are sex workers, it is not enough to focus on transphobic violence across gender differences: race and class must likewise be centered." Interestingly, Stock (2020) cites Bettcher (2014a) when arguing that the motivation for violence against trans people might not directly stem or stem only from transphobia, but perhaps racism or whorephobia. However, this is not in service of proposing a more intersectional approach.[5] Stock jumps over that critique and lands on a skepticism toward the idea of transphobia writ large (2020: chap. 7).

And of course, by presenting any analysis of trans health care or activism in which race and class are not factors, calls for more restrictive access to medical care ignore that any increased gatekeeping will disproportionately affect those who already have the least access to care. There is already a disproportionately small number of nonwhite patients in trans pediatric settings (see for example, Bercera et al. 2018 or Chodzen et al. 2018), and adding barriers makes it less accessible to those without reliable health coverage. Furthermore, analysis without race misses how white supremacy can promote adherence to normative gender roles (cf. Page and Richardson 2009). As M, a twenty-year-old genderqueer research participant of mine, put it, "Every day when I was fourteen or fifteen I really cared about what I was wearing, like always tried to be pretty all the time . . . for a lot of reasons, I feel like some of it tied into race too. Because I felt like an outsider by race . . . if I couldn't fit in that way, by being white, then I could fit in by being the girliest girl possible." For M, recourse to a normative gender presentation in childhood was a strategic—if unconscious—way to avoid being marginalized as one of the few people of color among their peer group. Since there are several factors that might prevent people of color from accessing transition services, especially in childhood, the concern over detransition presumes the whiteness of patients while functioning as a call to action that would exacerbate the already unequal access to health care that exists.

The Family

The biopolitics of insidious concern is centered on the protection of the nuclear family as a natural, stable, and moral social form. This is often voiced through the grievance that institutions like schools, therapists, or social groups have displaced the moral authority of parents in favor of accommodating a threatening few. One of the most striking examples of this is when Shrier (2020) relates the story of a child she calls "Gayatri,"[6] an Indian American teen born to immigrant parents. We are told that Gayatri found it hard to make friends until they joined their school's gay-straight alliance and began going by *they/them/their* pronouns. Their parents, apprehensive yet generally supportive, broke into tears of sadness after Gayatri announced their identity and pronouns during a school assembly, without any warning beforehand. Shrier frames this as an example of one of the many ways trans identity subverts parental authority, and a full three chapters—"The Schools," "The Parents," and "The Shrinks"—are dedicated to understanding the forces at play against parents in favor of "the transgender craze." While Shrier is supposedly concerned for the children at the center of her book, she also tells us that, after adopting a new name and *they/them* pronouns, Gayatri "had friends—lots of them" (21), and several other examples glossing over the apparent well-being of an actually existing child. By her own evidence, Shrier is not so much concerned with the well-being of actually existing children as she is with maintaining the family as the primary arena of moral education.

These are the biopolitics of insidious concern. Children are doubly rendered as a population-level symbol for a mode of heterosexual reproduction and ignored as individuals in need of particular forms of care. The biopolitical aim here is to foster the life of the nuclear family, so "children" are only relevant as parts for the reproduction of that social form. Parents are as much a population here too. Several parents I have interviewed are happy when institutions adopt gender inclusive policies, often because it alleviates some care work involved in trying to explain gender to every other parent or child at school. Actual parents are not under threat, but the parental authority exemplified in the heteronormative family is.

Insidious concerns do not necessarily contain all of these factors at once, but they all call for a moral policing of the reproductive order. As I argue below, they are being articulated the most loudly at a time when access to health care, public space, and public services is markedly precarious. This makes the exclusion of trans people from public central to an emerging trans-exclusionary feminist politics.

Being in Public

Insidious concerns target public accommodation, from gender inclusive bathroom policies to gender affirmative health care and school policies. In the following section, I argue that the biopolitical logic of insidious concern has enabled the production of reactionary publics with attendant notions of citizenship that exclude trans people from "the public." The public or publics can mean both an audience in which texts and ideas circulate as well as a political formation shared by those with citizenship status. Insidious concern creates a public, in terms of an audience for circulation, through a shared sentimental attachment to "norms" around the family and gender, while also advocating for a public, in the sense of a political formation, based on exclusion.

Trans youth themselves seem to be aware of this public, often engaging it as a political signifier. Ada, a then eighteen-year-old and soon to be nineteen-year-old trans woman I interviewed, was initially apprehensive about talking to a researcher when I reached out over email. When we talked, she seemed to have lost any hesitation since I first introduced myself. After detailing aspects of her family life, sexuality, and local politics, she tells me she wants multiple tattoos and piercings because she wants "to be the trans person that boomers are afraid of."

Most of the trans youth I have interviewed do not express an aspiration to instill fear in older generations, but Ada's statement highlights how sentiment is central to forming an insidiously concerned public. The privatization of citizenship (Berlant 1997) has brought with it a moralizing politics of sexuality and gender. Neoliberalism, meaning the sets of policies enacted over the past half century favoring entrepreneurialism and privatization over citizenship and public goods, has long accommodated reactionary moralism. Melinda Cooper (2017) identifies neoliberalism and neoconservativism as complementary rather than opposed ideologies, wherein neoliberal policies curtail access to public spaces of care and social conservatives double down on the importance of the patriarchal family as the primary institution for moral education, care, and social reproduction. This dynamic enables trans-exclusionary feminists to launch their various attacks on public accommodations, from gender inclusive school policies to bathrooms and health care. However, it diverges from neoliberal economizing through a "politics of sentiment," in which "rage and resentment has been taken to new levels of intensity" in contemporary politics (Maskovsky forthcoming). This is a point of convergence between trans-exclusionary politics and the right wing more generally, in which notions of biological sex and conservative conceptions of the family become political rallying points based in sentiment. Ada's desire to be feared plays off the perception that her appearance subverts the political and sentimental attachments to gender and the family that the right wing harbors.

The public politically structures citizenship, broadly understood as membership in the public and the right to politically engage therein. Insidious concern structures citizenship around shared sentimental attachment to hegemonic family structure, gender comportment, and sexuality. Neoliberalism famously economized citizenship, often by attaching it to labor. This was the case for welfare reform, or "workfare," in the 1990s, which brought with it a form of contractual citizenship in which "rights should be contingent on the performance of responsibilities" (Collins and Mayer 2010: 13). Insidious concern shifts the contingency of citizenship to adherence to a cisgender narrative about the relationship between the body and gender. Bodies that disrupt this narrative are excluded as political subjects and thus should not be accommodated by public institutions like bathrooms, classrooms, or medicine. The consequences of this narrative's instability are then offloaded onto "the individuals whose narratives, documents, and bodies reveal the mutability of the category [gender]" (Currah and Mulqueen 2011: 558).

These exclusionary politics commonly take the form of bathroom bills or restrictions on trans inclusive public school curricula and health care, essentially targeting any kind of occupation of physical space. Here, these policies share with neoliberalism a project of morally regulating public space. Lauren Berlant and Michael Warner (1998) have discussed this phenomenon in a different context, tracking how public spaces for queer people were targeted by rezoning laws. Berlant and Warner argue that, when areas like Christopher Street are rezoned to be more "family friendly" to the residents, the right to the city for queer people is effectively under attack. They point out that many of the young people who frequent Christopher Street could never afford to live there, but that "urban space is always host space. The right to the city extends to those who use the city" (563).

In the decades since, geographic restructuring has continued to accompany sex- and gender-based moralizing. Economic and municipal policies continue to impede access to care for trans people specifically and queer people more generally. Rereading this piece by Berlant and Warner, I am reminded of my first visit to a pediatric center in Manhattan. I am heading into a meeting of medical researchers and physicians. The center it takes place at is unique for being both cost free, able to provide some limited services without parental permission, and having a trans health project. It is located in a majority white neighborhood that is one of the most affluent neighborhoods in Manhattan, but the majority of the patients are young women and girls of color, "mostly for reproductive health," a physician tells me as he leads me down the hall. Most of the patients could not afford to live in the same neighborhood as the center. Nonetheless, this clinic is exceptional in some ways. Some early data from an internal survey suggests that there is a greater proportion of trans people of color receiving care here than in comparable private clinics, especially for mental health. Still, it exists in a contradictory state. While it provides free services to the uninsured, gentrification continues to push the core of its patients farther and farther away. So many of the demands this center advocates for come down to the right to exist in public.

Basic accommodations like access to bathrooms, protection from discrimination and harassment in public places like schools, and access to health care hinge on a notion of citizenship that is undergoing a radical renegotiation, such that "care" for trans kids entails barring them from public services. At the same time, simply ensuring access to institutional forms of care for individuals does not address the underlying economics of displacement from public facilities. Alternatively, Hil Malatino (2020: 2) imagines "trans care" as an inherently collective process that requires unlearning "the mythos of neoliberal, entrepreneurial self-making" as a model for navigating the politically uneven terrain of care. Malatino emphasizes that trans care relies on precarious networks that are rarely formalized and depend heavily on interpersonal relationships. At the same time, they exist in tandem with more institutionalized forms of care. They are grounded in material conditions at the same time that they reimagine social relationships through enacting care. The possibility of trans care informs the next section.

Situated Ambivalence

Insidious concern is a product of the same political-economic conditions in which we attempt to imagine alternative forms of trans care. Critiquing it on the basis that it is rooted in inherently oppressive structures is only the beginning of a counterdiscourse to it. By way of conclusion I want to contextualize recent theorizing on gender within the squeeze on social reproduction that many people face. In doing so I attempt to answer the question that Noah Zazanis (2021: 33) posits as the framework for theorizing trans reproduction: "if gender is a structure imposed onto its subjects, what does it mean to 'change' genders while remaining subjected to that structure?" To put it differently, Zazanis is asking how a social structure like gender can act as an essentialist, normalizing force, as it does for trans-exclusionists, without foreclosing the possibility of its reappropriation.

Before I started research I was initially concerned with how I could non-judgmentally represent parents that struggle to accept trans identity. Almost everyone is socialized into transphobic assumptions, but I was worried that trying to empathetically explain the position of mostly cis parents might result in excusing rather than analyzing them. What I quickly came to realize is that most of the parents and people with loved ones who are transgender that I came across were mostly looking for support in a generalized context of precarity, what Nancy Fraser (2016: 99) has called the "crisis of care." Unlearning transphobia, alongside other interpersonal struggles, certainly took place. But most parents, including the relatively well-to-do, were more worried about trying to accommodate their child while being in between jobs, trying to access health care, or trying to find access to any kind of transition services, among other struggles. This is the context in which both insidious concern and trans care came to be. Navigating this context can feed anxiety and grievance politics while it could also highlight the need for alternate forms of care.

For Fraser (2016), the crisis of care is characterized by the increasing difficulty in accessing care and the things necessary to socially reproduce oneself and others. A lack of resources like childcare, employment, and health care is the context within which scholars are theorizing gender and in which people are forming their own gendered subjectivities. In many ways, this has radically destabilized the material scaffolding of the patriarchal family, and by extension gender roles. Despite this, gender still has structural effects as an axis of social and economic differentiation. Social reproduction theory has time and again demonstrated how the burdens of the crisis of care disproportionately fall on women, especially working-class women and women of color (cf. Collins and Mayer 2010; Colen 1995). In short, gender works as an accumulation strategy for capital, as Kay Gabriel (2020) puts it, "Gender for capital assumes the form of an accumulation strategy, an ideological scaffolding that sustains an unequal division of labour, contours practices of dispossession and predation, and conditions particular forms of exploitation, including and especially in the form of un- and low-waged reproductive labour." However, gender is not reducible to the functions of capital. Gabriel ends her essay by asking, "What would it mean for gender to function as a source of disalienated pleasure rather than an accumulation strategy?" (2020). In other words, Gabriel is insisting that the meanings we associate with various gendered markers have an afterlife outside capital. That is to say, embracing masculinity or femininity is not always a direct effect of capital's needs alone.

The central contradiction Gabriel highlights is that, while the while gendered system we have is indeed rooted in the need for capital to segment the working class, both cis and trans people alike nonetheless often find much of the symbolism and embodied practices of that system to be a source of pleasure. When people like Stock articulate insidious concern in gender critical terms, they recapitulate a biologically essentialist theory of gender to posit that our pleasures are problematic. They insist that to say that a child is a trans boy instead of a masculine girl, or a trans girl instead of a feminine boy, reifies and reproduces a gendered essence rooted in an ideology that only ever functions as oppressive. This particular interpretation of gender as a system implies that it is often morally necessary to deny the pleasure derived from being fully seen, affirmed, or cared for on one's own expressed gendered terms. It reduces gender to an unchanging, biologically derived variable independent of social action.

In light of this, it is temping to embrace the sense of radical plasticity afforded by transgender pediatric care as ushering in a newly queer future. However, as Gill-Peterson (2018: 6, 4) argues, this grants "immense authority to medicine in making the trans child an ontological possibility," which historically, "at its institutional best . . . granted access to a rigid medical model premised on binary normalization. At its institutional worst, it allowed gatekeeping clinicians to reject black and trans of color children as *not plastic enough*." Phrased another way, embracing radical plasticity is akin to what Bettcher (2014b) calls the "beyond the binary" theory of gender without attention to how there are various levels of comfort within the binary.

A counterdiscourse to insidious concern is therefore situated between needing to account for diverse experiences of trans embodiment, while also accounting for how gender is both structured by but not limited to capital's needs. On the one hand, if gender is a system, we need to account for how it is enforced and reproduced. On the other, we need to account for how gendered markers can be appropriated without reproducing an ultimately cisnormative system of differentiation. Ethnographically, I have observed a situated ambivalence that grants access to institutions of care and social reproduction without commitment to its attendant ideological constraints. Oftentimes, this entails expressing grievances about a medical model of gender while using the vocabulary of medicine. I do not mean ambivalence in the sense of apathy; rather, it is a recognition that our subjectivities may indeed be structured in large part by capitalism and all of its disciplining institutions, but that they are also not reducible to those institutions' restraints. Similarly, these institutions regularly fail to produce manageable subjects without rendering them illegible. What we have instead is a bricolage of meanings that we can attempt to reappropriate.

For example, Rebecca, mother of a trans boy, has used "gender dysphoria" not as an explanation or diagnostic category legitimating her son's subjectivity but as a way of describing his experience with social and medical institutions themselves. "He hasn't had real dysphoria until recently when he was saying he wants to be like a 'normal boy'... he doesn't want to get shots every month. He doesn't want to worry about his implant having other effects... *that* brought on his dysphoria, *society*, in a way, brought on his dysphoria." Here, Rebecca uses what is usually a diagnostic requirement for treatment as instead a reflection of the effects of living in a transphobic society. Rather than using dysphoria as explanatory criteria or as a means of circumventing medical gatekeeping, she argues that the consciousness of one's body brought on by interaction with a medical institution is what created the presence of dysphoria in the first place, while also recognizing that medical interaction is necessary for her son's desired embodiment. A medical framework is not just a normalizing force geared toward creating a subject suitable for capitalist reproduction. Rebecca uses the vocabulary of dysphoria to explain exactly how medicine falls short of encapsulating her son's subjectivity.

Similarly, physicians sometimes circumvent the diagnostic criteria required for insurance approval through use of a different diagnosis altogether: endocrine disorder. In cases in which a patient already has access to mental health services or documenting gender dysphoria would prove problematic, some physicians opt to diagnose their adolescent patients with "endocrine disorder" instead. The implications of this diagnosis, as opposed to gender dysphoria, are surprisingly radical. Instead of construing the trans patient as having the "mind" or "soul" of one gender "trapped" in the body of another, this diagnosis construes a trans child's body as simply producing too much or too little of certain hormones. Rather than rejecting wholesale the young body, treating an endocrine disorder is a relatively minor alteration. Physicians themselves are not thinking about these political implications. Cultivating a greater ambivalence toward diagnosis allows trans kids to remain medically legible while producing potentially transformative understandings of trans embodiment.

These examples are incomplete and far from revolutionary, but they speak to the political valence of the quotidian that trans-exclusionary feminists and others who advocate for the exclusion of trans people from feminist theory seek to minimize, downplay, or eliminate. These examples are responses to the interpellation of medicine that reappropriates language with ambivalence and ambiguity. They take on a normative vocabulary without reproducing its entire logic. Recognizing the dual potential of "care" to recapitulate the social forms and violences of capitalism as well as its ability to produce something new is a productive way of both critiquing the normative order and recognizing nascent possibilities that lie ahead.

Mikey Elster is a PhD candidate in sociocultural anthropology at the City University of New York Graduate Center. Their current dissertation research is on the ethics and politics of care in transgender pediatrics in New York City. Their research interests include medical anthropology, North America, gender, and sexuality.

Notes

1. Names of research participants and locations are pseudonyms.
2. The text cited here is an epub, so it does not have consistent page numbers. Citations are based on the paragraph's distance from the subheading under which they appear.
3. In this section, moral panic and sex panic are used interchangeably because each panic under discussion represents a moment when sexuality was posed as primarily a moral and political threat. Gay panic and trans panic are used to refer to specific forms of moral panic where either homosexuality or being trans were the specific targets of a more general moral panic.
4. 109 Cong. Rec. House App. A34–A35 (January 10, 1963) (extension of statement by Albert S. Herlong Jr.).
5. There is a critique to be made here, such as Sarah Lamble's (2008) argument that the Trans Day of Remembrance can obfuscate racial and class inequalities by focusing on transphobia alone.
6. "Gayatri" is a pseudonym assigned by Shrier. Although we are told that they go by a different name than their parents gave them, Shrier does not create another pseudonym and continues to refer to them with feminine pronouns. Unfortunately, this entails that I continue to refer to them as "Gayatri" to avoid confusion.

References

Bauer, Heike. 2017. *The Hirschfeld Archives: Violence, Death, and Modern Queer Culture.* Philadelphia: Temple University Press.

Bercera-Culqui, Tracy A., et al. 2018. "Mental Health of Transgender and Gender Nonconforming Youth Compared with Their Peers." *Pediatrics* 141, no. 5: 1–11. https://doi.org/10.1542/peds .2017-3845.

Berlant, Lauren. 1997. *The Queen of America Goes to Washington City: Essays on Sex and Citizenship.* Durham, NC: Duke University Press.

Berlant, Lauren and Michael Warner. 1998. "Sex in Public." *Critical Inquiry* 24, no. 2: 547–66.

Bettcher, Talia Mae. 2014a. "Transphobia." *TSQ* 1, nos. 1–2: 249–51.

Bettcher, Talia Mae. 2014b. "Trapped in the Wrong Theory." *Signs* 39, no. 2: 383–406.

Bjork-James, Sophie. 2020. "White Sexual Politics: The Patriarchal Family in White Nationalism and the Religious Right." *Transforming Anthropology* 28, no. 1: 58–73.

CBS News. 2021. "Transgender Healthcare." *60 Minutes*, May 23. https://www.cbsnews.com /video/60minutes-2021-05-23/.

Chodzen, Gia, Marco A. Hidalgo, Diane Chen, and Robert Garofalo. 2019. "Minority Stress Factors Associated with Depression and Anxiety among Transgender and Gender-Nonconforming Youth." *Journal of Adolescent Health* 64, no. 4: 467–71. https://doi.org/10.1016/j.jadohealth .2018.07.006.

Colen, Shellee. 1995. "'Like a Mother to Them': Stratified Reproduction and West Indian Child-care Workers and Employers in New York City." In *Conceiving the New World Order: The Global Politics of Reproduction*, edited by Faye D. Ginsburg and Rayna Rapp, 78–102. Berkeley: University of California Press.

Collins, Jane, and Victoria Mayer. 2010. *Both Hands Tied: Welfare Reform and the Race to the Bottom in the Low-Wage Labor Market*. Chicago: University of Chicago Press.

Conservapedia. n.d. "Feminism." https://www.conservapedia.com/Feminism (accessed May 31, 2021).

Conservapedia. n.d. "Homosexual Agenda." https://www.conservapedia.com/Homosexual_Agenda (accessed May 31, 2021).

Cooper, Melinda 2017. *Family Values: Between Neoliberalism and the New Social Conservatism*. Brooklyn, NY: Zone.

Currah, Paisley, and Tara Mulqueen. 2011. "Securitizing Gender: Identity, Biometrics, and Transgender Bodies at the Airport." *Social Research* 78, no. 2: 557–82.

Davis, Dána-Ain 2019. *Reproductive Injustice: Racism, Pregnancy, and Premature Birth*. New York: NYU Press.

Fraser, Nancy. 2016. "Contradictions of Capital and Care." *New Left Review*, no. 100: 99–117.

Gabriel, Kay. 2020. "Gender as Accumulation Strategy." *Invert Journal* 1. https://invertjournal.org.uk/posts?view=articles&post=7106265#gender-as-accumulation-strategy.

Gill-Peterson, Jules. 2018. *Histories of the Transgender Child*. Minneapolis: University of Minnesota Press.

Lamble, Sarah. 2008. "Retelling Racialized Violence, Remaking White Innocence: The Politics of Interlocking Oppressions in Transgender Day of Remembrance." *Sexuality Research and Social Policy* 5, no. 1: 24–42.

Malatino, Hil. 2020. *Trans Care*. Minneapolis: University of Minnesota Press.

Maskovsky, Jeff. 2021. "Engendering White Nationalism." In *Race, Gender, and Political Culture in the Trump Era: The Fascist Allure*, edited by Christine A. Kray and Uli Linke. Milton Park, UK: Taylor and Francis.

Munce, Meghan. 2021. "Texas Senate Resumes Push to Ban Transition-Related Medical Care for Transgender Children, Days after Bill Failed in House." *Texas Tribune*, May 17. https://www.texastribune.org/2021/05/17/texas-transgender-children-medical-care/.

Page, Enoch H., and Matt U. Richardson. 2009. "On the Fear of Small Numbers." In *Black Sexualities: Probing Powers, Passions, Practices, and Policies*, edited by Juan Battle and Sandra L. Barnes, 57–81. New Brunswick, NJ: Rutgers University Press.

Payne, Daniel. 2016. "The Transgender Suicide Rate Isn't Due to Discrimination." *Federalist*, July 7. https://thefederalist.com/2016/07/07/evidence-the-transgender-suicide-rate-isnt-due-to-discrimination/.

Peters, Torey. 2021 *Detransition, Baby*. New York: Penguin Random House.

Roberts, Dorothy E. 1997. *Killing the Black Body: Race, Reproduction, and the Meaning of Liberty*. New York: Penguin Random House.

Salamon, Gayle. *The Life and Death of Latisha King: A Critical Phenomenology of Transphobia*. New York: New York University Press.

Serano, Julia. 2017. "Stop Pitting Detransitioners against Happily Transitioned People." *Whipping Girl* (blog), June 30. http://juliaserano.blogspot.com/2017/06/stop-pitting-detransitoners-against.html.

Shrier, Abigail. 2020. *Irreversible Damage: The Transgender Craze Seducing Our Daughters*. Washington, DC: Regnery.

Skousen, W. Cleon. (1958) 2014. *The Naked Communist*. Salt Lake City: Izzard Ink.

Snorton, C. Riley. 2017. *Black on Both Sides: A Racial History of Trans Identity*. Minneapolis: University of Minnesota Press.

Snorton, C. Riley, and Jin Haritaworn. 2013. "Trans Necropolitics: A Transnational Reflection on Violence, Death, and the Trans of Color Afterlife." In *The Transgender Studies Reader 2*, edited by Susan Stryker and Aren Z. Aizura, 66–76. New York: Routledge.

Stevenson, Lisa. 2014. *Life beside Itself: Imagining Care in the Canadian Arctic*. Berkeley: University of California Press.

Stock, Kathleen. 2021. *Material Girls: Why Reality Matters for Feminism*. London: Little Brown Book Group. Kindle.

Valentine, David. 2007. *Imagining Transgender: An Ethnography of a Category*. Durham, NC: Duke University Press.

Zazanis, Noah. 2021. "Social Reproduction and Social Cognition: Theorizing (Trans)gender Identity Development in Community Context." In *Transgender Marxism*, edited by Gleeson and O'Rourke, 33–46. London: Pluto.

Sympathy, Fear, Hate

Trans-Exclusionary Radical Feminism and Evangelical Christianity

C. LIBBY

Abstract A recent pastoral guide designed to help Christians better understand "transgender individuals and the broader ideological movement" took a seemingly bizarre turn when it urged readers to sympathize with radical feminist concerns about the safety of women and the increasing threat to their very identity. While the depiction of the dangerous trans subject as a potential source of injury is nothing new, the increasingly frequent evangelical reliance on affectively charged rhetoric mimicking trans-exclusionary radical feminist writing is surprising enough to merit further investigation. This essay analyzes and responds to the burgeoning connections between trans-exclusionary radical feminism, "gender critical" writing, and transphobic evangelical Christian rhetoric by arguing that their affective resonance, predicated on the proper cultivation of sympathy, fear, and hatred, is made possible by a shared commitment to a dimorphic conception of sex difference and the politics of injury.
Keywords transphobia, evangelical Christianity, gender critical, affect studies, transgender studies

Evangelical Christian leaders in the United States and the United Kingdom have spent the last decade compiling pamphlets, blog posts, and books designed to educate the broader evangelical community about the transgender movement, or what they call the newest "assault on the sexes" (O'Leary and Sprigg 2015). Typically, the argument against transgender rights in these texts proceeds as follows: first the authors assert that the modern transgender movement is attempting to radically change understandings of sex and gender; this is followed by a review of terminology such as *sex*, *gender*, *gender identity*, and the assertion that these new definitions undermine the divinely ordained, immutable, and transhistorical conception of dimorphic sex; finally the authors provide practical tips for dealing with transgender subjects including prohibiting gender affirming surgery and the use of hormone replacement theory, frequently encouraging misgendering so as to avoid deception, and recommending

TSQ: Transgender Studies Quarterly ★ Volume 9, Number 3 ★ August 2022 **425**
DOI 10.1215/23289252-9836078 © 2022 Duke University Press

reparative therapy to realign the subject's gender identity with their sex assigned at birth (O'Leary and Sprigg 2015; Evangelical Alliance 2018; Council on Biblical Manhood and Womanhood 2017; Family Policy Alliance n.d.; Focus on the Family 2015; Minnesota Family Council 2019; Sprinkle 2021). These manuals also typically include a brief discussion of intersex conditions, which are described as extremely rare and in no way related to the current debate regarding transgender subjects.[1]

The rhetorical and citational scaffolding of these documents mirrors earlier evangelical responses to gay rights activism and the broader LGBTQIA movement (Jordan 2011; Cobb 2006). The sources quoted are typically outdated, one-sided, and at odds with broader scientific and medical communities. The rhetoric is alarmist, stressing moral decay, contagion, and apocalypticism, and the use of biblical texts reflects a historical-grammatical hermeneutic reliant on a handful of verses and a specifically anti-LGBTQIA interpretive framework. However, what is unique in these specifically anti-transgender statements is the inclusion of trans-exclusionary radical feminist and "gender critical" writing as representative of the "feminist" perspective on transgender issues. For instance, the recent pastoral guide, "Transformed: A Brief Biblical and Pastoral Intro-duction to Understanding Transgender in a Changing Culture," takes a seem-ingly bizarre turn by citing gender critical author Germaine Greer's warning that biological women are "losing out everywhere" (Evangelical Alliance 2018: 23; Gilligan 2017). Even more surprising is Dale O'Leary and Peter Sprigg's (2015: 5) citation of trans-exclusionary radical feminist Janice Raymond to bolster their argument that transsexuality is a "rebellion against reality" or, as Raymond (1994: xxiii) puts it, "the falsification of reality." Later O'Leary and Sprigg (2015: 17) cite Raymond as an exemplar of the conflict between transgender women and les-bian feminists who view "men pretending to be women as 'invading women' by 'reducing the real female form to an artifact, appropriating this body for them-selves.'" Why evangelical leaders would incorporate a thinker who is purportedly responsible for what they earlier termed the first (feminist) and second (homo-sexual) waves of the "assault on the sexes" is perplexing indeed (1). However, these are by no means the only uses of trans-exclusionary radical feminist and gender critical writing by evangelical authors. In fact, it is almost impossible to find an evangelical opinion paper or book on transgender issues that doesn't make use of such writing.

The depiction of the dangerous transgender subject as a potential source of injury is nothing new, but the increasingly frequent reliance by evangelicals on the affectively charged rhetoric of trans-exclusionary radical feminist writ-ing is surprising enough to merit further investigation. This essay analyzes and responds to the burgeoning connections between trans-exclusionary radical fem-inism, gender critical writing, and transphobic evangelical rhetoric by arguing that contemporary transphobia is not merely a conceptual error that can be remediated through intellectual debate. Rather, this form of transphobia, undergirded by a shared commitment to a dimorphic sex difference and the politics of injury, is facilitated by an affective resonance of sympathy, fear, and hatred between these unlikely groups.

The task of examining the relationship between trans-exclusionary radical feminist rhetoric and evangelical Christianity is imperative, now more than ever, given the radical increase in anti-transgender legislation in the United States and United Kingdom, the devastating increase in transgender homicides, and the concerted attacks on transgender rights from Christian leaders and gender critical scholars. As Siobhan Kelly (2016) astutely notes, "The brand of transphobia located in some feminist religious discourses is now being repackaged into the rhetoric used by supporters of the legal exclusion of transgender people, such as by North Carolina's HB2." Responding to these threats, transgender studies scholars (Bettcher 2007; Stanley 2011; Salamon 2018) have written extensively about the ideological and political underpinnings of transphobia and anti-transgender violence. The monograph *TERF Wars: Feminism and the Fight for Transgender Futures* (Pearce, Erikainen, and Vincent 2020) focuses specifically on the recent proliferation of debates about transgender inclusion within feminism. Likewise, religious studies scholars have written broadly about conservative Christianity's acrimonious relationship with the LGBTQIA movement. For instance, R. Janet Jakobsen and Ann Pellegrini (2003: 4) explore how "quintessential American assumptions about religion, values, and public life are crucially connected to sexuality and its regulation." Mark D. Jordan's (2011) text, *Recruiting Young Love*, maps a rhetorical genealogy of Christian conceptions of homosexuality to demonstrate that, although claims of universalism are often made, these rhetorics are historically specific and inextricably entangled with the language of modern sexology, psychiatry, and social reform. Although Jordan's book concerns itself primarily with the church's response to white gay men, he offers a prescient warning when he notes that "some church voices define homosexuality as a sinful failure of gender, rather than of sex, and they respond to it by restoring what they regard as the right relation between male and female" (xviii). Emphases on right relations between the sexes and on the regulation of one's relationship to sex itself are now at the forefront of Christian anti-transgender rhetoric. Finally, in response to Kelly's (2016) and Max Strassfeld's (2018) calls to put transgender studies in conversation with religious studies, a handful of scholars have begun to theorize the relationship between transphobia and conservative Christianity (Blyth and McRae 2018) and to map the broader connections between radical feminism, transphobia, and religion (O'Donnell 2019; Partridge 2018). However, despite this robust field of scholarship, there has been little attention paid, thus far, to the prolific use of trans-exclusionary radical feminist writing by evangelical leaders or to the affective resonance between these two groups.[2]

Before exploring this connection further, it is important to mention that two terms used throughout this essay have contested and complicated histories: *trans-exclusionary radical feminism* (TERF) and *evangelical*. The acronym for trans-exclusionary radical feminists was coined in the 2000s to pinpoint a specific subset of radical feminists who articulated transgender exclusion as a fundamental component of their feminism (Pearce, Erikainen, and Vincent 2020; Smythe 2018). Radical feminists, including Mary Daly, her student Janice Raymond, Sheila Jeffreys, and Germaine Greer, depict transgender individuals and transgender women more specifically as a minacious presence bent on infiltrating feminist spaces and harming female bodies. These writers advocate for the wholesale exclusion of transgender women from feminist spaces, reaffirm a binary dimorphic understanding of sex difference, and use the rhetoric of mutilation, invasion, rape, and destruction to cultivate fear and hatred among their readers. Recently, there has been a move to eliminate the use of the acronym *TERF* by designating it as hate speech. Today, authors who affirm a similarly trans-exclusionary position prefer to be referred to as gender critical feminists or just feminists. In a recent interview, when asked about their position on the use of the term *TERF*, Judith Butler stated that in their opinion, *TERF* is a descriptive rather than a derogatory term (Ferber 2020). In concert with Butler, this article uses the phrase *trans-exclusionary radical feminist* descriptively to refer to authors whose understanding of transgender subjectivity aligns with the position above, but I avoid the use of the acronym. While I am sensitive to the fact that some consider the term offensive, I interpret the move to obfuscate the distinction between trans-exclusionary radical feminists and the broader feminist community as part of an ongoing effort by conservative and anti-transgender writers to enact a re-semantization of *feminism* in hopes of misleading readers by blurring the ideological differences between these trans-exclusionary writers and most feminist thinkers today. This re-semantization also appears in evangelical writing as authors consistently frame the anti-transgender vitriol expressed by a handful of trans-exclusionary radical feminists as representative of "feminism." This re-semantization of the term limits its purview while simultaneously making its corresponding conservative evangelical position more palatable to politically left-leaning subjects. This strategy is particularly apparent in the pamphlets and books designed to educate parents and laypeople about transgender issues (Evangelical Alliance 2018; Family Policy Alliance n.d.; Minnesota Family Council 2019). For example, the purportedly radical feminist group Women's Liberation Front (WoLF) explains their co-branding of the parent resource guide developed by the Minnesota Family Council (2019: ii) by claiming that the document highlights "the concerns of many parents on the political left who recognize the negative impact of gender identity ideology."

The second contested term that appears in this essay is *evangelical*. The difficulty of pinning down who or what counts as evangelical has been attested to by countless scholars (Kidd 2019; Worthen 2014). For the purposes of this article, following historian Molly Worthen (2014: 4), I use what she refers to as a historian's definition of evangelical, one that uses the term to refer to the wide range of Christians who share a historical lineage in the "revivals and moral crusades of the eighteenth and nineteenth centuries." Pointing to this historical lineage offers a capacious definition while also drawing attention to the long history of affective formation within evangelicalism.[3] As religious studies scholar Elizabeth B. Clark (1995: 476) notes, "In America, evangelicalism became the popular locus for the affective style; the conversion experience offered an immediate, personal connection with God forged in moments of heightened emotional sensibility. This emphasis on affect has subsequently played a pivotal role in conservative evangelical moral and political formations. Finally, because it would be impossible to represent the multitudinous viewpoints of the approximately 24.5 percent of the US population that identify as evangelical, I do not suggest that all individual evangelicals hold the views espoused by the leaders referenced in this article (Pew Research Center 2021). Rather, when I refer to evangelicals, I am specifically talking about conservative evangelical leaders. To understand the viewpoints of these contemporary evangelical leaders and their position on transgender issues, I examined a wide range of materials including brochures, position statements, pamphlets, books, blog posts, newspaper and magazine articles, and educational materials. I leave it to other scholars to extend this work by exploring how these official publications are being implemented on the ground in churches, Christian schools, pastoral counseling sessions, and home-school curricula.

Despite their distinct historical and ideological lineages, contemporary evangelical and trans-exclusionary radical feminist positions on transgender issues share an affective resonance. An important component of this affective resonance emerges in the grouping of transgender individuals together with what is called transgender ideology, or simply gender ideology. Anti-trans rhetoric today positions transgender rights as part of a larger "transgender agenda" that threatens to endanger women and children and to strip Christians of their civil rights (Family Policy Alliance n.d.). Much like the earlier panic over the "homosexual agenda," transgender activism is framed as part of a wide-ranging social disease sweeping across the United States. Michael K. Laidlaw, in his endorsement of the Minnesota Family Council's *Parent Resource Guide* (2019: iii), advises parents to use the guide to educate themselves about the new "unscientific gender paradigm" so they can acquire "the true medical facts of this social contagion." Fear mongering around the metaphor of social contagion is extended to an outright call to arms in service of the protection of binary gender on the Focus on the Family website, which states, "We believe that this is a cultural and theological challenge that we must engage and win. The modern 'transgender' movement is systematically work-ing to dismantle the reality of two sexes—male and female—as the Bible and the world have always known this to be" (Focus on the Family 2015). This tactic of positioning transgender rights as an attack on the divinely ordained, immu-table, and historically verifiable understanding of sex as binary appears in offi-cial documents such as the Nashville Statement, on evangelical websites, and in Christian educational materials. For example, Colin Smothers's blog post response to Joe Biden's commitment to transgender protections under US law relies on the presumed immutability of binary sex. Smothers's (2020) post, "Trans-gender Tide Rising," endorses a rudimentary "common sense" understanding of the imperativeness of binary sex difference, asserting that it is "one of the most basic, indisputable, scientifically-verifiable, essential for-the-continuation-of-the-human-race-indispensable facts of our existence." Alarmingly, these appeals to history, common sense, and science are based on a myopic understanding of historical and scientific writing on sex and gender. And, importantly, this posi-tioning of transgender individuals as contagious vectors of a new dangerous gender ideology renders them unsympathetic to evangelical audiences.

Sympathy for Women

Sympathy has played a formative role in evangelical moral and political forma-tion since the antebellum period. Clark (1995: 476) explains that evangelical reli-gious practice "made popular a style of moral reasoning from sympathy and compassion." During the Great Awakenings in the United States, many evan-gelicals envisioned "the good society as a network of benevolent believers, united by ties of sentiment, their hearts quivering with affectionate regard for the well-being of others" (477). Subsequently, affective appeals have undergirded a wide array of evangelical political campaigns including abolitionism, temperance, anti-pornography, anti–sex trafficking, and the antiabortion movement. This type of affective appeal often relies on the juxtaposition between a sympathetic innocent victim and a pernicious threat. In modern anti-transgender writing, those who espouse the conservative ideology of binary sex difference are the vic-tims, while transgender people are figured as the threat to be feared and hated.

Conservative Christian leaders have spoken with a unified voice about the perils of transgender identity and have positioned "gender ideology" in direct opposition to their understanding of a Christian worldview. Their refusal to

sympathize with transgender subjects is justified by foregrounding a patholo-
gizing interpretation of transgender subjectivity in concert with an emphasis
on the dangers of gender ideology. This refusal of sympathy is equally prevalent
among trans-exclusionary radical feminists. For instance, Raymond (2021: 232)
cautions against sympathizing with transgender people, warning that "misplaced
sympathy will only strengthen a society in which new sex roles are the norm, where
gender crises become subject to medicalization, and where self-declaration of
sex is epidemic." Reflecting on these refusals of sympathy, I argue that the rigid
understanding of sex difference espoused by these groups delimits the proper
objects of sympathy to cisgender, typically white women and positions transgender people as the locus of fear and hatred.

Trans-exclusionary radical feminists, gender critical writers, and evangelical leaders vehemently defend a dimorphic understanding of sex difference.
For instance, gender critical author Sheila Jeffreys (2014: 6) reifies biological sex
difference and opposes concepts such as gender identity because, as she states, "it
disappears biology and all the experience that those with female biology have of
being reared in a caste system based on sex." This interpretation should sound
familiar to those who have read earlier trans-exclusionary radical feminist writing
by Daly, Greer, and Raymond. In fact, Jeffreys (2014: 6, 11) lauds Raymond's book,
The Transsexual Empire (1994), as a "deservedly well-known tour de force" and
"ground-breaking." Although these authors claim to reject essentialist conceptions of gender, their writing reflects both gender realism (the view that women
have some feature in common that makes them women) and a rigid understanding of sex dimorphism (Mikkola 2009). Linda Alcoff (1988: 408–9) offers
a brilliant analysis of this trend in her essay, "Cultural Feminism versus Post-
structuralism: The Identity Crisis in Feminist Theory," where she demonstrates
that despite Daly's "warnings against biological reductionism" she consistently
depicts "women's identification as female as their defining essence."[4] This understanding of sex difference and gender realism is undergirded by an exclusionary imperative that refuses to incorporate transgender women into the category
of woman.

Although these exclusionary tactics have historically targeted transgender
women, recent anti-transgender writing has turned its attention to transgender
men and nonbinary transgender subjects. Here the broader transgender movement is figured as an ominous threat designed to ostracize those assigned female
at birth from their bodies and their communities. This argument appears in Janice
Raymond's (2021) latest foray back into the topic of transgender subjectivity,
Doublethink: A Feminist Challenge to Transgenderism. Raymond's new book offers
a comprehensive compendium of anti-transgender writing alongside a reiteration
of her earlier project, *The Transsexual Empire*. Unfortunately, she does not engage

with transgender scholars in any meaningful way, choosing rather to ignore the nearly half-century of writing on the topic. Nonetheless, she claims that "recent research has indicated that the majority of those who are transgendering currently are young girls on a path to becoming trans-identified men" (94). According to Raymond, the increasing number of transgender men is directly related to the disdain "both society and the trans movement hold [for] women who are lesbians" (100). In her estimation, this crisis can be solved only by returning to a clear articulation of binary sex difference as biologically based and immutable (26).

Because evangelicals draw so heavily on trans-exclusionary radical feminist and gender critical writing about sex and gender, their conception of sex dimorphism is almost identical. To affirm the givenness of binary sex, evangelical writers weave a mix of scientific and "feminist" writing into their arguments. For example, evangelical writer Preston M. Sprinkle (2021: 32) offers a seemingly cut-and-dried description of sex dimorphism in his most recent book, *Embodied: Transgender Identities*, where he writes, "A person is biologically male or female based on four things: presence or absence of a Y chromosome, internal reproductive organs, external sexual anatomy, and endocrine systems that produce secondary sex characteristics." This straightforward list is representative of Sprinkle's larger claim that his book relies on scientific facts and established feminist interpretations of sex difference to guide Christians toward a proper response to the transgender movement. Unfortunately, *Embodied* is riddled with incoherent arguments and blatant misrepresentations of feminist writing. For example, when Sprinkle cites Hilary M. Lips's book *Gender: The Basics* to support his interpretation of sex difference, he claims she says that "sex refers to 'a person's biological maleness or femaleness' and 'is reserved for discussion of anatomy and the classification of individuals based on their anatomical category'" (32). However, as far as I can tell, the second phrase never appears in her book. As for the first quote, what she says is, "People who study the differences and similarities between women and men have sometimes made a distinction between sex and gender. They may use the term sex to refer to biological femaleness and maleness, and the term gender to refer to culturally mediated expectations and roles associated with masculinity and femininity" (Lips 2014: 2). Later she adds another caveat to this point, writing, "Although we tend to think of female and male as two distinct, non-overlapping categories, the fact that sex develops through a series of sequential steps shows that there are some possibilities for these categories to be fuzzy" (7). This is a very different understanding of biological sex difference than Sprinkle would lead his readers to believe. Things only get more problematic when he turns to his next "feminist" expert, Rebecca Riley-Cooper. Riley-Cooper is part of the growing number of UK-based writers who claim the moniker *gender critical*. These writers believe that sexual dimorphism is an undisputed biological fact and that transgender women should not be permitted to claim the category of woman, and they argue that allowing them to do so harms women by evacuating the category of meaning. This presentation of a gender critical position as indicative of feminism more broadly is common in evangelical writing and dangerously misleading. Furthermore, it ignores the robust conversation within feminist writing on the categorization of woman (Jenkins 2016; Stryker and Bettcher 2016; Watson 2016). Sprinkle (2021: 32) concludes this section with the assertion, "Sexual dimorphism among non-intersex humans is an established, observable, objective, scientific, the-earth-is-round-and-not-flat sort of fact." This type of jocular posturing is designed to foreclose debate and reify dimorphic sex difference over and against gender ideology.

Despite evangelical and trans-exclusionary radical feminist certainty regarding the universal givenness of sex dimorphism, this understanding of sex difference is highly contested. As Leah DeVun (2021: 201) elegantly demonstrates in *The Shape of Sex: Nonbinary Gender from Genesis to the Renaissance*, "sexual binarism was neither a natural nor a timeless phenomenon." Historians of premodern Europe have explored the variegated nature of medieval understandings of sex difference from a wide range of perspectives, and what is clear is that the idea that humans are distinctly "binary-sexed" was in no way "self-evident to all premodern thinkers" (38).[5] A similar argument against the ubiquity of binary sex difference can be made by examining Indigenous, non-Western, and other non-Christian sources.[6] So, when did this idea of biologically fixed dimorphic sex emerge?

Scholars have traced the emergence of Western scientific descriptions of "male and female anatomies as radically different" to the late eighteenth and early nineteenth centuries (Mikkola 2016: 38). The historical and cultural specificity of this understanding of sex difference is significant insofar as it forms the basis of trans-exclusionary radical feminist and evangelical conceptions of sex. Kyla Schuller (2018) offers insight into the scientific and cultural origins of sex difference by exploring the development of what she terms the "biopolitics of feeling." In this framework, sexual differentiation is understood as a unique achievement of the civilized and embedded in the burgeoning field of race science. Schuller writes, "A flurry of new and long-lasting tactics of sex difference emerge in this period, including policed dress; sex- and race-segregated bathrooms; restrictions on abortion and contraception; sex- and race-based admission policies to newly established educational and professional institutions; the gradual consolidation of modern sexuality; and feminist claims for women's political rights" (16). In this context "race stabilizes the economic and biological health of the populations, which enables the development of civilization, while sex difference stabilizes civilization" (16). In other words, the rhetoric of sexual dimorphism cannot be disentangled from the development of the biopolitics of race.

Transgender studies scholar Jules Gill-Peterson (2018) traces this phenomenon into the twentieth century, foregrounding the racial history of medicine, to explore how the racialized genealogies of transsexuality and transgender medicine impacted transgender children specifically (2018). Hil Malatino's (2019) incisive writing on the biopolitics of gender links the development of the concepts of sex and gender back to sexologist John Money's problematic work on intersex conditions. According to Malatino, what is discovered is that the idea of an "essentialized, transhistorical, acultural medical understanding of gender" is anything but that (179). Rather, like sex, it is deeply embedded in a biopolitics steeped in race science and heteronormativity. Ultimately, an investment in a dimorphic conception of sex difference is an investment in a biopolitics of gender rooted in white supremacy.

Contextualizing the Evangelical Christian Worldview

The affective resonances of sympathy and fear between trans-exclusionary radical feminists and evangelicals are undergirded by a commitment to a dimorphic conception of sex difference. However, despite this agreement, there are innumerable ideological differences between these two groups. The radical feminist authors quoted in these Christian texts frequently argue elsewhere for the proliferation of lesbianism, the destruction of patriarchal foundations in society and in Christianity specifically, and for the dissolution of hierarchical family formations. Clearly, these goals are at odds with evangelical conceptions of sexual morality, society, and family life. Nevertheless, evangelical reliance on trans-exclusionary feminist writing is undeniable. In light of this dissonance, it is tempting to suggest that the quotations from trans-exclusionary radical feminists may simply be another example of the anti-intellectual practice of proof texting, or taking a portion of text (usually biblical) out of context and displaying a willful disinterest in the broader argument of the passage, the genre, or the historical context.

This practice of proof texting has been a cornerstone of anti-LGBT arguments propounded by conservative evangelical leaders. However, Worthen (2013: 2) problematizes this beguiling oversimplification in her text, *Apostles of Reason*, where she argues that it is the persistent crisis of authority, rather than simply anti-intellectualism, that has rendered evangelicalism a "minefield for independent thought." Worthen deftly maps a genealogy of this crisis, linking it to an intellectual milieu characterized by rampant separatism, pseudohistory, and the rise of the religious right. Beginning with the exaltation of the concept of Weltanschauung, or worldview, during the 1940s, Worthen examines how Weltanschauung offered evangelicals a solution to the problem of authority, by positing a unifying "Christian worldview," and provided a common enemy, the burgeoning "non-redemptive religion called 'modernism' or 'liberalism'" (31). Ultimately, Worthen concludes that the rhetorical strategy of the Christian worldview is to "curtail debate, justify hardline politics, and discourage . . . moderation or compromise" (261). Evangelical anti-transgender writing replicates this strategy by positioning "liberal" gender ideology in direct opposition to a Christian worldview that defends sex dimorphism. Although this adaptable worldview claims to offer universal epistemological and moral guidance for Christians, it is ultimately imbricated in the specific historical, cultural, and theological milieu in which it developed. Challenging these claims of unbiased universalism, scholars (Curtis 2021; Butler 2021) have demonstrated that, much like most of US evangelicalism, the contemporary evangelical Christian worldview is damningly inflected by race science, white supremacy, and xenophobia.

A staunch commitment to a worldview that upholds dimorphic sex difference as the only possible reality makes it necessary for both conservative evangelical Christians and trans-exclusionary radical feminists to deny the empirical facts of historical variability and the racist origins of sex difference in the name of gender realism. This leads them to espouse an incoherent combination of claims, simultaneously attesting to the value of "facts" above all else while denying large swaths of historical reality. Despite this position's logical incoherence, the repeated articulation of binary sex difference as the Christian alternative to gender ideology endows it with the affective power to sustain a fear and hatred of transgender people while cultivating sympathy for those who adhere to a binary conception of sex difference. This affective power is further enhanced by the claim that gender ideology is not only anti-Christian but also a source of injury.

Evangelicals have not only incorporated trans-exclusionary radical feminist writing into their anti-transgender positions, but they also claim that their partnership with this group highlights the unprecedented nature of the "transgender threat." The recent cooperation between an evangelical lobbying group, Family Policy Alliance, and a self-declared radical feminist organization, WoLF, in filing a Supreme Court brief opposing bathroom and locker room access for transgender students highlights this collaboration. After filing the brief, the Family Policy Alliance's (2017) website declared, "How wrong does something have to be for a Christian pro-family organization and a self-described radical-feminist group to oppose it together at the Supreme Court?" In fact, this is not the first time these groups have worked in concert. Beginning with the Reagan administration, many radical feminists found common ground with evangelicals on issues of sex trafficking and pornography (Duggan and Hunter 2006; Bernstein 2007, 2010; Bernstein and Jakobsen 2010; Jackson, Reed, and Brents 2017). After losing ground in the battles against domestic pornography and sex work, in 1988 the radical feminist group Women Against Pornography (WAP) decided to shift their focus toward international sex trafficking (Jackson, Reed, and Brents 2017: 70). As a result of this new direction, WAP leaders Laura Lederer, Janice Raymond, and Doris Leidholdt created the Coalition Against Trafficking in Women (CATW), which subsequently partnered with evangelicals to promote the Trafficking Victims Protection Act of 2000. Nonetheless, it is important not to overstate the participation of radical feminists in current evangelical efforts to promote their anti-transgender worldview. Aside from WoLF, a group with close ties to evangelicals, there has been little indication that radical feminists have authorized or are even aware of the use of their work in these new, anti-transgender evangelical texts.[7] In summary, despite their historical coalition around pornography and sex trafficking, single-issue ideological alignment can't fully explain evangelical leaders' prolific use of trans-exclusionary radical feminist writing, given the diametrical opposition of the two groups on almost every other issue. So, what else is driving evangelicals' promiscuous use of trans-exclusionary radical feminist writing?

The Politics of Injury

Modern anti-transgender writing purports to defend a universal, commonsense, biologically based understanding of dimorphic sex difference. This claim allows writers to position what they call the new gender ideology as both a threat and as a source of injury. For example, the Evangelical Alliance's (2018: 23) pamphlet, *Transformed*, aligns itself with gender critical writers, noting that "some Christians have agreed with concerns being raised by women's groups and others about the safety of women, but also more fundamentally that their very identity is being challenged." According to this logic, gender ideology introduces novel definitions for the supposedly established categories of sex and gender. In turn, these new formulations threaten to destabilize the traditional meaning of the category "woman" and thereby eliminate the grounds to fight sex-based violence and discrimination. This destabilization is depicted as a threat to the "Christian worldview" and women's rights more broadly. As a result, two groups emerge as victims of gender ideology: evangelical Christians and (white) women.

The politics of injury is a political and affective strategy utilized by both liberal and conservative groups. According to Janet Halley (2005: 68), the politics of injury foregrounds "the concept of harm" as "central both to the feminist understanding of women's experience in patriarchy, and to the optimal approach of feminism to law." This appeal to injury is prominent in trans-exclusionary radical feminist writing and in evangelical anti-transgender documents. Given the vast array of scholarship that addresses the contested nature of the category of woman (Jenkins 2016; Stryker and Bettcher 2016; Watson 2016) and details the shortcomings of legal rights arguments based on sex difference (Brown 1995), it is noteworthy that both trans-exclusionary radical feminist writers and evangelical leaders continue to utilize a politics of injury to fortify their anti-transgender position. This appeal to injury works to further consolidate affective resonance between these groups by drumming up sympathy for cis women broadly while denigrating transgender subjects.

Describing how an appeal to injury can be used to garner undeserved sympathy, journalist Samantha Schmidt (2020) explains that the "feminist" group WoLF position themselves as victims of martyrdom and silencing to facilitate the group's image as under attack, even though they are "being platformed by the largest, most-funded legal organizations in the world."[8] This reliance on a politics of injury also undergirds religious rhetoric that falsely positions Christians as victims of secular culture. Michael Cobb (2006: 5) describes the Christian Right's use of this tactic in his book *God Hates Fags*, where he explains that "followers portray themselves as religious victims in a secular world" and claim to be "some of the most persecuted people in a world that devalues their strong religious faith." Both groups also consistently foreground claims of white female vulnerability to argue against transgender rights (Patel 2017; Koyama 2020).

Wendy Brown (1995: xi) describes how a reliance on wounded attachments forms the basis for what she terms "ungrounded persistence in ontological essentialism and epistemological foundationalism, for infelicitous formulations of identity rooted in injury, for litigiousness as a way of political life, and for a resurgence of rights discourse." This resonates with the strategies utilized by both evangelical and trans-exclusionary radical feminists against transgender rights. Although Brown is addressing the limitations of injury as a political strategy for the Left, her insights are relevant here as well. This emphasis on wounding and exclusion results in a stultifying political position that limits freedom while further solidifying exclusionary logics. As she writes, "Politicized identity thus becomes attached to its own exclusion because it is premised on this exclusion for its very existence" (72–73).

The politics of injury utilized by conservative Christian writers and 'gender critical' feminists to justify their anti-transgender animus is powered by a regime of negative affects aligned under the broader affective category of fear. Writing about religious affects, Donovan O. Schaefer (2015: 146) describes how these often emerge as exclusionary, violent affects. This tendency can be seen in the rhetorical use of panic-inducing terms such as *contagion*, *rape*, *invasion*, and *deception* to describe transgender subjects. For example, Raymond spends an entire chapter of her new book arguing that transgender women are responsible for high numbers of sexual assault within LGBTQIA communities. Likewise, James Dobson's response to the "Dear Colleague Letter on Transgender Students" swiftly moves into an endorsement of transphobic violence. Dobson (2016) writes, "If you are a married man with any gumption, surely you will defend your wife's privacy and security in restroom facilities. . . . If you are a dad, I pray you will protect your little girls from men who walk in unannounced, unzip their pants and urinate in front of them. If this had happened 100 years ago, someone might have been shot." Dobson's appeal to a fictitious historical moment when the sanctity of gender-segregated public restrooms could be defended with vigilante justice acts as a rallying cry for modern-day violence based on ahistorical nostalgia and a politics of injury.

Conclusion

Overwhelming statistical data makes it clear that anti-transgender violence far outstrips violence enacted by transgender folks. Additionally, transgender individuals suffer from higher rates of depression and suicide than either evangelicals or trans-exclusionary radical feminists. Despite these facts, in the documents referenced in this essay, cisgender women and evangelicals, not transgender people, are consistently portrayed as sympathetic, endangered, vulnerable, and subject to injury. The resilience of this transphobic position signals that transphobia is not merely a conceptual error but also a form of affective resonance predicated on a binary conception of sex difference and the politics of injury. Because the affects of sympathy, fear, and hate resonating between these groups are grounded in exclusion, a step toward combatting this form of transphobia is to foreground inclusive affects that facilitate compassion over fear and hatred and a capacious relationality over insularity. It is my hope that this essay's project of tracing the affective resonances between evangelicals and trans-exclusionary radical feminists will be the first step toward creating new affective realities that support transgender subjects and resist transphobia.

C. Libby is an assistant teaching professor in women's, gender, and sexuality studies at Penn State University.

Notes

1.   There are no explicit treatment protocols recommended for intersex conditions in these documents.
2.   Sophie Lewis (2017) brilliantly maps the connections between anti-surrogacy advocates, trans-exclusionary feminists, and conservative religious groups. There are also several newspaper and online articles detailing this connection (Gleeson 2018; Michaelson 2016; Parke 2016).
3.   Although the term *evangelical* has become almost synonymous with theological and political conservatism, historically it represented a much more expansive category than, for example, *fundamentalist*; see Balmer 1993.

4.   See O'Donnell 2019 for an analysis of the theological basis for Daly's understanding of sex difference.

5.   See Laqueur 1987 for an explanation of the one sex mode based on genital homology. Joan Cadden (1993) takes issue with the narrowness of Laqueur's investigation and offers a variety of different models of sex in the medieval period. Rhonda McDaniel (2018) proposes a third gender or a divine metagender, while others imagine there to be five or six sexes (Long 2019: 122). DeVun (2021) explores the concept of nonbinary gender in the premodern period by analyzing the theological debate about primal androgyny.

6.   For Indigenous conceptions of two-spirit, see Pyle 2018. See Tudor 2021 for decolonizing trans studies. For Jewish interpretations of nonbinary sex, see Strassfeld 2022.

7.   In an email correspondence (June 28, 2021) I had with Janice Raymond, she indicated that she was not aware that evangelicals were using her writing.

8.   Following a 2020 change to US Treasury regulations, nonprofits are no longer required to disclose donor information on their 990 tax documents. This makes it difficult, if not impossible, to identify WoLF's funding sources. However, what is clear is that, following the $15,000 grant they received from the conservative evangelical group Alliance Defending Freedom, in 2017 WoLF's funding profile has increased exponentially ($18,551 in 2018, $57,073 in 2019, $250,804 in 2020).

References

Alcoff, Linda. 1988. "Cultural Feminism versus Post-structuralism: The Identity Crisis in Feminist Theory." *Signs* 13 no. 3: 405–36.

Balmer, Randell. 1993. *Mine Eyes Have Seen the Glory: A Journey into the Evangelical Subculture in America*. Oxford: Oxford University Press.

Bernstein, Elizabeth. 2007. "The Sexual Politics of the 'New Abolitionism.'" *differences* 18, no. 3: 128–51.

Bernstein, Elisabeth. 2010. "Militarized Humanitarianism Meets Carceral Feminism: The Politics of Sex, Rights, and Freedom in Contemporary Antitrafficking Campaigns." *Signs* 36, no. 1: 45–71.

Bernstein, Elisabeth, and Janet R. Jakobsen. 2010. "Sex, Secularism, and Religious Influence in US Politics." *Third World Quarterly* 31, no. 6: 1023–39.

Bettcher, Talia Mae. 2007. "Evil Deceivers and Make-Believers: On Transphobic Violence and the Politics of Illusion." *Hypatia* 22, no. 3: 43–65.

Blyth, Caroline, and Prior McRae. 2018. "'Death by a Thousand Paper Cuts': Transphobia, Symbolic Violence, and Conservative Christian Discourse." In *Rape Culture, Gender Violence, and Religion*, edited by Caroline Blyth, Emily Colgan, and Katie B. Edwards, 111–33. London: Palgrave Macmillan.

Brown, Wendy. 1995. *States of Injury: Power and Freedom in Late Modernity*. Princeton, NJ: Princeton University Press.

Butler, Anthea. 2021. *White Evangelical Racism: The Politics of Morality in America*. Chapel Hill: University of North Carolina Press.

Cadden, Joan. 1993. *Meanings of Sex Difference in the Middle Ages: Medicine, Science, and Culture.* Cambridge: Cambridge University Press.

Clark, Elizabeth B. 1995. "'The Sacred Rights of the Weak': Pain, Sympathy, and the Culture of Individual Rights in Antebellum America." *Journal of American History* 82, no. 2: 463–93.

Cobb, Michael. 2006. *God Hates Fags: The Rhetorics of Religious Violence*. New York: New York University Press.

Council on Biblical Manhood and Womanhood. 2017. "Nashville Statement." https://cbmw.org
/nashville-statement.

Curtis, Jesse. 2021. *The Myth of Colorblind Christians: Evangelicals and White Supremacy in the Civil Rights Era*. New York: New York University Press.

DeVun, Leah. 2021. *The Shape of Sex: Nonbinary Gender from Genesis to the Renaissance*. New York: Columbia University Press.

Dobson, James. 2016. "Protect Your Kids from Tyrant Obama." *WND*, May 30. https://www.wnd.com/2016/05/protect-your-kids-from-tyrant-obama/.

Duggan, Lisa, and Nan D. Hunter. 2006. *Sex Wars: Sexual Dissent and Political Culture*. London: Routledge.

Evangelical Alliance. 2018. *Transformed: A Brief Biblical and Pastoral Introduction to Understanding Transgender in a Changing Culture*. www.eauk.org/resources/what-we-offer/reports/transformed-understanding-transgender-in-a-changing-culture.

Family Policy Alliance. 2017. "Unlikely Allies for Privacy and Safety: A Radical Feminist Group and Christian Pro-Family Group." January 9. https://familypolicyalliance.com/issues/2017/01/09/unlikely-allies-for-privacy-and-safety-a-radical-feminist-group-christian-pro-family-group/.

Family Policy Alliance. n.d. "Transgenderism and Gender Dysphoria." https://familypolicyalliance.com/issues/sexuality/transgender/ (accessed May 1, 2021).

Ferber, Alona. 2020. "Judith Butler on the Culture Wars, JK Rowling, and Living in 'Anti-intellectual Times." *New Statesman*, September 22. www.newstatesman.com/uncategorized/2020/09/judith-butler-culture-wars-jk-rowling-and-living-anti-intellectual-times.

Focus on the Family. 2015. "Transgenderism—Our Position." Last modified February 1, 2018. https://www.focusonthefamily.com/get-help/transgenderism-our-position/.

Gilligan, Andrew. 2017. "No Sex, Please, This Is the Census." *Sunday Times*, October 8. https://www.thetimes.co.uk/article/no-sex-please-this-is-the-census-sswntgs5z.

Gill-Peterson, Jules. 2018. *Histories of the Transgender Child*. Minneapolis: University of Minnesota Press.

Gleeson, Jules Joanne. 2018. "Trans Ethics, Not Gender Ideology: Against the Church and the Gender Critics." Verso blog, June 27. https://www.versobooks.com/blogs/3894-trans-ethics-not-gender-ideology-against-the-church-and-the-gender-critics.

Halley, Janet. 2005. "The Politics of Injury: A Review of Robin West's Caring for Justice." *Unbound* 1, no. 65: 65–92.

Jackson, Crystal A., Jennifer J. Reed, and Barbara G. Brents. 2017. "Strange Confluences: Radical Feminism and Evangelical Christianity as Drivers of US Neo-abolitionism." In *Feminism, Prostitution, and the State the Politics of Neo-abolitionism*, edited by Eilis Ward and Gillian Wylie, 66–85. New York: Routledge.

Jakobsen, R. Janet, and Ann Pellegrini. 2003. *Love the Sin: Sexual Regulation and the Limits of Religious Tolerance*. New York: New York University Press.

Jeffreys, Sheila. 2014. *Gender Hurts: A Feminist Analysis of the Politics of Transgenderism*. New York: Routledge.

Jenkins, Katharine. 2016. "Amelioration and Inclusion: Gender Identity and the Concept of Woman." *Ethics* 126, no. 2: 394–421.

Jordan, Mark D. 2011. *Recruiting Young Love: How Christians Talk about Homosexuality*. Chicago: University of Chicago Press.

Kelly, Siobhan. 2016. "Feminist Transphobia, Feminist Rhetoric: From Trans-Exclusive Radical Feminism to HB2." *Journal of Feminist Studies in Religion* blog, August 30. http://www.fsrinc.org/feminist-transphobia-rhetoric/.

Kidd, Thomas S. 2019. *Who Is an Evangelical? The History of a Movement in Crisis.* New Haven, CT: Yale University Press.

Koyama, E. 2020. "Whose Feminism Is It Anyway? The Unspoken Racism of the Trans Inclusion Debate." *Sociological Review* 68, no. 4: 735–44.

Laqueur, Thomas. 1987. "Orgasm, Generation, and the Politics of Reproductive Biology." In *The Making of the Modern Body: Sexuality and Society in the Nineteenth Century*, edited by Catherine Gallagher and Thomas Laqueur, 1–41. Berkeley: University of California Press.

Lewis, Sophie. 2017. "Defending Intimacy against What? Limits of Antisurrogacy Feminisms." *Signs* 43. no. 1: 97–125.

Lips, Hilary M. 2014. *Gender: The Basics.* New York: Routledge.

Long, Kathleen P. 2019. "Intersex/Transgender." In *The Bloomsbury Handbook of Twenty-First-Century Feminist Theory*, edited by Robin Truth Goodman, 121–41. London: Bloomsbury.

Malatino, Hil. 2019. *Queer Embodiment: Monstrosity, Medical Violence, and Intersex Experience.* Lincoln: University of Nebraska Press.

McDaniel, Rhonda. 2018. *The Third Gender and Ælfric's "Lives of Saints."* Kalamazoo, MI: Medieval Institute.

Michaelson, Jay. 2016. "Radical Feminists and Conservative Christians Team Up against Transgender People." *Daily Beast*, September 4. Last modified April 23, 2018. https://www.thedailybeast.com/radical-feminists-and-conservative-christians-team-up-against-transgender-people.

Mikkola, Mari. 2009. "Elizabeth Spelman, Gender Realism, and Women." *Hypatia* 21, no. 4: 77–96.

Mikkola, Mari. 2016. *The Wrong of Injustice.* New York: Oxford University Press.

Minnesota Family Council. 2019. *Responding to the Transgender Issue: Parent Resource Guide.* Ebook. https://genderresourceguide.com/wpcontent/themes/genderresource/library/documents/NPRG_Full_Document_Links_V18.pdf.

O'Donnell, Katherine. 2019. "The Theological Basis for Trans-Exclusionary Radical Feminist Positions." In *Lesbian Feminism: Essays Opposing Global Heteropatriarchies*, edited by Niharika Banerjea, Kath Browne, Eduarda Ferreira, Marta Olasik, and Julie Podmore, 81–102. London: Zed.

O'Leary, Dale, and Peter Sprigg. 2015. "Understanding and Responding to the Transgender Movement." Family Research Council. https://www.frc.org/transgender.

Parke, Cole. 2016. "The Christian Right's Love Affair with Anti-trans Feminists." Political Research Associates, August 11. https://www.politicalresearch.org/2016/08/11/the-christian-rights-love-affair-with-anti-trans-feminists.

Partridge, Cameron. 2018. "'Scotch-Taped Together': Anti-'Androgyny' Rhetoric, Transmisogyny, and the Transing of Religious Studies." *Journal of Feminist Studies in Religion* 34, no. 1: 68–75.

Patel, N. 2017. "Violent Cistems: Trans Experiences of Bathroom Space." *Agenda* 31, no. 1: 51–63.

Pearce, Ruth, Sonja Erikainen, and Ben Vincent. 2020. "TERF Wars: An Introduction." *Sociological Review* 68, no. 4: 3–24.

Pew Research Center. 2021. "Religious Landscape Study: Evangelical Protestants." https://www.pewforum.org/religious-landscape-study/religious-tradition/evangelical-protestant/.

Pyle, Kai. 2018. "Naming and Claiming: Recovering Ojibwe and Plains Cree Two-Spirit Language." *TSQ* 5, no. 4: 574–88.

Raymond, Janice. 1994. *The Transsexual Empire: The Making of the She-Male.* New York: Teachers College Press.

Raymond, Janice. 2021. *Doublethink: A Feminist Response to Transgenderism*. North Geelong, VIC: Spinifex.

Salamon, Gayle. 2018. *The Life and Death of Latisha King: A Critical Phenomenology of Transphobia*. New York: New York University Press.

Schaefer, Donovan O. 2015. *Religious Affects: Animality, Evolution, and Power*. Durham, NC: Duke University Press.

Schmidt, Samantha. 2020. "Conservatives Find Unlikely Ally in Fighting Transgender Rights: Radical Feminists." *Washington Post*, February 7. www.washingtonpost.com/dc-md-va /2020/02/07/radical-feminists-conservatives-transgender-rights/.

Schuller, Kyla. 2018. *The Biopolitics of Feeling: Race, Sex, and Science in the Nineteenth Century*. Durham, NC: Duke University Press.

Smothers, Colin. 2020. "Transgender Tide Rising." The Council on Biblical Manhood and Womanhood blog, October 21. https://cbmw.org/2020/10/21/transgender-tide-rising/.

Smythe, V. 2018. "I'm Credited with Having Coined the Word 'Terf.' Here's How It Happened." *Guardian*, November 28. https://www.theguardian.com/commentisfree/2018/nov/29/im -credited-with-having-coined-the-acronym-terf-heres-how-it-happened.

Sprinkle, Preston M. 2021. *Embodied: Transgender Identities, the Church, and What the Bible Has to Say*. Colorado Springs, CO: David C. Cook.

Stanley, Eric. 2011. "Near Life, Queer Death: Overkill and Ontological Capture." *Social Text*, no. 107: 1–19.

Strassfeld, Max. 2018. "Transing Religious Studies." *Journal of Feminist Studies in Religion* 34, no. 1: 37–53. https://muse.jhu.edu/article/690604.

Strassfeld, Max. 2022. *Trans Talmud: Androgynes and Eunuchs in Rabbinic Literature*. Oakland: University of California Press.

Stryker, Susan, and Talia M. Bettcher. 2016. "Editors' Introduction." *TSQ* 3, nos. 1–2: 5–14.

Tudor, Alyosxa. 2021. "Decolonizing Trans/Gender Studies? Teaching Gender, Race, and Sexuality in Times of the Rise of the Global Right." *TSQ* 8, no. 2: 238–56.

Watson, Lori. 2016. "The Woman Question." *TSQ* 3, nos. 1–2: 248–55.

Worthen, Molly. 2013. *Apostles of Reason: The Crisis of Authority in American Evangelicalism*. New York: Oxford University Press.

Pulpit of Performative Reason

Kathryn Lofton

Abstract This essay observes that a hostile relationship to religion is an elemental component of contemporary debates about gender and sexuality, and this hostility has its origin in a specific movement, freethought. A long line of Anglophone self-described freethinkers argues that human beings embrace religions because they cannot think without direction. TERF voices echo this explanation as they seek to right what they determine are wrong figurations of gender. The free-thinker's ritual presentation requires standing at a pulpit determined by their claimed associations with and commitment to reason, and then correcting someone else's view of themselves with a red pen in front of a crowd. Understanding TERFs, and their ability to declare what gender is and is not, requires a foray into the history of religions to perceive why this is such a tenacious prejudicial rite of modernity.

Keywords freethought, secularism, ritual, New Atheism, religion

I n November 2021 evolutionary biologist and atheist provocateur Richard Dawkins (2021d) asked his Twitter followers to sign on to a declaration by the UK-based anti-transgender advocacy group the Women's Human Rights Campaign (WHRC). Dawkins's Twitter feed is a repeating churn of topics appealing to his audience, an audience that has, for decades, consumed his self-promoted "free-thinking" political ideas. Followers hear him announce with pride the number of languages his books have been translated into (forty-two) and how much he enjoys meeting readers at his book signings. They witness him honoring the invention of the internet, since it "gives hope for parts of the world benighted by ignorant religion & superstition" and they follow his defense of those people who, by his appraisal, bravely stand against the woke mob. Included among those he defends are Kathleen Stock, the philosophy professor who resigned from a UK university amid accusations of transphobia, whom Dawkins refers to as "a brave hero of reason," and nineteenth-century evolutionary theorist Charles Darwin, as well as the Ex-Muslims of North America and the Women's Human Rights Campaign (Dawkins 2021a, b).

This essay considers why anti-trans positions coordinate so well with the politics propounded by Dawkins and his atheist brethren. Trans-exclusionary

TSQ: Transgender Studies Quarterly ∗ Volume 9, Number 3 ∗ August 2022 **443**
DOI 10.1215/23289252-9836092 © 2022 Duke University Press

radical feminists (TERFs) and gender critical feminists are among those public figures associated most often with transphobic thought and rhetoric. Yet a third significant source of transphobic rhetoric are proclaimed atheists that frame their transphobia as a defense of the rights of "women." Trans studies has not attended to these atheist expositors of transphobia, but these atheist voices are loud, expert at public battle, and engaged with both trans-exclusionary radical feminists and gender critical feminists. "Kathleen Stock is wonderfully sensible," Dawkins (2021c) elsewhere tweets, "If her arguments seem laboured, it's because she's daily surrounded by obscurantist logomachists. They, sadly, are paid to harangue students who feel obliged to take them seriously. Dear students, please refresh your minds with science." This essay takes up a somewhat unexpected tension: although atheist thinkers like Dawkins locate their opposition to religion in what they describe as religion's denigration of women, these anti-religious warriors in fact share more with religious people, including conservative Catholics and evangelicals who refuse the reality of trans experience, than their atheism may suggest.

Scholars in the field of religious studies have spent the last two decades working to describe those boundaries between the religious and the secular as powerful, consequential fiction. What societies delineate as the secular is not irreligious but an expression of religion.[1] The figure of the atheist is one with an imbricated relationship to religious forms and power. Atheists, who also often self-describe as freethinkers, derive a great deal of their rhetorical suasion from their pulpit of performative reason. The public atheist uses their available mediated pulpits—whether printed pamphlets in the nineteenth century or Twitter in the twenty-first—to offer sermons about subjects they render of high moral interest, including encroachment on academic freedom, scientific research, and biological determinism. "Women" have long been a subject of moral concern for freethinkers.

Discussions of trans-exclusionary feminists and gender critical feminists sometimes seem to imply that perpetrators of transphobia are religious and defenders of trans people are not. Yet there is no meaningful distinction between religious and nonreligious iterations of transphobia. Tracking the freethought tradition from which atheist public advocates emerge makes clear that contemporary gender critical feminism finds one of its roots in the fight by putatively anti-religious persons to protect "women" from patriarchal harm in religions. This article shows that freethinkers understand the embrace of gender diversity and trans liberation as a form of secular dogma requiring their critique. That these speakers do so from an anti-religion stance that is itself dogmatic is, for students of religious studies, less surprising than it might be for those new to understanding religion as a socially constructed classification. Freethought criticizes and thus seeks to undermine religious adherence by pointing to instances in which religion undermines female-identified subjects. This is how religion and anti-religion remain in a codependent tango, each reifying the power of the other through their attentive dislike.

In this essay I introduce the idea of "the pulpit of performative reason" to convey from where freethinkers derive their explanatory power. For Dawkins, his performative reason is at its strongest when he is resisting the accusation that he may be racist, sexist, or dogmatic. He is not, he repeats, transphobic or Islamophobic. "No!" he writes, speaking to the charge of Islamophobia. "I'm phobic about"

> FGM
> Whipping women for being raped
> Pushing gays off buildings
> Honour killing
> Death for apostasy, extramarital sex, etc
> Teaching children anti-scientific nonsense
> I'm NOT Muslimophobic. Muslims are main victims of the above.
> (Dawkins 2021f)

This list is an unsourced account of extremist Islam, an account Dawkins authored and, for the last many years, has repeated to any audience he has. This list focuses on what he understands fundamentalist Islam to support, yet its insults apply to how he describes any bad occupiers of an identity, whether they are those he decries as bad Muslims or bad activists. Bad Muslims and the bad trans activists share, by his account, ungrounded knowledge, or belief, which is the basis of the action he labels irrational. "There's only one way of knowing: science," he writes (Dawkins 2021e). Heron Greenesmith has reflected on how Dawkins's transphobia reflects a broader embrace of "right-wing rhetoric" by pro-science intellectuals. "Atheism has a long history of exclusionary gate-keeping," Greenesmith (2021) writes, underlining that the post-9/11 New Atheists are becoming the next wave of recruits to transphobia, "slingshotted by their extreme anti-Muslim rhetoric into irrelevance and bigotry." The New Atheists were early twenty-first-century public intellectuals, largely British, who promoted atheism and, in the process, indicted religion. Greenesmith underlines that the form this indictment often takes is a "non-tolerant calling-out and attacking people," directly paralleling the rhetorical form taken in public by many trans-exclusionary feminists (Burns 2019).

I agree with Greenesmith that calling out, an ineluctable feature of relational life, is a defining reflex of TERF practice. Without suggesting all TERFs are atheists like Dawkins, nor suggesting all atheists are trans-exclusionary, I'd like to think about the alignment Greenesmith encourages scholars and trans activists to perceive, namely, that there is easy company between trans-exclusionary feminists and those atheists who seek the public spotlight for their missionary operations. Standing in a pulpit of performative reason is how many trans-exclusionary thinkers understand themselves as precisely not cissexist, but fighters for truth.

A scholar of trans life might decide that conservative religious outlooks are the major source for trans-exclusionary politics. Yet many people who espouse trans-exclusionary speech are neither Catholic nor evangelical, even as they may, at times, sound as if they are motivated by religious fervor. Observing the religious fervor of transphobic atheists contributes to what Susan Stryker (2019: 281) describes as a "new wave of trans studies scholarship" that "parallels the critique of secularism to be found in religious studies, in that it refuses the secular/religious dichotomy, as well as the science-versus-religion framework." Studying trans politics in the contemporary period requires seeing why the secular is not a safe shelter for trans recognition. Perhaps, however, this perception already occurs in the religious decision making of trans people. As a Muslim, queer, trans person illustrates, "There is so much stigma, so I keep my identity pretty quiet in religious spaces" (Sumerau, Mathers, and Lampe 2019: 191). A Buddhist, queer nonbinary person took a similar approach: "It is too hard. I generally don't discuss my identities with religious people anymore" (191). What these words suggest is that trans people don't find their identities understood well by those who seem to be religious kin, or by the standard sociological classifications for religious identity. Nascent data suggests a prevalence of non-Judeo-Christian-Islamic religious identities among trans persons. In response to one survey instrument about religion, a trans person replied, "Many of the questions were more applicable to conventional western monotheistic spirituality and many didn't make sense for my belief system" (Kidd and Witten 2008: 46). Among the few studies of transgender religious lives, two things are clear: it isn't easy to declare yourself as trans within a specific religious space, and the number who identify as atheist is not a demographically significant portion of trans individuals (Mathers 2017: 2). Trans people trouble the gender-rescue justification that suffuses freethought's most ardently expositors. As trans activists work to resist the prejudices of secular reason, understanding its religious location will assist resistance to freethought's regime.

* * *

Freethought is an Anglophone idiom defined by the questioning of received opinion and traditional customs. Its history emphasizes the boldness of its representatives: libertines, deists, family limitation advocates, and atheists who refused the social norms of society, especially insofar as those norms emerged from dominant religious systems.[2] The words *free* and *reason* string together a disparate set of individuals and publishing efforts toward the freethinking cause. Early British freethought texts, John Toland's *Christianity Not Mysterious* (1696) and Anthony Collins's *Discourse of Freethinking* (1714), were provocatively intolerant of any sentimental ideas about religion and any other dominating system of thought. The first openly anti-Christian book published in North America was Ethan Allen's *Reason the only Oracle of a Man* (1787). A little under a century later, the founding of the National Secular Society in 1866 was a key moment in British working-class freethought and remained the most powerful British freethought organization until the British Humanist Association in 1963. In the United States Elihu Palmer edited an early deist newspaper, *The Temple of Reason* (1800–1801), and admirers of Thomas Paine's writings founded the Free Press Association in 1825. A spate of new freethought societies formed in the antebellum period, including the United Moral and Philosophical Society for the Diffusion of Useful Knowledge in 1836; the Society of Free Inquirers, founded in 1842; and the Infidel Society for the Promotion of Mental Liberty founded in 1845. Most of these societies rose and fell in fewer than three years. In the nineteenth century, atheists and freethinkers produced grassroots newspapers to provoke a movement: *The American Nonconformist, The Freethought Ideal, Freethinker's Magazine,* and *The Truth Seeker* among scores of others. Publishing presses (like Truth Seeker Company, Freidenker Publishing Company, J.P. Mendum, and Peter Eckler Company) were incorporated, and associations begun. The sectarianism of freethought was not as bounteous as the many schismatic breaks of Protestant Christianity, but it possessed many of the same habits of modern religious organization, including the development of parachurch associations and deploying all available media distribution.

In this section I situate the transphobic public cultures I discuss above within a broader genealogy of freethought in order to demonstrate the persistent relationship between disbelieving in religion and negating certain gender expressions. From the beginning, freethought expression included worries about women-identified persons in religious systems. Such thinking largely emerged from the pens of male-identified authors, though female-identified freethinkers existed as a powerful minority: British feminist Mary Wollstonecraft repudiated religious orthodoxy, and Scottish-born Frances Wright declared churches the most formidable enemy of world progress. Ernestine L. Rose was the first publicly declared female atheist in the United States, and Matilda Joslyn Gage's bestselling *Woman, Church, and State* (1893) traced the oppression of women by religion, especially Christianity. Work by women in freethought and atheist circles invariably highlighted religion's disrespect of women as one of the major reasons to disavow religion. Gage's book (subtitle: *The Original Exposé of Male*

Collaboration against the Female Sex) worked through the history of Christianity as a series of women's restrictions and degradations. Gage indicted Christianity for its role in foreclosing women's freedom through marriage and its connected tax and property laws. "The most stupendous system of organized robbery known has been that of the church towards woman, a robbery that has not only taken her self-respect but all rights of person; the fruits of her own industry; her opportunities of education; the exercise of her own judgment, her own conscience, her own will," Gage (1893: 238) writes. Women-identified persons engaged in freethought centered religion as a problem for their freedom. Here is Ernestine Rose, in her 1851 address on woman's rights. Observe the continuity between how she figures the "woman" relative to priestcraft, and how she valorizes sense and intelligence against bigotry and intelligence:

> It has been said, that "The voice of the People is the voice of God." If that voice is on the side of justice and humanity, then it is true, if the term God means the principle of Truth and of Right. But if the public voice is oppressive and unjust, then it ought to be spurned like the voice of falsehood and corruption; and woman, instead of implicitly and blindly following the dictates of public opinion, must investigate for herself what is right or wrong-act in accordance with her best convictions and let the rest take care of itself, for obedience to wrong is wrong itself, and opposition to it is virtue alike in woman as in man, even though she should incur the ill will of bigotry, superstition, and priestcraft, for the approval of our fellow-being is valuable only when it does not clash with our own sense of right, and no further.
>
> The priests well know the influence and value of women when warmly engaged in any cause, and therefore as long as they can keep them steeped in superstitious darkness, so long are they safe; and hence the horror and anathema against every woman that has intelligence, spirit, and moral courage to cast off the dark and oppressive yoke of superstition. But she must do it, or she will ever remain a slave, for of all tyranny that of superstition is the greatest, and he is the most abject slave who tamely submits to its yoke. Woman, then, must cast it off as her greatest enemy. (Rose 1851)

Rose suggests that those who cling to superstition enslave themselves. She also suggests those who cling to superstition are enslaved to tyrannies that encourage intolerance. She specifies who is specifically responsible for such intolerance, namely, those who "keep them steeped in superstitious darkness." These priests, male-identified enslavers of "women" to the superstition of religion, are the subject of sharpest indictment by freethinkers, both male- and female-identified. Freethought is a push not only against religion but also against the form of patriarchy that they argue propels religion. Perhaps because freethinkers rightly perceived that women-identified people predominated in religious observance, their specific gendered experience became a primary exhibit in the freethought survey of what they perceived as religion's demeaning and deluding attributes.

David Tribe (2007: 343), past president of the UK-based National Secular Society and editor of the *Freethinker*, explains how historians decide who to include and not: "In naming freethinkers in histories and biographical dictionaries, compilers usually adopt a relative standard: that is the degree of heterodoxy detected is inversely proportional to the power of orthodoxy in the freethinker's environment." And since religious membership declined in the United States and England across the twentieth century, the "orthodoxy" freethinkers combated shifted from the Protestant establishment in those countries to other kinds of adherence freethinkers could resist. The mid-twentieth-century counterculture included criticisms of the family economy and sentimental morality, often including recommendations of new spiritual systems and healing rites. In the first decade of the twenty-first century, atheists formed grassroots social groups in growing numbers, and existing organizations witnessed significant growth in membership. The Freedom From Religion Foundation (FFRF), for example, nearly tripled its membership in the first decade of the twenty-first century, while American Atheists almost doubled theirs in the eighteen months after appointing David Silverman, an outspoken, publicity-seeking, and self-described "trouble-making" atheist as its executive director in 2010. While membership in these organizations is still small—FFRF and American Atheists combined barely have twenty thousand members—the increase suggested an increased number of people felt aligned with an oppositional relationship to religion (Guenther, Mulligan, and Papp 2013: 458–59).

Any explanation for this growth must include the increasing presence of male-identified atheist public intellectuals, who collectively authored more than a dozen bestselling books in this epoch decrying religion and promoting the atheist belief system. The public output of the New Atheists comprised a media sensation, and a robust counter–New Atheist response by theists followed (Ward 2008; Haught 2008; Berlinski 2009; Markham 2010; McGrath 2010). A parallel set of writers tackled the shallowness of their scientific and philosophical knowledge.[3] Reflecting on this discursive explosion, philosopher Whitley Kaufman (2019) argued that the long-term significance of the New Atheists is minimal, especially "from an intellectual or scholarly perspective," bearing little on the rise of religiously unaffiliated Americans—sometimes called the rise of the "nones"—in the United States and distinctive, if at all, for their rhetorical skill, not their philosophical insights. Kaufman notes how that rhetoric is an inheritor of traditions of freethought that preceded the New Atheists, and that

New Atheist's skewering description of orthodoxies was something they would pass on to subsequent British and American public intellectuals seeking a platform for their resistance.

Grace Davie (2012) has noted that New Atheists could not exist apart from their fundamentalist counterparts. That is, New Atheists "in many ways adopt the characteristics of the forms of religion that they most dislike" (6). It is old hat to say that atheism is just another literalism, defined less by the content of its complaint than by the style of its conveyance. Writing about Richard Dawkins, literary critic Terry Eagleton (2006) remarked that he had more in common with American TV evangelists than the refereed scientists to whom he claimed frequent recourse. Political scientist Stuart McAnulla (2014: 140) resists, slightly, "It can be tempting to view new atheism as a secular mimic of religious fundamentalism, particularly as both 'sides' of this equation often seek to gain from the clashes generated between them." He refuses such a dualism, however, because he thinks religious fundamentalism engages a deep relationship to a philosophical tradition, whereas the only tradition New Atheists propound is to give "a new prominence to anti-religious sentiment," which they usually only source as far back as David Hume (1711–76), Charles Darwin (1809–82), or Friedrich Nietzsche (1844–1900) (140).

Historians of freethought root the tradition in the figure of the philosophe, a term that designated thinkers of eighteenth-century France who were united, despite divergent personal views, in their conviction of the supremacy and efficacy of human reason. Inspired by the philosophic thought of René Descartes; the skepticism of the *Libertins*, or freethinkers; and the popularization of science by Bernard de Fontenelle, the philosophes supported social, economic, and political reforms, including most importantly a deconstruction of the church and (what they understood as) its wrongful epistemological hold on society. For McAnulla, however, the polarizing rhetoric New Atheists use does not deserve the label *religion*; it deserves only the label *prejudice*. McAnulla's resistance to the New Atheists as a tradition of substantive thought makes sense if focusing on their specific epoch and textual horizons. But atheists have had a long-standing social role in the Anglophone West, one in which their social and political minoritization is well known (Edgell, Gerteis, and Hartmann 2006). What I seek to describe here is how this political minoritization did not equal marginalization in the public sphere. Rather, freethinkers craft a pulpit of performative reason to mirror and combat the pulpits of policing virtue that Christians establish everywhere they claim a majority.

"Performative" is a practice that produces that which it names. There is no "reason" discernible in the freethought corpus but what it expounds as its expertise. A person tweets an article about a Hindu boy in Pakistan charged with blasphemy for urinating in a library. A self-declared freethinker and free speech advocate re-tweets the piece, commenting, "The rule of law, and ascendancy of reason, are low in Pakistan. Alas" (Christakis 2021). The performative function of the piece is to make the speaker the authority on reason—they charge themselves as evaluators of its lack and so possess its power. The pulpit of performative reason is the method by which freethinkers—from philosophes to TERFs—ritualize their stances. Freethought survives outside organization through this ritual of public speech that recenters the freethinker's power over and against other ideologies or organizations.

"Debunking begets more debunking," Emily Ogden (2018: 47) writes in her study of nineteenth-century mesmerism, "The task of deploring credulity is perennially incomplete and must always be repeated." Ogden is a part of a group of scholars who have thought about how public entertainments in the eighteenth and nineteenth century offered a kind of ritual theater for the evaluation of what is true and false, what is reason and what is belief. James Delbourgo (2006), for example, describes how public exhibitions of electrical implements afforded an opportunity to think through the meaning of "useful knowledge" and "common sense." He argues that the controlled experimental display of electric power offered audiences a mechanism through which to think about the powers of the human mind to decide what was sensible to believe. David Walker (2013) has explained how Lyceum and circus amusements became ritual theaters of reason, focusing on how entrepreneur P. T. Barnum brought proclaimed spiritualists to the center ring to include audiences in the evaluation of their veracity under the term *humbug*. Humbug is, in Walker's evaluation of Barnum's public displays, a "set of claims or acts designed to arouse excitement around a particular good (55)." Ogden, Delbourgo, and Walker describe a ritualized infotainment, one that starred freethought figures tangling with audience's suppositions about what was and was not credible to compel them to believe in reason. What they perceive in circus tents and Lyceum circuits can be found now in Twitter handles and *Guardian* op-eds.

Freethought disavows religion yet creates an epistemic frame in which belief is not discarded. Rather, belief converts its devotional energies to a new object. New Atheists confidently rebuked religion because it was, to them, anti-reason. They sought to enjoin audiences to learn reason through the debunking performances they staged.[4] Dawkins (2006: 308), for example, chided that "faith is an evil precisely because it requires no justifications and brooks no arguments." New Atheists want to grab control of public education and press something they understood as "science" and "facts" into everyone's palms. Religious belief was irrational (they wagered); what people needed was faith in science. Victor J. Stenger (2014: 445) offers a typical New Atheist metaphor when he analogizes religion to primitive society: "If human civilization is to survive and thrive, faith in Bronze Age myths must yield to reasoning based on scientific evidence." At some point people must depart the Bronze Age, the New Atheists press. Religion is irrational, it is emotional, and it is instinctual. Religion entraps its believers; it enslaves them with its wiles, then forgets to remove the handcuffs.

Freethinkers do not want to ban religion, exactly; they just want to evacuate it from the public sphere. New Atheists tolerate religion's private practice; what they condemn is the publicizing of religion in political action, whether in terrorist acts or curricular revision. Notably, as McAnulla observes, the New Atheists took their argumentative cues from feminist consciousness raising. I quote at length from McAnulla's (2012: 96) work:

> Feminists argued that the difficulties women experienced in their daily lives (such as domestic violence) were often self-understood as "personal" issues, which were rooted either in their own personality or the contingent nature of relationships they were in. Feminists perceived it as important that women should become aware of the widespread, perhaps systematic nature of problems afflicting women. This could potentially be achieved through processes of "consciousness-raising."[5] Through discussion and campaigning women could come to perceive their own experience as part of a wider picture of sex discrimination that was perpetuated through dominant cultural attitudes and political institutions. One example concerned the use of language, and the argument that everyday expressions could be "gendered" in ways which, often unwittingly, might reinforce stereotypes concerning the appropriate roles for men and women, for example terms such as "chairman."
>
> New atheists have taken lessons from feminist consciousness-raising about language. For example, Dawkins [2006: 338] suggests that the special status accorded to religious beliefs is reflected in some common language use. For example, a child who has parents who are Roman Catholic in their religious beliefs, and who is sent to a Catholic school at age six, is often referred to as a "Catholic child." Yet Dawkins asks in what sense it is legitimate to label a six-year-old child a "Catholic," when at this stage of their life the child can have grasped little of Catholic theology, let alone reflected on how far they wish to endorse it. He points out that we would be unlikely to label the child of Marxist parents as a "Marxist child."

McAnulla suggests New Atheists understand their work as a form of identity politics, inspired in part by feminist models of political reeducation. The example Dawkins provides from the Roman Catholic context is indicative of how the worrisome objects of New Atheists and TERFs are the same. Both groups sensationalize the classroom as a site of ideological incursion, whether in the form of creationist education or promotions of sexual health. Among New Atheists there was conflict about whether religion should be taught in public schools— Dawkins (2015) was opposed to it, whereas Daniel Dennett (2006) argued that all religions, including the position of the nonreligious, should be taught factually in schools. The agreement is that the schools are the fighting space. In this the New Atheists seem less sophisticated in their interpretive apparatus than the feminists from whom they learned the power of linguistic revisionism. "The striking element in the identity politics of the New Atheists," Teemu Taira (2012: 105) writes, "is that while it imitates the strategies used by gays and feminists and while it has partially overlapping cause in their opposition to the bigotry of conservative religion, the New Atheists distance themselves from some of the associated theoretical repertoire." New Atheists aren't feminist or queer-positive; they borrow rhetoric but do not sympathize or ally.

Much has been written from within Islamic studies and beyond to repudiate the ignorance of New Atheist racist Islamophobia and their related sexism (Abu-Lughod 2002; Hidayatullah 2014; Khalil 2018; Trzebiatowska 2019; Werleman 2015). What is incontrovertible is that bigotry is to New Atheist thinking as light is to photosynthesis: their thought process cannot be animated without it. The "free" in freethought is a comparative claim: someone else is not. Invariably the unfree person is a gendered subject who is prone to patriarchal power: the Muslim woman, the Hindu widow, the Catholic altar boy, the evangelical girl— freethought exists to liberate those assumed to be oppressed. Scholars have pointed out that prominent figures in New Atheism see multiculturalism and gender equality as a threat to the hegemonic white, male-identified atheist community (Amarasingam and Brewster 2016: 118). From its beginning, freethought had a particular eye for indicting religion, as it restricted the sovereignty of white men to reign as free speakers with access to free love. Whatever "community" it developed was in service of shoring up support for legal action and activism toward this purpose. In her work on the contemporary New Atheist movement, Katya M. Guenther (2019) shows how the atheist movement maintains a very gendered movement culture in support of gender inequality. Guenther's work supplements earlier research that suggested being atheist was socially risky for women-identified persons, since it situated them in a presumptively aggressive discursive space (Edgell, Frost, and Stewart 2017). Guenther (2019: 47) explains that "a culture of men's dominance—which extends to men making claims about women's rights and criticizing women who speak out against men's abuses of power—has contributed to women respondents feeling shut out and silenced." Female-identified persons, drawn to the movement because they want to resist the role of religion in legislating against stem cell research, marriage equality, abortion rights, or women's rights, find that gender issues are sidelined within the atheist movement, where women also remain underrepresented among both leadership and rank-and-file.

The significant increase of female-identified presence in the atheist movement over the last thirty years does not correlate to increase respect for "women," either within the atheist movement or beyond. As Marta Trzebiatowska (2019): 483) explains, atheism and feminism are both devalued identities when embraced by women-identified persons. Identifying as an atheist affords the participants an impetus to invent a new vocabulary to account for their identity, and for female-identified atheists this means that "they engage in a balancing act of domesticating atheism and feminism and neutralizing the perceived threat both (but mostly the latter) might pose to the public gender regime." Gender critical feminists—some who identify as atheists, most who understand themselves as freethinkers—participate in an interpretive space that claims to combat gender inequality for women, especially women trapped in religious systems imagined to be controlled by men. Yet gender critical feminists sustain gender inequality in their weaponization of science, reason, rationality, and critical thinking as forms superior to religion, feeling, and belief. "By failing to examine and interrogate these concepts as gendered ideas," Guenther (2019: 54) writes, "the [atheist] movement reproduces gender hierarchies embedded in the broader culture, and reifies science, reason, and rationality as masculine domains and faith, emotionality, and irrationality as the inferior feminine."

What I seek to underline is that atheist movements contribute a gendered culture of public reason that is wholly righteous, correcting how other people live and think about their lives as gendered persons. In this environment trans-exclusionary and gender critical feminisms find easy affinity with atheist debunking. Sara Ahmed describes a pamphlet distributed by trans-exclusionary radical feminists at a Reclaim the Night march in London in November 2014. Its text begins by redescribing the purpose of Reclaim the Night as "protesting male violence against women." It then describes trans women as "male transgenders" and suggests that "male transgenders" commit violence against women "at exactly the same rate as non-transgender males." This misgendering enables trans women to be positioned as perpetrators unwelcome at a march about gendered violence, and as people who have no experience as victims of gendered violence themselves. On the other side of the pamphlet are four photographs of trans women who are given a story that is not theirs: they have committed violence against women; they have tried to hide that violence by describing themselves as trans or not men (Ahmed 2016: 25). This TERF pamphlet seeks to render violence against women-identified persons as an inevitable result of a gender identity, maleness, that it understands as immutable. The TERF pamphlet is a mirror of the gendered account of religion in which the problem is patriarchate priests, who can only ever be instruments of gendered violence. In the annals of atheism and free-thought, "women" are useful as testimonies to the suffering wrought by religious control and submission to superstition.

Women-identified persons who align with TERF interpretations of trans lives do so as a continuation of a battle not only over their embodiment but also as an expression of their claim to injury. The pulpit of performative reason is one long occupied by gendered figures of disproportionate authority. Being on that stage, with that regard, is its own kind of drag. Who might hunger to perform it? In their thoughtful symptomatic reading of Sheila Jeffreys's *Gender Hurts: A Feminist Analysis of the Politics of Transgenderism* (2014), Patricia Elliot and Lawrence Lyons (2017: 363) suggest that a key element of transphobia is the relief it provides from ambiguity:

> This uncanny feeling of uncertainty creates a sense of loss of the bodily basis for sexual difference and identity. At a time when gender identity is regarded—either positively or negatively—as performative, as social construction, sexual identity must be rooted somewhere else: in a bodily difference taken to be given or natural. The trans project, however, makes the presumably natural unnatural, and the presumably essential merely contingent.
>
> Social science research demonstrates repeatedly that individuals with a low tolerance for ambiguity are more likely to express bias against bisexual and transgender people. This "lower ambiguity tolerance" is often correlated with those identified with conservative religion [see Garelick et al. 2017; Greenesmith n.d.]. Yet, as has been demonstrated, low ambiguity tolerance also is an indicating trait of freethinking exposition. The history of revival preaching is one that includes many efforts to terrify listeners with tales of how confused the world out there is, how caught it is in ambiguity when there are truths to be found and named.[6] Calling listeners home to gender facts and gendered reason ought to be understood as another bid to clarify confusion through the practice of religion, whether in the form of familiar orthodoxy or dissenting heresy.

At the outset of this essay, I observed that the TERF position is one that shows the intimacy between religion and opposition to religion. I conclude with a broader hope to see how analyzing the history of religion helps scholars of gender and sexuality identify how religion operates internal to the terms of public debate. In the study of religion, secularism studies worked to diminish knee-jerk understandings of the boundary between religion and nonreligion. Understanding that religion is inlaid in claims on behalf of scientism, or that secular life is not divested of religion, will not become scholarly common sense overnight. Yet trans experiences of transphobia push on scholars to move quicker in their reckoning with the damage caused by both the misogynistic and transphobic violence of religion and the misogynistic and transphobic violence of those scholars and intellectuals, many claiming atheism and freethought, seeking to clean up religion's effects. It is impossible to carve a space of "irreligion" that is not complicit with a formation of religion. The story of trans religious lives may yet include many conservative pasts and futures; work addressing their experiences should preoccupy the next generations of scholars. As this work unfolds, trans studies will do well to relinquish dichotomies between what is religious and what is not, instead asking, as it does with gender, to whose advantage it is to make such distinctions the interpretive and literal laws of the land.

Kathryn Lofton is the Lex Hixon Professor of Religious Studies and American Studies, professor of history and divinity at Yale University. She is the author of *Oprah: The Gospel of an Icon* (2011) and *Consuming Religion* (2017).

Notes

1. Among the large number of works contributing to secularism studies, see Anidjar 2006; Asad 2003; Blankholm 2014; Cannell 2010; Connolly 1999; Fessenden 2007; Modern 2011; Mufti 2004; and Wenger 2017.
2. See Jacoby 2004; Mullen 1987; Schmidt 2016; and Turner 1985.
3. For helpful summary of New Atheist critiques, see Admirand 2020; Berlinksi 2008; Eagleton 2009; Hart 2009; Feser 2008; Plantinga 2011; and Ward 2008.
4. The New Atheist text titles underline this summary: Hitchens 2009; Dawkins 2006; Dennett 2007; and Harris 2004.
5. Here McAnulla cites Sarachild 1978.
6. For a trans history of this rhetorical presence, see Larson 2019.

References

Abu-Lughod, Lila. 2002. "Do Muslim Women Really Need Saving? Anthropological Reflections on Cultural Relativism and Its Others." *American Anthropologist* 104, no. 3: 783–90.

Admirand, Peter. 2020. "Atheist Critiques of the New Atheists: Advancing Atheist-Theist Dialogue." *Interreligious Studies and Intercultural Theology* 4, no. 2: 176–200.

Ahmed, Sara. 2016. "An Affinity of Hammers." *TSQ* 3, nos. 1–2: 22–34.

Amarasingam, Amarnath, and Melanie Elyse Brewster. 2016. "The Rise and Fall of the New Atheism: Identity Politics and Tensions within Us Nonbelievers." In *Annual Review of the Sociology of Religion: Sociology of Atheism*, edited by Roberto Cipriani and Franco Garelli, 118–36. Leiden: Brill.

Anidjar, Gil. 2006. "Secularism." *Critical Inquiry* 33, no. 1: 52–77.

Asad, Talal. 2003. *Formations of the Secular: Christianity, Islam, and Modernity*. Stanford, CA: Stanford University Press.

Berlinski, David. 2009. *The Devil's Delusion: Atheism and Its Scientific Pretensions*. New York: Basic.

Blankholm, Joseph. 2014. "The Political Advantages of a Polysemous Secular." *Journal for the Scientific Study of Religion* 53, no. 4: 775–90.

Burns, Katelyn. 2019. "The Rise of Anti-trans 'Radical' Feminists, Explained." *Vox*, September 5. https://www.vox.com/identities/2019/9/5/20840101/terfs-radical-feminists-gender-critical.

Cannell, Fenella. 2010. "The Anthropology of Secularism." *Annual Review of Anthropology* 39: 85–100.

Christakis, Nicholas A. 2021. "Eight year old Hindu boy charged with blasphemy for urinating in library." Twitter, August 9, 11:24 a.m. https://twitter.com/NAChristakis/status/14247534317 30925578.

Connolly, William. 1999. *Why I Am Not a Secularist*. Minneapolis: University of Minnesota Press.

Davie, Grace. 2012. "Belief and Unbelief: Two Sides of a Coin." *Approaching Religion* 2, no. 1: 3–7.

Dawkins, Richard. 2006. *The God Delusion*. Boston: Houghton Mifflin.

Dawkins, Richard. 2015. "Don't Force Your Religious Opinions on Your Children." *Time*, February 19. https://time.com/3711945/children-religion-parents-school-policy/.

Dawkins, Richard. 2021a. "Hume, Huxley, Fisher . . . will they come for Darwin next?" Twitter, November 25, 1:04 a.m. https://twitter.com/RichardDawkins/status/1463750520603131907.

Dawkins, Richard. 2021b. "Kathleen Stock is a brave hero of reason." Twitter, December 3, 7:56 a.m. https://twitter.com/RichardDawkins/status/1466753162673598466.

Dawkins, Richard. 2021c. "Kathleen Stock is wonderfully sensible." Twitter, December 2, 8:17 a.m. https://twitter.com/RichardDawkins/status/1466396206880497668.

Dawkins, Richard. 2021d. "Please sign the Declaration on Women's Sex-based Rights." Twitter, November 29, 9:17 a.m. https://twitter.com/RichardDawkins/status/1465324057277173772.

Dawkins, Richard. 2021e. "There's only one way of knowing: science." Twitter, December 15, 7:55 a.m. https://twitter.com/RichardDawkins/status/1471101687444160520.

Dawkins, Richard. 2021f. "'You're Islamophobic.' No!" Twitter, December 10, 11:43 a.m. https://twitter.com/RichardDawkins/status/1469347127629340678.

Delbourgo, James. 2006. *A Most Amazing Scene of Wonders: Electricity and Enlightenment in Early America*. Cambridge, MA: Harvard University Press.

Dennett, Dan. 2006. "Let's Teach Religion—All Religion—in Schools." TED video, February 2006. https://www.ted.com/talks/dan_dennett_let_s_teach_religion_all_religion_in_schools.

Dennett, Daniel C. 2007. *Breaking the Spell: Religion as a Natural Phenomenon*. New York: Penguin.

Eagleton, Terry. 2006. "Lunging, Flailing, Mispunching." *London Review of Books*, October 19.

Eagleton, Terry. 2009. *Reason, Faith, and Revolution: Reflections on the God Debate*. New Haven, CT: Yale University Press.

Edgell, Penny, Jacqui Frost, and Evan Stewart. 2017. "From Existential to Social Understandings of Risk: Examining Gender Differences in Nonreligion." *Social Currents* 4, no. 6: 556–74.

Edgell, Penny, Joseph Gerteis, and Douglas Hartmann. 2006. "Atheists as 'Other': Moral Boundaries and Cultural Membership in American Society." *American Sociological Review* 71, no. 2: 211–34.

Elliot, Patricia, and Lawrence Lyons. 2017. "Transphobia as Symptom: Fear of the 'Unwoman.'" *TSQ* 4, nos. 3–4: 358–83.

Feser, Edward. 2008. *The Last Superstition: A Refutation of the New Atheism*. South Bend, IN: St. Augustine's.

Fessenden, Tracy. 2007. *Culture and Redemption: Religion, the Secular, and American Literature*. Princeton, NJ: Princeton University Press.

Gage, Matilda Joslyn. 1893. *Woman, Church, and State: The Original Exposé of Male Collaboration against the Female Sex*. New York: Truth Seeker.

Garelick, Angela S., Gabrielle Filip-Crawford, Allison H. Varley, Craig T. Nagoshi, Julie L. Nagoshi, and Rosalind Evans. 2017. "Beyond the Binary: Exploring the Role of Ambiguity in Biphobia and Transphobia." *Journal of Bisexuality* 17, no. 2: 172–89.

Greenesmith, Heron. n.d. "Grey Areas." https://www.herongreenesmith.com/single-post/2019/06/03/forthcoming-grey-areas-how-intolerance-of-ambiguity-makes-bisexual-and-transgender-people (accessed June 10, 2022).

Greenesmith, Heron. 2021. "Atheist Richard Dawkins Swings to Anti-trans Right in Grasp at Broader Intellectual Relevance." *Religion Dispatches*, November 30.

Guenther, Katja M. 2019. "Secular Sexism: The Persistence of Gender Inequality in the US New Atheist Movement." *Women's Studies International Forum*, no. 72: 47–55.

Guenther, Katja M., Kerry Mulligan, and Cameron Papp. 2013. "From the Outside In: Crossing Boundaries to Build Collective Identity in the New Atheist Movement." *Social Problems* 60, no. 4: 457–75.

Harris, Sam. 2004. *The End of Faith: Religion, Terror, and the Future of Reason*. New York: W. W. Norton.

Hart, David Bentley. 2009. *Atheist Delusions: The Christian Revolution and Its Fashionable Enemies*. New Haven, CT: Yale University Press.

Haught, John F. 2008. *God and the New Atheism: A Critical Response to Dawkins, Harris, and Hitchens*. Louisville, KY: Westminster John Knox Press.

Hidayatullah, Aysha A. 2014. *Feminist Edges of the Qur'an*. New York: Oxford University Press.

Hitchens, Christopher. 2009. *God Is Not Great: How Religion Poisons Everything*. New York: Twelve.

Jacoby, Susan. 2004. *Freethinkers: A History of American Secularism*. New York: Metropolitan.

Kaufman, Whitley. 2019. "New Atheism and Its Critics." *Social Compass* 14, no. 1: e12560.

Khalil, Mohammad Hassan. 2018. *Jihad, Radicalism, and the New Atheism*. Cambridge: Cambridge University Press.

Kidd, Jeremy D., and Tarynn M. Witten. 2008. "Understanding Spirituality and Religiosity in the Transgender Community: Implications for Aging." *Journal of Religion, Spirituality and Aging* 20, nos. 1–2: 29–62.

Larson, Scott. 2019. "Histrionics of the Pulpit: Trans Tonalities of Religious Enthusiasm." *TSQ* 6, no. 3: 315–37.

Markham, Ian. 2010. *Against Atheism: Why Dawkins, Hitchens, and Harris Are Fundamentally Wrong*. Hoboken, NJ: Wiley-Blackwell.

Mathers, Lain A. B. 2017. "Expanding on the Experiences of Transgender Nonreligious People: An Exploratory Analysis." *Secularism and Nonreligion* 6, no. 3.

McAnulla, Stuart. 2012. "Radical Atheism and Religious Power: New Atheist Politics." *Approaching Religion* 2, no. 1: 87–99.

McAnulla, Stuart. 2014. "Secular Fundamentalists? Characterising the New Atheist Approach to Secularism, Religion, and Politics." *British Politics* 9, no. 2: 125–45.

McGrath, Alister. 2010. *Dawkins' God: From "The Selfish Gene" to "The God Delusion."* Hoboken, NJ: Wiley-Blackwell.

Modern, John Lardas. 2011. *Secularism in Antebellum America*. Chicago: University of Chicago Press.

Mufti, Aamir R., ed. 2004. "Critical Secularism." Special issue, *boundary 2* 31, no. 2.

Mullen, Shirley A. 1987. *Organized Freethought: The Religion of Unbelief in Victorian England*. London: Routledge.

Ogden, Emily. 2018. *Credulity: A Cultural History of US Mesmerism*. Chicago: University of Chicago Press.

Plantinga, Alvin. 2011. *Where the Conflict Really Lies: Science, Religion, and Naturalism*. Oxford: Oxford University Press.

Rose, Ernestine L. 1851. "Address on Woman's Rights." October 19. Archives on Women's Political Communication, Iowa State University. https://awpc.cattcenter.iastate.edu/2017/03/21 /address-on-womans-rights-october-19-1851/.

Sarachild, Kathie. 1978. "Consciousness-Raising: A Radical Weapon." In *The Feminist Revolution: The Struggle for Women's Liberation*, edited by Bonnie J. Morris and D-M Withers, 144–50. New York: Random House.

Schmidt, Leigh Eric. 2016. *Village Atheists: How America's Unbelievers Made Their Way in a Godly Nation*. Princeton, NJ: Princeton University Press.

Stenger, Victor J. 2014. *God and the Multiverse: Humanity's Expanding View of the Cosmos*. Amherst, NY: Prometheus.

Stryker, Susan. 2019. "General Editor's Introduction." *TSQ* 6, no. 3: 279–82.

Sumerau, J. E., Lain A. B. Mathers, and Nik Lampe. 2019. "Learning from the Religious Experiences of Bi+ Trans People." *Symbolic Interaction* 42, no. 2: 179–201.

Taira, Teemu. 2012. "New Atheism as Identity Politics." In *Religion and Knowledge: Sociological Perspectives*, edited by Matthew Guest and Elisabeth Arweck, 97–113. Burlington, VT: Ashgate.

Tribe, David. 2007. "Freethought." In *The Encyclopedia of Unbelief*, 343–46. Amherst, NY: Prometheus.

Trzebiatowska, Marta. 2019. "'Atheism Is Not the Problem. The Problem Is Being a Woman': Atheist Women and Reasonable Feminism." *Journal of Gender Studies* 28, no. 4: 475–87.

Turner, James. 1985. *Without God, without Creed: The Origins of Unbelief in America*. Baltimore: Johns Hopkins University Press.

Walker, David. 2013. "The Humbug in American Religion: Ritual Theories of Nineteenth-Century Spiritualism." *Religion and American Culture: A Journal of Interpretation* 23, no. 1: 30–74.

Ward, Keith. 2008. *Why There Almost Certainly Is a God: Doubting Dawkins*. Oxford: Lion.

Wenger, Tisa. 2017. *Religious Freedom: The Contested History of an American Ideal*. Chapel Hill: University of North Carolina Press.

Werleman, C. J. 2015. *The New Atheist Threat: The Dangerous Rise of Secular Extremists*. Great Britain: Dangerous Little Books.

Introduction

Trans-Exclusionary Politics by Other Means

SERENA BASSI and GRETA LAFLEUR

Trans-exclusionary dogma is the political quicksilver of our moment. Impossibly dynamic, these politics can assume the shape of any container—policies, religious beliefs, nationalist sentiment, laws—they inform. Indeed, it is the deeply mercurial nature of trans-exclusionary perspectives that makes them so pernicious. They can undergird, at once, calls for a putatively stabilizing return to traditional gender roles in the home and the state *and* demands for greater legal and policy-based protections for girls and women in sport, employment, and state services; anti-colonial critique *and* imperialist nationalisms; and biological essentialisms *and* the explosion of gender norms. To account for the breadth and diversity of trans-exclusionary politics of various kinds would require several years' worth of additional special issues, but even then, because these politics are so labile, so responsive to the conservative political whims of the moment, we have no doubt but that they will continue to take new form and shape new and emergent ideological entrenchments.

We thus decided to conclude this special issue with a "forum," a collection of shorter pieces that we hoped would broaden the scope of the questions, movements, and histories that this special issue addresses. We received many proposals in response to this special issue's call for papers that were not quite article length but that brought important breadth and depth to the qualitative and lived experience of trans-exclusionary politics. In what follows we present readers with an assemblage of what we have come to think of as important one-offs, which offer both short and more sustained opportunities to think about the landscape of these politics in different grounded contexts. Mat Thompson's piece, "Choosing Threat, Embodying the Viral," homes in on the rhetoric of contagion that pervades trans-exclusionary political rhetoric.[1] Instead of asking how trans people might resist any association with the epidemic, especially during times of a global

TSQ: Transgender Studies Quarterly ★ Volume 9, Number 3 ★ August 2022
DOI 10.1215/23289252-9836106 © 2022 Duke University Press

pandemic, they argue that we should embrace the viral and the dangerous as a means of politics. Hidenobu Yamada narrates the fortunes of trans-exclusionary feminist politics in Japan, elaborating how gender identity disorder—GID—came to be hallowed as a state-sponsored form of experience supplanting other, differently capacious understandings of gender diversity that more directly challenge nationally codified norms around family and kinship. On a related note, Ezra Berkley Nepon offers a report from their longtime work in LGBT philanthropy, detailing the development of global philanthropic organizing specifically aimed at accounting for and circumventing the growing power of trans-exclusionary politics in both state-based and private forums. Jo Krishnakumar and Annapurna Menon's dialogue addresses similar concerns on a more local level, offering a dialectical reflection on each of their experiences of more implicit forms of transphobia or trans-exclusionary politics in feminist organizing spaces in their home of the United Kingdom, even or especially in political movements that do not specifically dedicate themselves to trans politics. Gina Gwenffrewi, on the other hand, reflects on the experience of being an academic and journalist seeking to interrupt implicitly and explicitly trans-exclusionary narratives in the UK press within the context of a media culture that has been famously unwilling to consider perspectives by trans people or anyone else advocating for trans political justice. Finally Sophie Lewis and Asa Seresin offer a critical meditation on some of the not incidental but rather crucial historical sympathies between feminisms and fascisms, drawing critical attention to the fact that these politics are not so strange, as bedfellows, as we might want them to be.

Together, these pieces represent a widening and diversifying of the conversation around global trans-exclusionary politics and their imbrication in right-wing movements of various stripes that this special issue seeks to establish with its seven article-length pieces. We hoped that, by including a forum, we could encourage the inclusion of a wider range of topics, as well as a series of responses that would provide a place for casual, colloquial, first-person, experiential understandings of the long arm of trans-exclusionary politics on a global scale. The short pieces that follow represent an extremely eclectic series of responses: some informational, some more theoretical, some reflecting on past experiences, some calling for specific models of future action. What unites them, to our mind, is how they import a more granular and emplaced understanding of the fortunes of trans-exclusionary politics in specific places, forums, and communities. Unfortunately, what also unites them is that, taken as a whole, they truly reveal the terrifying extent, reach, and hydra-headed evils of these politics. From Japan to Croatia, England to the United States, trans-exclusionary coalitional politics have exploded beyond the fairly tight range of sites where, for many years, we expected to find them, such as certain radical lesbian communities, university philosophy departments, and proposals for legal protections for lesbian, gay, and bisexual people. We find trans-exclusionary politics—whether they take the form of trans-exclusionary feminisms, "gender critical" feminisms, or anti-gender approaches to the organization of family and state—in local, domestic, national, and international structures all over the world: in local and state ordinances regulating health care; in anti-imperial and anti-colonial writing; in nationalist propaganda; in local and national education policy; in international religious and anti-religious doctrine; in right-wing movements of all stripes; and, of course, in some feminisms, just to name a few. This forum represents only a handful of possible approaches to the vast global rhizome of trans-exclusionary politics. While the pieces that follow will not, of course, settle these questions, they importantly broaden the scope of the inquiry and lay important foundations for future strategizing.

Serena Bassi is assistant professor of Italian studies at Yale University. Their work interrogates modern racial, gendered, and sexual formations by focusing on literature in translation. They have published in journals including *Translation Studies, Comparative Literature Studies*, and *Signs*.

Greta LaFleur is associate professor of American studies at Yale University. They are the author of *The Natural History of Sexuality in Early America* (2018) and coeditor of *Trans Historical: Gender Plurality before the Modern* (2021) and "The Science of Sex Itself," a forthcoming special issue of *GLQ*.

Note

1.   For an example of this rhetoric, see Marchiano 2017.

Reference

Marchiano, Lisa. 2017. "Outbreak: On Transgender Teens and Psychic Epidemics." *Psychological Perspectives* 60, no. 3: 345–66.

Fascist Feminism

A Dialogue

SOPHIE LEWIS and ASA SERESIN

Repudiations of trans-exclusionary radical feminism often take the form of a call to strip from TERFs the name *feminist*. TERFism, it is often argued, is not "real feminism," and in this same vein it is sometimes argued that lesbian exponents of transmisogyny are not a "real" part of queer history. Asa Seresin and Sophie Lewis—both of us transplants from "TERF Island," living in the United States—here advance a different approach. In this critical dialogue, we suggest that, if some feminisms are patriarchal, and some lesbianisms are invested in whiteness, then queer feminists must become comfortable positioning some feminists—even queer ones—as their enemies. With reference to minoritarian sections of the archive of early twentieth-century British lesbian suffragism and, equally, of 1970s US lesbian separatism (both of whose contemporary heirs we locate in the "gender critical" movement), the discussion attends to *fascisant* themes within Anglophone feminism past and present, such as the sacralization of cis female fertility and the homoerotics of sameness. What if certain feminisms, historically, have not simply colluded with white-supremacist projects but actually amounted to fascisms themselves? How might ceasing to deny that feminisms can be fascist actually strengthen antifascist transfeminist organizing in this moment?

Sophie Lewis: Hello Asa. I am delighted to get this opportunity to think about fascist feminisms and their erotics with you. To date, there has been a substantial amount of scholarly work on the nexus of fascism and male homoeroticism, but very little, as far as we know, on the libidinal economy of the equivalent formation in women's history. Likewise, we've seen a great deal of excellent archival work coming out lately on the anti-liberatory endeavors of women (eugenics, "mothers of massive resistance," female slave-owning, etc.), but not so much on

TSQ: Transgender Studies Quarterly ∗ Volume 9, Number 3 ∗ August 2022   **463**
DOI 10.1215/23289252-9836120   © 2022 Duke University Press

the sometimes specifically feminist character of these white supremacisms and how we might apprehend it. We both perceive a kind of Eros running through the archive of the far-right wing of women's rights: it appears palpable to us in the pleasures people take in exercising maternalist authoritarianism, in the euphoria of the womanhood-as-suffering worldview, in the wounded attachment under-girding same-sex cis separatism. You have commented—on the UK context specifically—that "the commitment to misery, to being a 'bloody difficult woman,' is one of the main affective drives of the stubborn British insistence on an anti-trans and anti-sex work position" (Seresin 2021). For me, this really pinpoints the self-satisfaction of the national feminism in question, which is, incidentally, conservative even when it is cultivated among Labour supporters, say. You helped bring into focus a brand of smugness that is, once named, pretty unmistakable to many of us with close ties to Britain: Unapologetic Englishwomanhood™, a populism so grandiose it verges on auto-eroticism. (I'm thinking of all the TERF hashtags that evoke a defiant brandishing of wombs, of vaginas, of breasts, of XX chromosomes in terms redolent, for me, of the romance of the Blitz.) I think I was feeling in this direction when I speculated about the "no-nonsense" fetish that centrally drives British TERFs (Lewis 2019), and I am grateful to you for filling out my mental picture.

Asa Seresin: Hi Sophie! I am likewise thrilled to be having this conversation with you.

SL: I anticipate pit-stops at everything from neopaganism to leatherdykes; from "civilizing" suffragists to antiporn lawyers; from Mrs. Pankhurst to Posie Parker; and from the women's KKK to "TAnon" (the analog of the more famous QAnon network, which focuses specifically on the "globalist" conspiracy to, er, trans-genderize America's children).

In case of doubt, we are not talking about the long archive of reactionary action that happens to have been creatively undertaken and overseen by women (e.g., eugenics, pro-segregation, pro-lynching, settler-genocidal, pro-life). We are talking about the times when this action was lived and framed as feminism.

I will briefly give two examples of the discomfort that attaches immediately to instances when scholars take fascist declarations of feminism at their word. Kathleen Blee (1991), in her research on 1920s Klanswomen, found that feminism actually played a major role in their ideology. Reviewers of Blee, however, hastened to explain that this feminism was "insincere" or "false." Similarly, in *Hurrah for the Blackshirts!*, Martin Pugh (2006: 144) discloses how Emmeline Pankhurst's personality cult, the Women's Social and Political Union (WSPU), foreshadowed the interwar dictatorships, and he documents how the British Union of Fascists (BUF) (to which many suffragettes flocked) "couched much of its propaganda in distinctly feminist terms." But he then backtracks by insisting, "All of this amounted to a feminine expression of fascism, rather than feminism" (144). We're not so sure. We think Pugh is too quick to purify and absolve "feminism" here.

AS: Right. We want to take a different approach. What if certain forms of feminism, historically, have not simply colluded with white-supremacist projects but have actually been fascist themselves? How might ceasing to deny that feminisms can be fascist actually strengthen antifascist organizing in this moment?

SL: OK, before we dive into this conversation, should we briefly indicate our working definitions of both *feminism* and *fascism*—these apparently antithetical terms? Are you happy to call "feminism" any project that seeks to enlarge the sphere of action for a human (individual or collective) female, feminine, or gender-oppressed subject? Are you okay with understanding fascism as a fundamentally colonial matrix of domination, whose cults seek to impose, among other things, right reproduction upon human populations via both positive and negative eugenics? If so, how should we go about broaching the subject of their overlap? I am keen, as well, to hear you describe the contours of your evolving commitment (or not) to this internally riven rubric, feminism, from your standpoint.

AS: When it comes to our definition of feminism, I think it's clear that we've already run into a problem: agitating on behalf of women and agitating on behalf of gender-oppressed subjects are two quite different projects—and this is before we even get into the problem of who is permitted entry to the category of womanhood. As you've mentioned, part of what we are trying to do here is resist a purifying impulse when it comes to feminism. It is politically and theoretically unhelpful to dismiss all white-supremacist, or transphobic, or otherwise oppressive feminisms as "not real feminism." This is particularly true, given that the imposition of a normative gender regime from which nonwhite people are coded as deviating has been a part of so many colonial projects. Already, then, we have illuminated a closer connection between fascism and feminism than is usually acknowledged, based on Aimé Césaire's (2000: 36) understanding of fascism as the application "to Europe of colonialist procedures which until then had been reserved exclusively for the Arabs of Algeria, the 'coolies' of India, and the 'n——s' of Africa." I think it's useful to hold this definition of fascism alongside your 2019 *New York Times* opinion piece, "How British Feminism Became Antitrans." There, you write,

> Imperial Britain imposed policies to enforce heterosexuality and the gender binary, while simultaneously constructing the racial "other" as not only fundamentally different, but freighted with sexual menace; from there, it's not a big

leap to see sexual menace in any sort of "other," and "biological realities" as essential and immutable. (Significantly, many Irish feminists have rejected Britain's TERF-ism, citing their experience of colonialism explicitly as part of the reason.) (Lewis 2019b)

Historians who work on the role of women in fascist movements often express surprise that women would be invested in a political ideology that is inherently anti-feminist and misogynistic. Yet female fascists themselves expressed a strong belief that fascism had something to offer women, and I don't think we should rush to dismiss this as false consciousness. Fascism did have much to offer certain subsets of white women who were invested in upholding white supremacy as well as conservative social norms surrounding the family, religious morality, and social purity. Martin Durham (1998: 11–12) notes that at its founding meeting, "the Italian fascist movement adopted a programme which included a call for women to have both the vote and the right to hold office. . . . By the end of 1921, some 2,000 women belonged to the movement and the Bologna party paper was already referring to 'Fascist feminism' in describing local militants." Benito Mussolini doubled down on this promise to offer women the vote at the 1923 Rome Conference of International Alliance of Women—an organization founded by Millicent Fawcett and Susan B. Anthony, among others—where he was the opening speaker. Meanwhile, during the interrogation following his arrest in 1940, Oswald Mosley stated his belief in the "complete equality of men and women" (29). This rhetoric echoes earlier fascist literature, such as a 1934 article from *Blackshirt* magazine, which asserts that "fascism sees women as complementary and equal to man" (qtd. in Gottlieb 2021: 102).

It perhaps won't come as a surprise that fascist movements generally failed to deliver on their promises to offer social and political "equality" to women. Historically, to announce your intention to advocate for gender equality via an entrenchment of gender roles has been a way of signaling disingenuousness. But recently TERFs have picked up this trope in earnest. In his 1932 book *The Greater Britain*, Mosley argued, "*We want men who are men, and women who are women*" (qtd. in Durham 1998: 29; emphasis in the original). This statement sounds like an anticipatory refutation of the common assertion that "trans women are women." In this sense, it foreshadows the rhetoric of the gender critical movement, whose most fervent desire is, in their terms, the state's acknowledgment of the "reality" of sexual difference and the impossibility of sex/gender transition.[1] TERFs love to fixate on the phrase "trans women are women"; Helen Joyce (2021: 10) writes, "What first intrigued me about gender-identity ideology was the circularity of its core mantra, 'transwomen are women,' which raises and leaves unanswered the question of what, then, the word 'woman' means. What led me to think further was the vilification of anyone who questioned it." Here, Joyce projects the "circularity" and incoherence of transphobic thought onto trans people themselves. This is an important point of convergence between fascism and TERFism: an anti-intellectual celebration of intuitive perception and a celebration of epistemic incoherence as if it were a virtue.[2] (A related point of convergence— anti-Semitism—has flared up in relation to Joyce's book in particular, which claims that the trans "global agenda" is funded by a sketchy cabal of Jewish billionaires.)[3] I have to admit I laughed out loud at the moment when Joyce (2021: 7) claims, "Since evolution has equipped humans with the ability to recognise other people's sex, almost instantaneously and with exquisite accuracy, very few trans people 'pass' as their desired sex." Her rapturous celebration of evolutionary instinct (that word *exquisite!*) perfectly aligns with fascism's anti-intellectual intellectual tradition.

SL: As you know, your point here is in line with the published, then egregiously censored, argument Judith Butler made in an interview with *Transgender Marxism* editor Jules Gleeson on no less a platform than the *Guardian*, the venerable liberal newspaper with the notoriously trans-antagonistic UK office. (Members of the US office of the *Guardian* have even denounced their counterparts in London because of the latter's TERFism.) Butler (2021) was circumspect: they merely said that "the anti-gender movement is one of the dominant strains of fascism in our times." So, we might pause here and spell out that, while all TERFs are gender criticals, not all gender criticals are TERFs. However much the two constituencies seem to blur in practice, the *RF* part of *TERF*—that is, the radical feminist argument for trans exclusion—marks TERFism as distinct from the wider, nonfeminist, and indeed often anti-feminist position that deems "gender ideology" to be detrimental to society or evil. However, we are adding, explicitly, that we cannot assume a priori that there are no feminists—even radical feminists—within the "anti-gender" strain of contemporary fascism.

It was a small minority of straight and lesbian radical feminists who, historically, promulgated and then doubled down on a trans-exclusionary account of sex-class's primacy (meaning: dyadic at-birth sexuation is a primary axis of human oppression relative to class, and also relative to racialization). Radical feminism is by no means represented by this minority. Nevertheless, the racial politics of that minority's feminism are worth taking seriously. As a number of scholars at this point have argued—María Lugones, Emi Koyama, and Marquis Bey are the names that, for me, immediately spring to mind—there is an unspoken whiteness to this dyadic, cissexualist account of the world. I would like to see even more work in this vein, focused, for instance, on putting TERFist ideological mechanisms into historical context, specifically in terms of their racial interests. We might recall how white women in Europe and America for centuries simultaneously analogized their cause to, and differentiated it from, antislavery and antiracism, popularizing the notion that "woman is the n——r of the world," for example, and fighting tooth and nail against the idea (I'm looking at you, Elizabeth Cady Stanton) that it might be "the hour of the Negro." For decades, as Alyosxa Tudor (2002) has argued, TERFS have timed their organizing in such a way as to distract (and detract) from the movement for Black lives. I certainly noticed many people on social media remarking upon something that had also struck me very forcefully at the time: the day J. K. Rowling (2020b) tweeted incendiarily, "'People who menstruate.' I'm sure there used to be a word for those people. Someone help me out. Wumben? Wimpund? Woomud?," was more or less the day the media finally realized that the worldwide insurrection sparked by the murder of George Floyd was no mere flash in the pan. It was as though Rowling wanted to pull attention away from anti-Blackness and foster worry, instead, about "female erasure."

I'll add one final suggestion. In addition to paying greater attention to this potentially anti-anti-racist dynamic, left anti-capitalists might profit from remembering that the belief in the primacy of sex-class was one salient (though by no means sufficient, it goes without saying) ingredient of fascist identity. Klaus Theweleit (1987: 169) shows exhaustively in *Male Fantasies* that "one of the primary traits of fascists is assigning greater importance to the battle of the sexes than to the class struggle." As your points about Mussolini and Mosley remind us, it is quite possible to be a white-supremacist advocate of gender equality.

AS: There is an interesting moment in Julie Gottlieb's (2021: 5) *Feminine Fascism* where she blames communist class reductionism for "stunting the development" of feminist antifascism. I think this does an injustice to the long tradition of feminist antifascism while simultaneously scapegoating communist movements for the fact that some women were drawn to fascism. Anyway, to return to your earlier question concerning my commitment to feminism, I'm glad we're writing this together because mine is not as durable as yours, I think. I grew up in the exact tradition of British feminism that we're critiquing—I went to the same suffragette-founded high school as Maya Forstater, the TERF fired for transphobia, whose case famously gained the support of Rowling. As a teenager I remember hearing a teacher making disparaging comments about another student for wearing a niqab because ours was a feminist institution. A year after I left, the student feminist club successfully lobbied the Tesco petrol station opposite the school to stop selling "lad's mags" (softcore pornography). The rage I feel as someone formerly interpellated by this form of feminism is something you share, I think. It's made me especially attentive to intellectual and political moves to innocence, whether that be the "memeification" of queer ethical superiority or casualized "men are trash" misandry (Seresin 2019). Sophie, could you tell me more about your relationship to feminism?

SL: Like most queer scholars, I've wrestled long with dis/identification with "feminism." Neither Monique Wittig's suggestion that lesbians are not women, nor Lugones's lesbian-informed denunciation of the coloniality of woman-centered politics, struck me as particularly shocking when I first encountered them. At the same time, my father's anti-feminist taunting made me feel like a feminist at the most elemental level, ever since I can remember. You can tell I'm agonizing over this answer! Especially since it's you—my friend Asa—asking me whether I am a feminist in the pages of *TSQ*, my answer could run very long. I could first disclaim that opposing feminism (which sometimes takes the form of calling feminism "fascist") is itself a fascistic move. I might then talk about my total opposition to femonationalism, maternalism, femocracy, misandry, sexual moralism, and liberal feminism. I could describe the alienation (at best) and aversion (at worst) I've experienced with regard to feminisms encountered in the wild, since adolescence. I could affirm my, nonetheless, gut-deep anti-anti-feminism. But you're right: in other contexts and moods, the matter is less equivocal for me than it is for you. I'm a "feminist against the family," after all; a feminist against cisness (as Heaney has it);[4] a partisan of Beth Richie's "abolition feminism." I sniff misogyny a mile away. My whole white queer middle-class European girlhood was awash in red-hot antipatriarchal emotion! Lastly, I think I actually see "feministness" as partly outside individuals' choice and control, as a relation of social recognition. For example, my feministness has often been ascribed to me, for me, just from looking at me on the street. The ascription isn't wrong. I mean: I do "identify." The raging, righteous pleasures of feministness are potent. The addictiveness of that righteous feeling prevented me for many years from becoming attuned to (and learning to fight) feminist femmephobia, feminist whorephobia, feminist anti-Blackness, ableism, cissexism, Orientalism, and so on. But, also, fat, bra-less, hairy-armpitted AFABs like me (and many TERFs . . .) are widely "read" as feminists, in public, regardless of our speech.

AS: Earlier you brought up "wounded attachments." I want us to zero in now on the question of erotics and why we're trying to illuminate the specifically erotic pull of fascist feminism. Given that fascism defines itself so vehemently against sexual freedom, queerness, and the erotic, it might surprise some people that we are choosing to think via the term *erotics*. What do you think this framing illuminates about the fascist impulse within feminism?

SL: I think naming the erotic frisson in fascist and *fascisant* feminisms is useful because it tells the truth about that "commitment to misery" these actors vaunt, right? There is an excited, sacrificial kind of doom that attends the condition of being so-called women-born women, in the eyes of participants in eugenic feminism. This doom (which they pretend to want to fend off but actually hungrily seek after, for instance in cis misogyny apocalypses like *The Handmaid's Tale*) is epically beautiful, to them. There are homo-, hetero-, and autoerotic payoffs to be had here, in spades. Jules Joanne Gleeson (2021b) recently speculated about "an addiction to disgust reflex triggers" in the feminists swarming her Twitter account. This is well put. The promise of libidinal rewards following enlistment in TERFery is a bit of an open secret. Fun times are implied quite clearly in the popular idiom *Prosecco Stormfront*, for example (which refers to the British webforum and hotbed of TERF organizing Mumsnet). Tudor (2020), similarly, defines TERFism as "an activity you do for pleasure." A piece of biopolitical property is being defended, indignantly—lustily. I will try to paraphrase: Mother's sacrosanct body is beset on every side by thieves and liars, only to be additionally caricatured by impostors, an imposture that governments then enshrine in law, making laws that honor this impostor, this travesty, in the way that Woman ought to be honored!! And only other bona fide wombyn can possibly understand the gruesomeness of this indignity. But men like Derrick Jensen and Graham Linehan can be fulsomely praised for sticking up for women . . .

As an extinction fantasy narrative, it is all quite gothic. Which reminds me: do you remember the internet meme circa 2016 (whose origins are unknown to me, honestly) whereby the quasi-murderous arch TERF Cathy Brennan was derided as a "fake goth"? I have a pet theory that fascist feminists, in their capacity as (fake) goths, fundamentally agree with Edgar Allan Poe (1846: 165) that "the death of a beautiful woman is, unquestionably, the most poetical topic in the world." I suppose what I am claiming is that the millenarian emergency of "female erasure"[5] imagined by Mary Daly, Sheila Jeffreys, and Janice Raymond is an imminent disaster the cisterhood loves, Cassandra-like, to hate.

Uncovering the presence of this apocalyptic intoxication or self-martyring titillation in some feminist discourses can be useful simply because it makes it easier to understand the draw these mythologies exert upon feminized (usually white, but not always) human beings. In the *Trouble with White Women: A Counterhistory of Feminism*, I was gratified to find that Kyla Schuller (2021: 200) agrees with us: "TERF politics has an erotics." Kyla parses the textual intercourse between Daly and Raymond as charged with yearning and eroticism. But it is a chastity-fetishizing eroticism, I think, and it is not unrelated to the feverish fits of collective maternal prudery organized by TAnon, with its fantasies of child trafficking and "rapid-onset" contagions of transgenderism among America's juveniles (Gill-Peterson 2021; Leveille 2021). The scope for falling in love with the romance of one's own stalwart moral courage, and that of one's feminist sisters, resonates for me with the romance of eugenic feminism more generally, which includes figures like Charlotte Perkins Gilman, Margaret Sanger, Kathleen Mayo,

Sarojini Naidu, and Indira Gandhi (Nadkarni 2014; Ziegler 2008). Eugenic feminism rests on a stirring story about woman's redemptive, all-important role as the author and guardian of the reborn and regenerated race: a story whose loudest proponents are sometimes, paradoxically, lesbians.

On which note: tell me more about the lesbian fascist suffragettes.

AS: Earlier I mentioned that for many women the draw of fascism lay in its promise to enshrine their identity as mothers, to protect the family, and to promote social purity. In early 2021 I became interested in a group of women who found fascism appealing for quite different reasons. I've called them lesbian fascists, but this is really something of a misnomer, not only because in this early twentieth-century moment "lesbian" was still an emergent category and not a term these people necessarily applied to themselves, but also because many of them might be closer to what we now think of as transmasculine (not that the two are always mutually exclusive). The British aristocrat and BUF member Rotha Lintorn-Orman, for example, would dress up as male figures (such as Father Christmas and "a grandfather") at fascist social events; the French athlete and later Nazi Violette Morris got a double mastectomy so she could better fit inside her cyclecar (at least, this was her stated reason). Others, such as Mary Sophia Allen, who served as a police officer alongside her partner, Margaret Damer-Dawson, were masculine, butch women who publicly foregrounded their womanhood, even if their private lives were another story (Allen was called Robert and "Sir" by people she knew personally). Allen's fascist politics revolved around her belief that society was in drastic need of "women police"—she traveled to Germany to speak with Adolf Hitler himself about it—and she wrote a three-volume autobiography with *woman* and *lady* in every title (*The Pioneering Policewoman, A Woman at the Crossroads*, and *Lady in Blue*).

For Allen, women police were vital for the enforcement of social purity feminism in public. She believed that "women police, in patrolling parks and streets, could protect children" (Durham 1998: 44), a task for which men were presumed to be intrinsically unsuitable. There's such a strange convergence of desires at work here, which is typical of the archive of lesbian and feminist fascism. On the one hand, Allen's rabid eagerness to serve as a police officer (for years she did so voluntarily, to the point of actually being sanctioned by the state) does seem at least somewhat rooted in her queer masculine identity—I'm thinking of her desire to be called "Sir." At the same time, she grounds her argument about the need for women police in family ideology, in protecting the innocence of the child. This is your area of expertise, so I'm going to turn it over to you now. Clearly, fascism is deeply invested in white reproductive futurity and in the unit of the white nuclear family. We are accustomed to pitting queerness in comfortable opposition to this kind of politics. What do you make of the women police movement, propelled by the mix of family ideology and queer (trans)masculinity? Do you see a relation to the way in which lesbian TERFs in the present are fixated on defining womanhood via reproductive capacity even where lesbianism itself often precludes women from conceiving children biologically?

SL: You raise an important point. The concept of homonationalism, with its white-supremacist freight of "family values," is practically always illustrated with reference to gay male (white) married couples like Pete and Chasten Buttigeig. Why not Cressida Dick, the commissioner of the London Metropolitan Police, and her partner (police officer) Helen Ball? Speaking of whom: the women's police movement is far from dead. During the anti-police uprising of 2020, a slew of op-eds (from *Ms.* magazine to *CNN*) called for police departments to hire more women because policewomen, it is erroneously supposed, do not murder Black people. In particular, by virtue of their sex, they have children's best interests at heart. In October 2020 the National Fraternal Order of Police tweeted a photo of a white Philadelphia policewoman, her eyes half-closed in maternal pity, with her arms clasped around a tiny Black two-year-old. The caption read, "This child was lost during the violent riots in Philadelphia, wandering around barefoot in an area that was experiencing complete lawlessness. The only thing this Philadelphia police officer cared about in that moment was protecting this child."[6] This was blatantly fascist propaganda, made even more egregious by the fact, as it later emerged, that the Philadelphia police itself had ripped the child in question away from his mother earlier in the day (that woman, Rickia Young, has been awarded $2 million in damages). This circular tale is such a perfect encapsulation of the irreducible class antagonism between racialized and proletarianized caregivers and what could equally be called, in the carceral-eugenic tradition, the National Maternal Order of Police.

As you notice, there is so much apparent tension and contradiction in this female cop archive, notably between the policewomen's identifications with state masculinity and their vindications of the principle of feminine maternal authority over a populace. But perhaps motherhood (the institution) was always simply the other side of the coin of paternal fascism, the "good cop" to fatherhood's bad one. The genre certainly extends to today's transphobic military lesbians and white lesbian femonationalists: women like Miriam Ben-Shalom, a former staff sergeant in the US Army and contributor to the pagan anti-gender *Female Erasure* anthology, whose statements of loyalty to "apple pie, motherhood and the American flag" are a matter of record. While researching the historical roots of the explosion of Islamophobic governmental feminism in Germany—feminism that seized upon an incident of mass sexual assault that took place in Cologne on New Year's Eve 2015 in order to peddle anti-Muslim border policies—I discovered that Cologne was in fact where the Prussian Weibliche Kriminalpolizei (WPK) first began in 1923. The WPK was Germany's female criminal police department, whose officers were responsible for children and adolescents. It expanded hugely under Nazism. Learning about the WPK gave me an added perspective, shall we say, on the adulation that Germany's transphobic second-waver-in-chief, the lesbian feminist Alice Schwarzer, heaped on the Cologne Police Department in early 2016, for having defended the bodies of native German women and girls from the groping hands of what the new neo-Nazi feminists in Pegida (Patriotic Europeans Against the Islamicization of the Occident) were calling "Islamist rapefugees."[7]

For avoidance of doubt, let us stress again that there are many vital and liberatory strains of lesbian politics. The majority of 1970s lesbian organizing seems to have been trans inclusive (Heaney 2016), and much of it was also family abolitionist, in the sense of commune-oriented, anti-state, anti-capitalist, poly-maternalist, and children's liberationist (I'm thinking here of contributions by Kay Lindsey to Toni Cade Bambara's *Black Woman* anthology, published in 1970). I am, as you know, extremely fond of the Wages Due Lesbians, a mothering-against-motherhood moment in history.

And that is precisely why I am so repelled when certain radfems, today, deploy lesbianism (whether or not they are themselves lesbians) as a family-values, think-of-the-children type of conservatism. "Gender critical"–identified straight feminists who say they are fighting lesbophobia, in particular, seem to utter online the most gender-traditional appeals to the moral authority of motherhood one could ever imagine. They typically call for carceral state powers to back this authority. Meanwhile, Britain's massively popular message-board Mumsnet is a self-declared "army of mothers," whose percentage of lesbian combatants is notoriously tiny, but where feminists nevertheless constantly air concerns about "lesbian erasure." (One could witness this same dynamic in Rowling's (2020a) infamous anti-trans open letter, which worried about lesbians being "called bigots for not dating trans women with penises.") I cannot say what proportion of contemporary TERFism is really waged by lesbians, as opposed to heterosexual women using lesbians as their flagship endangered species, but my distinct impression is that the proportion is tiny. Alas, it is not zero (viz. "Get the L Out"). I have myself witnessed avowed lesbian socialist feminists tie themselves in knots at Marxist events, mounting fundamentalist defenses of a definition of femaleness as "cyclical secretion of luteinizing hormone." Kathleen Stock, the depressingly influential lesbian academic, is very invested in purifying the definition of lesbian sexuality to exclude kink, as well as cocks (be they flesh or silicone).

Amid all this awfulness, though, my question to you is: how do we avoid trivializing the analytic charge (so dear to Stock) of societal "lesbophobia," while fighting neo-social-purity-feminism? Do you agree that lesbians have good reasons to be reticent to see themselves or their forebears as implicated in fascism?

Could you reflect a little about the distinction we are drawing between an individual's or even a subculture's fascist drives, and the rather different matter of the fascism of a state or government apparatus? Secondly, could you unpack for us this concept of a homoerotics of sameness and what it helps us do here?

AS: As I mentioned earlier, I felt conflicted about the title I chose for the short essay I wrote about Lintorn-Orman, Allen, and others, which was "Lesbian Fascism on TERF Island." I don't want to imply that I have uncovered some massive archive of lesbian fascism or to further stoke the impression of lesbians and trans people being at war with one another. At the same time, in choosing such a provocative title I did want to push back against the reflexive framing of lesbians as intrinsically progressive and innocent, an idea that has quite powerful currency right now. More and more, my work is oriented toward critically interrogating the work that "queer" is doing in contemporary culture as a totem of political purity. As Kadji Amin (2017) points out, this "idealizing impulse" exists within queer theory too, and I've been deeply inspired by the heuristic of de-idealization that he lays out in *Disturbing Attachments*. I'm really drawn to de-idealizing projects like Huw Lemmey and Ben Miller's (2019–present) *Bad Gays* (first a podcast, soon to be a book), which traces the histories of messy, cruel, and even straight-up evil queer people—including quite a few fascists. At the same time, it's telling that it took them until season 3—after twenty-six episodes!—before they featured a lesbian. Writing "Lesbian Fascism on TERF Island," which I called *Bad Gays* fan fiction, was also a loving form of dissent from the idea that lesbians are intrinsically better people or that lesbianism and fascism are incompatible.

In a 1992 essay, "Of Catamites and Kings," Gayle Rubin describes a subcultural tendency toward exclusionary and even fascistic practices within lesbian culture:

> Despite theoretically embracing diversity, contemporary lesbian culture has a deep streak of xenophobia. When confronted with phenomena that do not neatly fit our categories, lesbians have been known to respond with hysteria, bigotry, and a desire to stamp out the offending messy realities. A "country club syndrome" sometimes prevails in which the lesbian community is treated as an exclusive enclave from which the riffraff must be systematically expunged. . . . Over the years, lesbian groups have gone through periodic attempts to purge male-to-female transsexuals, sadomasochists, butch-femme lesbians, bisexuals, and even lesbians who are not separatists. FTMs are another witch hunt waiting to happen. (249)

It is no accident that the terms Rubin uses here—*xenophobia, bigotry, stamp out, expunge,* and *purge*—evoke far-right inclinations. At the same time, you are totally right that there is an important distinction between a subcultural tendency and fascism outright. However exclusionary their communities might at times be, lesbians are not well positioned to marshal the resources of the state in their favor. (Indeed, they are more likely to be targets of state persecution.) Similarly, I think you are right to question "what proportion of contemporary TERFism is really waged by lesbians" and to point out the injustice of lesbians having to answer for the bioessentialist and queerphobic nonsense committed by transphobes in their name.[8]

With all that said, I hope it's clear that I'm not interested in going after lesbians because I think they are especially fascistic, but rather that I'm invested in dispelling the myth that there is something inherent within lesbian culture that insulates it from harboring fascism. As I mentioned above, the historical co-implication of fascism and white male homosociality/homoeroticism is quite widely acknowledged. One crucial trope of this co-implication is what we have been calling the homoerotics of sameness. In gay male culture, this takes the form of valorizing a kind of cookie-cutter, hypermuscular, white male form as the gay ideal. We can also recognize it in the phenomenon of twinning: when two men who look exactly the same date each other. Bobby Benedicto (2019: 283) has written about the morbid narcissism of gay twinning and the fact that, "by definition, twinning cannot accommodate racial difference; its narcissism necessarily colludes with another prohibition: the prohibition against interracial desire."

Lesbian culture does not really have a comparable investment in twinning, but as a concluding thought I want to read the history of lesbian feminist bigotry against butch/femme as part of this tradition of the homoerotics of sameness. In quarantine I watched a 1992 documentary, *Framing Lesbian Fashion*, and was struck by what a couple of interviewees were saying about the 1970s frumpy lesbian feminist aesthetic, which several of them called a "uniform."[9] Of course, wearing a uniform in itself is not indicative of fascism. But the way that the wearing of this uniform was enforced—and dissenters, particularly butch/femme lesbians, condemned—is worth pausing over. In *Pleasure and Danger*, Joan Nestle (1984: 236) writes, "The message to fems throughout the 1970s was that we were the Uncle Toms of the movement. If I wore the acceptable movement clothes of sturdy shoes, dungarees, work shirt and back pack, then I was to be trusted." I think the policing of those who deviated from the "uniform" of "acceptable movement clothes" betrays an investment in sameness, to the idea that one can and should broadcast their commitment to a social/political position via aesthetics. Perhaps more importantly, it betrays a narrowness of imagination around what lesbian identity would be. As many people have pointed out, there is an indelible connection between the femmephobia found within certain lesbian communities and the transmisogyny of straight cis women who code trans women as regressive traitors to the cause of feminism. You see this in writing like Elinor Burkett's (2015) *New York Times* op-ed about Caitlin Jenner, "What Makes a Woman?," in which she disdainfully indicates that Jenner is wearing the wrong kind of uniform: "A new photo spread and interview in Vanity Fair . . . offered us a glimpse into Caitlyn Jenner's idea of a woman: a cleavage-boosting corset, sultry poses, thick mascara and the prospect of regular 'girls' nights' of banter about hair and makeup."

Speaking of uniforms—I want to end on a less bleak note, by bringing up what I know, Sophie, is one of your favorite films. *Mädchen in Uniform* (*Girls in Uniform*) is a boarding school lesbian love story that, rather extraordinarily, was made in Germany in 1931.

SL: Leontine Sagan's (1931) film is a vision of queer Jewish antiauthoritarianism, sapphic solidarity, and children's liberation. It skillfully discusses the affective and aesthetic seductions of fascism, argues for the urgency (amid the crumbling Weimar Republic!) of an antiheroic politics, and culminates in a finale in which, symbolically speaking at least, the girls take off their uniforms and embody a politics of what Ewa Majeswka (2021: 151) in *Feminist Antifascism* calls "contingent universality," mindful that love by itself is not, as it were, enough, because after all, "there is [also] love at the core of fascist mobilization." I think this is perhaps as good a note as any upon which to end this dialogue: honoring the history of feminist and/or lesbian anti-fascism even as we—indeed because we—insist on being attentive to the non-synonymity of feminism and anti-fascism and the collective arts by which they are, always contingently, made synonymous. Thank you, again, Asa, for engaging in this mutual exploration with me.

AS: Thank you, Sophie!

Sophie Lewis is a writer living in Philadelphia, teaching courses on feminism, utopian theory, and antiwork politics at the Brooklyn Institute for Social Research. Her first book was *Full Surrogacy Now: Feminism against Family* (2019), and her second, published in October 2022, is *Abolish the Family: A Manifesto for Care and Liberation*. Sophie's essays—on subjects ranging from "mothering against motherhood" to octopus eros—have been published in academic journals such as *Signs* and *Feminist Theory* as well as nonacademic ones such as *Boston Review*, the *New York Times*, *n+1*, *Dissent*, the *Baffler*, *Harper's*, and the *London Review of Books*. Sophie studied English literature (BA) and subsequently environmental policy (MSc) at Oxford University, followed by politics (MA) at the New School for Social Research and Human Geography (for her PhD) at the University of Manchester. She is now informally a visiting scholar at the Alice Paul Center for Research in Feminist, Queer and Transgender Studies at the University of Pennsylvania, subsists thanks to a Patreon, and tweets at @reproutopia.

Asa Seresin is a writer and PhD student in English at the University of Pennsylvania, where he is also pursuing a certificate in gender, sexuality, and women's studies. His research primarily focuses on heterosexuality and cultures of heteronegativity. He holds a BA in comparative literature from Harvard and an MPhil in English from Cambridge and lives between Philadelphia and London.

Notes

1. In *Trans: Where Ideology Meets Reality*, Helen Joyce (2021: 96) writes, "Even as the class of 'women' becomes 'some males and some females, with no objective traits in common,' female bodies continue to exist." Later, she adds, "The words 'male' and 'female' cannot mean both biology and identity. And setting aside the thorny question of what it might mean to feel male or female, why would such a feeling matter, if being male or female does not?" (139). Kathleen Stock (2021: 149), meanwhile, asserts, "If trans women are women, they are not 'women' in the same sense in which adult human females are 'women.' If trans men are men, they are not 'men' in the same sense in which adult human males are 'men.'" Undergirding all this pontification we can read an echo of Moseley's desire: men who are men, and women who are women.

2. Mark Hayes (2014: 21) describes these qualities as distinctive markers of English fascist thought: "What was required, the fascists believed, was a return to sounder and more trustworthy instincts—instincts which had been dulled by years of lifeless contemplation. . . . Fascist 'ideas' could be contradictory and confusing, and the fascists themselves not only acknowledged and accepted their theoretical incoherence, it was positively celebrated as a sign of their vitality."

3. Christa Peterson (2021) and Jules Joanne Gleeson (2021a), among others, have unearthed evidence of Joyce publicly acknowledging the influence of Jennifer Bilek, an anti-Semitic conspiracy theorist. Meanwhile, Bilek (2021) herself has accused Joyce of plagiarizing her.

4. Heaney's forthcoming second book, *Feminism against Cisness*, is an edited collection of essays by trans studies scholars who use anti-colonial, Marxist, and Black feminist methods to address the many legacies of the historical emergence of the idea that sex determines sexed experience.

5. "Female erasure," according to the Dianic cleric Priestess Ruth Barrett, "continues to be propagated through gender identity politics today and through continuing efforts to define and enforce oppressive gender constructs on the female sex." See femaleerasure. com, the homepage of *Female Erasure*, an anthology of gender critical radical feminism edited by Ruth Barrett (2019).

6. For news coverage of this incident see, for instance, Shepherd 2020.

7. For more on Alice Schwarzer and her femonationalist pronouncements about Muslim men, refer to Hark and Villa 2020.

8. In *Trans*, Joyce (2021: 63)—a straight "gender critical" woman—presents herself as representing an intellectual vanguard to which gay people are catching up: "A growing number of gay people are waking up to the link [between transition and homophobia], however. I have heard gender affirmation described as 'postmodern gay conversion therapy.'" Like most of the evidence on which her book rests, there is no citation for this quote, allowing Joyce the rhetorical sleight of hand of placing words into a gay person's mouth. In reality, the reader has no evidence of whether a straight or gay person said this or no reason to believe that Joyce herself didn't just make it up.

9.   One interviewee, Sally Gearhart, observes, "It was almost a uniform. Everybody had their shit-kicking boots and everybody had their jeans, and usually their unironed shirts and usually their 'Free Angela' buttons hanging from the shirts and the hair was usually short . . . that was pretty much the costume or the uniform." Another, Carmen Daria Morrison, claims, "In the 70s when the lesbians had sort of a 'uniform,' I was just coming out, so of course, I wore that uniform too" (Everett 1992).

References

Amin, Kadji, 2017. *Disturbing Attachments: Genet, Modern Pederasty, and Queer History*. Durham, NC: Duke University Press.

Barrett, Ruth, ed. 2019. *Female Erasure*. n.p.: Tidal Time.

Benedicto, Bobby. 2019. "Agents and Objects of Death: Gay Murder, Boyfriend Twins, and Queer of Color Negativity." *GLQ* 25, no. 2: 273–96.

Bilek, Jennifer (@bjportraits). 2021. "Your interview of me in 2020, for this book, proved fruitful, I see." Twitter, July 21, 10:17 p.m. https://twitter.com/bjportraits/status/1418032364798754816.

Blee, Kathleen. 1991. *Women of the Klan: Racism and Gender in the 1920s*. Berkeley: University of California Press.

Burkett, Elinor. 2015. "What Makes a Woman?" *New York Times*, June 6. https://www.nytimes.com/2015/06/07/opinion/sunday/what-makes-a-woman.html.

Butler, Judith. 2021. "Judith Butler: 'We Need to Rethink the Category of "Woman."'" Interview by Jules Joanne Gleeson. *Guardian*, September 7. https://theguardian.com/lifeandstyle/2021/sep/07/judith-butler-interview-gender.

Césaire, Aimé. 2000. *Discourse on Colonialism*. Translated by Joan Pinkham. New York: Monthly Review Press.

Durham, Martin. 1998. *Women and Fascism*. London: Routledge.

Everett, Karen, dir. 1992. *Framing Lesbian Fashion*. San Francisco: Frameline. Alexander Street. https://search.alexanderstreet.com/preview/work/bibliographic_entity%7Cvideo_work%7C1854235.

Gill-Peterson, Jules. 2021. "From Gender Critical to QAnon: Anti-trans Politics and the Laundering of Conspiracy." *New Inquiry*, September 13. https://thenewinquiry.com/from-gender-critical-to-qanon-anti-trans-politics-and-the-laundering-of-conspiracy.

Gleeson, Jules Joanne (@socialrepro). 2021a. "@HjoyceGender please don't sue me, but is it true you interviewed Jennifer Bilek in 2020?" Twitter, July 22, 5:27 p.m. https://twitter.com/socialrepro/status/1418321817304027144.

Gleeson, Jules Joanne (@socialrepro). 2021b. "Please don't row with people in my mentions." Twitter, September 11, 7:09 p.m. https://twitter.com/socialrepro/status/1436829162623455235.

Gottlieb, Julie. 2021. *Feminine Fascism: Women in Britain's Fascist Movement, 1923–1945*. London: Bloomsbury.

Hark, Sabine, and Paula-Irene Villa. 2020. *The Future of Difference: Beyond the Toxic Entanglement of Racism, Sexism, and Feminism*. Translated by Sophie Lewis. London: Verso.

Hayes, Mark. 2014. *The Ideology of Fascism and the Far Right in Britain*. London: Red Quill.

Heaney, Emma. 2016. "Women-Identified Women: Trans Women in 1970s Lesbian Feminist Organizing." *TSQ* 3, nos. 1–2: 137–45.

Joyce, Helen. 2021. *Trans: Where Ideology Meets Reality*. London: Oneworld.

Lemmey, Huw, and Ben Miller. 2019–present. *Bad Gays*. Podcast. https://badgayspod.com/.

Leveille, Lee. 2021. "The Mechanisms of TAnon: What Is 'TAnon'?" *Health Liberation Now*, April 12. https://healthliberationnow.com/2021/04/12/the-mechanisms-of-tanon-what-is -tanon.

Lewis, Sophie. 2019. "How British Feminism Became Anti-trans." *New York Times*, February 7. https://nytimes.com/2019/02/07/opinion/terf-trans-women-britain.html.

Majewska, Ewa. 2021. *Feminist Antifascism: Counterpublics of the Common*. London: Verso.

Nadkarni, Asha. 2014. *Eugenic Feminism: Reproductive Nationalism in the United States and India*. Minneapolis: University of Minnesota Press.

Nestle, Joan. 1984. "The Fem Question." In *Pleasure and Danger: Exploring Female Sexuality*, edited by Carol S. Vance, 232–41. Boston: Routledge.

Peterson, Christa (@christapeterso). 2021. "In her new book, the Economist's Helen Joyce claims the trans 'global agenda' is 'shaped' by three Jewish billionaires." Twitter, July 17, 11:25 p.m. https://twitter.com/christapeterso/status/1416599964214448130.

Poe, Edgar Allan. 1846. "The Philosophy of Composition." *Graham's Magazine* 28, no. 4: 163–67.

Pugh, Martin. 2006. *Hurrah for the Blackshirts! Fascists and Fascism in Britain between the Wars*. London: Penguin.

Rowling, J. K. 2020a. "J. K. Rowling Writes about Her Reasons for Speaking Out on Sex and Gender Issues." June 10. https://www.jkrowling.com/opinions/j-k-rowling-writes-about -her-reasons-for-speaking-out-on-sex-and-gender-issues/.

Rowling, J. K. 2020b. "'People who menstruate.'" Twitter, June 6, 5:35 p.m. https://twitter.com/jk _rowling/status/1269382518362509313.

Rubin, Gayle. 2012. "Of Catamites and Kings" In *The Gayle Rubin Reader*, 241–53. Durham, NC: Duke University Press.

Sagan, Leontine. 1931. *Mädchen in Uniform*. Berlin: Bild und Ton.

Schuller, Kyla. 2021. *The Trouble with White Women: A Counterhistory of Feminism*. New York: Bold Type.

Seresin, Asa. 2019. "On Heteropessimism." *New Inquiry*, October 9. https://thenewinquiry.com /on-heteropessimism.

Seresin, Asa. 2021. "Lesbian Fascism on TERF Island." Asa Seresin website, February 11. https:// asaseresin.com/2021/02/11/lesbian-fascism-on-terf-island.

Shepherd, Katie. 2020. "Police Took a Black Toddler from His Family's SUV." *Washington Post*, October 30. https://washingtonpost.com/nation/2020/10/30/philadelphia-fop-posts -toddler.

Stock, Kathleen. 2021. *Material Girls: Why Reality Matters for Feminism*. London: Little, Brown.

Theleweit, Klaus. 1987. *Male Fantasies*. Vol. 1. Translated by Stephen Conway. Minneapolis: University of Minnesota Press.

Tudor, Alyosxa. 2020. "Terfism Is White Distraction: On BLM, Decolonising the Curriculum, Anti-gender Attacks, and Feminist Transphobia." *Engenderings* (blog), June 19. https:// eprints.soas.ac.uk/33114.

Ziegler, Mary. 2008. "Eugenic Feminism: Mental Hygiene, the Women's Movement, and the Campaign for Eugenic Legal Reform, 1900–1935." *Harvard Journal of Law and Gender* 36, no. 1: 211.

Choosing Threat, Embodying the Viral

Trans* Endemics in Times of Pandemic

MAT A. THOMPSON

In 2020 trans* organizations across global contexts found government and state support during the coronavirus pandemic to be considerably lacking (Summers 2020; Goshal 2020) and thus sought to provide the absent financial, social, and health-care support for trans* people (APTN 2020; ILGA World 2020).[1] At the same time, trans* people all over the world have identified a prominent rise in transphobic rhetoric and legislation (Reid 2021; Deliso 2021). In the United Kingdom, the *Bell v. Tavistock* (2020) high court ruling, which asserted that under-sixteens were not able to consent to prescribed puberty blockers, and the governmental failure to amend the 2004 Gender Recognition Act were codifications of a deeply transphobic political atmosphere (BBC 2020; Murphy and Brooks 2020).[2]

In this atmosphere—the pandemic, on the one hand, and the increase in the official writing of transphobia into state and public policy, on the other—we see a consolidation of trans*-exclusive feminist, or TERF, discourse expressing themselves through the tropology of viral and toxic threat, most evident in rhetoric that explicitly refers to transness in viral terms. In this brief and formative essay, I endeavor to examine the contextual and discursive positioning of transness as a parallel to, or vector of, viral threat. I propose that transness is figured as an endemic threat to feminism by TERFs in attempts to draw from the affective resonances of the pandemic. What does it mean for transness to be endemic during a pandemic? Rather than refusing the positioning of transness as threat, I argue that threat is foundational to a revolutionary politics and that trans* scholarship might instead embrace and embody the viral threat it is already figured to be as a means to destabilize trans*-exclusive feminism.

Fears of a "social contagion" of "rapid onset gender dysphoria" among young people are widespread in TERF spaces (Littman 2018; Shrier 2020). Online

TSQ: Transgender Studies Quarterly * Volume 9, Number 3 * August 2022
DOI 10.1215/23289252-9836134   © 2022 Duke University Press

forums such as Mumsnet are filled with concerns over the "colonisation" (Datun 2021) of "female only" spaces, the "infiltration" of feminist spaces by trans rights activists (Terfragette69 2018), and the "transmission" of and possible "vaccination" against "trans ideology" (Barracker 2021). Assertions that "feminism isn't the right place for" (Patrickharviesorganicmuesli 2018) trans rights advocacy work hand in hand with declarations that gender studies, trans*, and queer scholars aim to "poison" (LGB Alliance 2021b) public discourse and "directly target children" (Davies-Arai 2018: 26). These concerns derive from a belief that the legislation of trans* rights violates and threatens women's human rights, undoing over a century of feminist work (LGB Alliance 2021a). In these viral and contagious terms, transness is figured as an imagined entity unto itself, manifested through the trans* body, which haunts and plagues feminism.

In a famously antagonistic essay, Andrea Long Chu declared trans* studies to be "over," calling it out to be little more than an ancillary notion to queer theory (Chu and Harsin Drager 2019: 103).[3] Taking issue with Chu's pronouncements, many trans* scholars have called "bullshit" on her "wilful misreadings of trans studies, queer studies [and] feminism," and have instead argued that trans* studies isn't actually here yet (Halberstam 2020: 325; Adair, Awkward-Rich, and Marvin 2020). While criticizing tendencies for trans* people to be "exceptionalised by a certain strand of queer theory, serving as figures for a kind of anti-binary subversion of gender," Gabby Benavente and Jules Gill-Peterson (2019: 24) point toward trans* studies' antagonistic start in works such as Susan Stryker's "My Words to Victor Frankenstein" (1994) or Sandy Stone's "Posttransexual Manifesto" (1992). Radical abstractions of bodily matter and reality by trans* studies scholars as monstrous (Barad 2015; Koch-Rein 2019; Stryker 1994), alien (Puig 2019), cellular (Brown 2015), alchemical (Lewis and Irving 2017), and viral (Chen 2015) have repeatedly demonstrated trans* studies' propensity toward aggressive and wild conceptualizations of trans* being, as opposed to a placating politics as Chu might suggest. It is this bleeding edge of imagining the body as a site of politics, while also abstracting metaphor from bodily experience, that makes trans* studies aggressive and assertive.

As such, scholarly considerations of trans* in viral terms are not new but rather stem from histories of AIDS that beset trans and queer subcultures (Sedgwick 1991; Chen 2011). Jules Gill-Peterson, as a means to explain such haunting, highlights Michel Foucault's distinction between the epidemic and the endemic to show that, in an endemic, "death [is] no longer something that suddenly swoop[s] down on life—as in an epidemic. Death [is] now something permanent, something that slips into life, perpetually gnaws at it, diminishes it and weakens it" (Foucault 2003: 244, in Gill-Peterson 2013: 279). For Gill-Peterson, AIDS shifts from epidemic to endemic as it becomes less immediate threat and more underlying. The endemic, if we understand it through Gill-Peterson's articulation of Foucault, is better thought of as an ongoing threat to life that never actually destroys but continually weakens.

That trans rights activism, or trans ideology, is considered an ongoing and pervasive infiltrating threat to feminism demonstrates perhaps most effectively the appropriateness of the endemic metaphor. The figuration of transness as an endemic and underlying threat to feminism by TERFs indexes the cleavage between a specter of trans* threat and the lived reality of being trans*. In positioning transness as an infiltration, usurpation, and corruption of feminism, inasmuch as transness is considered a "social contagion" (Littman 2018; Shrier 2020) and "poison" (Davies-Arai 2018), transness comes to exist as an endemic threat to women's rights and, by extension, women's bodies.

When we return this figuration to the context of the pandemic and align such threat with a model of toxicity and virality, we can see how this discourse of a trans* social contagion is made meaningful. Even prior to the context of a pandemic, the language of the endemic directly invoked the history of disease and contagion. As Alyosxa Tudor (2020) and Jacob Breslow (2020) have argued, TERFs exploit concerns over national security, such as during a global pandemic or a political landscape of increasing antimigrant sentiment, to codify a transphobic agenda. Assuring national security by way of securing women's rights at the expense of a racialized or, in this case, trans other is what has been described as femonationalism (Farris 2017), positioning that which is a threat to women as a threat to the nation (Sager and Mulinari 2018). In the case of UK transphobes, aligning a trans* threat with disease and virality in times of pandemic draws on such significance as a means to catch public and government attention.

What happens, then, when we take the positioning of transness as an endemic threat to feminism as a site of politics? Can we embody threat in productive ways, and why is this significant?

To answer such questions, we must pay attention to the decolonial and transnational critiques of theorizations of the inhuman. Trans*, queer, and posthuman studies have been rightly criticized for their failure to attend to the ways in which toxicity, virality, and animality have historically been used to discern a racialized other (Chen 2011; Roen 2001; Stryker 2019). Jin Haritworn (2015: 212) expresses concern over the ease with which metaphors of inhumanism have been adopted by queer and feminist scholars and asks, "How do inhuman 'orientations' intersect with different proclivities toward life and death? For whom might identifying with the nonhuman be too risky a move?" Zakiyyah Iman Jackson warns that movements beyond the human risk moving beyond race (2015) while also ignoring interrogations of the human made by Black studies (2013). It is thus that, in considering transness as threat, we must be mindful of for whom an embodiment of viral threat is a choice and a privilege, and for whom it is a process of subjectivization.

At the same time, it remains necessary to engage with threat as a site of politics. Threat, I would argue, is at the heart of any transgressive, resistive, or revolutionary action and underlines all activism and scholarship that seeks to dismantle hegemonic power. To shy away from threat would be to shy away from the essence of seeking change. While understandings of transness as inherently transgressive have been criticized for erasing the complexity of trans* experience and refusing transness's non-transgressive sides (Prosser 1998), it is perhaps too rash to overlook the threatening potential of transness. At an inaugural moment of queer theory, Leo Bersani (2010) expressed a desire for gay politics to celebrate its potential for death and radicalism rather than placate a normative structure of rights discourses (Ahuja 2015). Trans* studies, as it seeks to change and disrupt structures and institutionalizations of transphobia, should not discount the value of such a stance.

Trans* threat is what makes trans* studies a ground for a radical politics. While Chu and Drager (2019: 104) ask of trans* scholars, "why are we so nice to each other?," others declare that we "must be willing to turn away from the comfort zone of polite exchange" in order to "fail, to make a mess, to fuck shit up, to be loud, unruly, impolite, to breed resentment, to bash back, to speak up and out, to disrupt, assassinate, shock, and annihilate" (Halberstam 2006: 824). For Jack Halberstam (2020: 324), to be nice to one another is "not to draw hard lines between trans studies and queer studies but to recognize the shared spaces of study, practice, activism, and theory and to build on the work that has already been done." Trans* studies, then, is a space in which aggression and respect may go hand in hand; certainly, Halberstam's own hostile rebuttal to Chu is in itself a sign of respect for her assertions.

If we follow Mel Chen's (2011: 281) work on animacies, we might be able to generate a conceptualization of the virality of trans* threat as not only a political positioning of disruption but also a tool with which we can map the interactions between race, gender, sexuality, ability, and environment as they are invoked by discourses of toxicity. Such an acceptance of the viral may, in fact, "propel, not repel, queer love." A model of toxicity and virality helps us engage with transness's threatening nature and offers space to consider the positioning of transness as endemic, as well as the interplay between such figurative viral status and the very tangible effects of a devastating global pandemic that has been felt along existing lines of race, coloniality, and nation. Embracing threat invites an aggressive politics that carves out a space for trans* politics and survival within a feminism that rejects transness. Indeed, it is only by such assertive politics and graft as Stryker's (2020) and Halberstam's that trans* studies has found a place within the academy.

It is, of course, controversial and potentially dangerous to purposefully align transness with toxicity, particularly in times of pandemic, when trans* organizations are fighting hard to counter the institutional, financial, and social impacts of transphobia and the pandemic. Moreover, when capitalist structures work constantly to assume abjected bodies into forms of normativity as a means of nationalism and profit making, it becomes increasingly difficult to make room for threat. Trans-nationalist and homonationalist systems are prevalent and powerful, and many might consider an embodiment of threat futile, needlessly antagonistic, and regressive.

However, it is perhaps because of this very contention that identifying and embodying trans* threat is a worthwhile exercise. In doing so, we may highlight our own tendencies toward assimilative and placating politics that render transness yet another normativity. Being a threat makes space for nonnormative bodies and refuses their consolidation into a category of other to be disposed of, staking a claim to the power that has been refused them. Being a threat rejects a generalization and normalization of transness. Transness is threatening not only as it figures in TERF rhetoric, but also because, at some level, transness threatens logics of gendered essentialism. Perhaps we need to pay further critical attention to the implications of the political strategies we use that might, in fact, neutralise the power of the threat we pose as trans* people and, instead, embrace and embody the threat we are already figured to be. At our very core, we trannies threaten everything held dear by a structure of normative sex and gender, and we are never nice about it.

Mat A. Thompson holds a master's degree in gender and sexuality studies from the London School of Economics and Political Science. Their main research interests pertain to trans*, crip, and queer theories and applications of neurodivergency and autism, as well as decolonial approaches to sexuality and trans* studies.

Notes

1. I refer to *trans** in this article as a moniker to signify the broad scope of possible meaning that can be inferred from the term. *Trans** not only serves to name those subjectivities and identities of trans*-identified people but also the theories and affective forces that overflow bodies and subjectivities, as highlighted by Marquis Bey (2017). *Trans** is thus identity and subjectivity, and figuration, abstraction, and concept.
2. While, in September 2021 the ruling was overturned by the Court of Appeals, the atmosphere around the case was indicative of a hostile landscape for trans* people.
3. Indeed, queer's acquisition of trans* has been critiqued for erasing trans* complexity, focusing on trans* as an imaginative function of radicalism rather than a lived reality (Chaudhry 2019).

References

Adair, Cassius, Cameron Awkward-Rich, and Amy Marvin 2020. "Before Trans Studies." *TSQ* 7, no. 3: 306–20.

Ahuja, Neel. 2015. "Intimate Atmospheres: Queer Theory in a Time of Extinctions." *GLQ* 21, nos. 2–3: 365–85.

APTN (Asia Pacific Transgender Network). 2020. "#SeeUsSupportUs: Recognise the Needs of Trans and Gender Diverse Communities During COVID-19 Pandemic." https://weareaptn.org/wp-content/uploads/2020/03/APTN-Statement-on-COVID-19_.pdf (accessed August 2, 2022).

Barad, Karen. 2015. "Transmaterialities: Trans*/Matter/Realities and Queer Political Imaginings." *GLQ* 21, nos. 2–3: 387–422.

Barracker. 2021. Comment on Twistiesandshout, "Trans Social Contagion More Likely in Single Sex School?" Mumsnet (forum), January 29, 10:13 a.m. January 28, 2021. https://www.mumsnet.com/Talk/womens_rights/4149823-trans-social-contagion-more-likely-in-single-sex-school?msgid=104127410.

BBC. 2020. "Puberty Blockers: Under-Sixteens 'Unlikely to Be Able to Give Informed Consent.'" December 1. https://www.bbc.co.uk/news/uk-england-cambridgeshire-55144148.

Benavente, Gabby, and Jules Gill-Peterson. 2019. "The Promise of Trans Critique: Susan Stryker's Queer Theory." *GLQ* 25, no. 1: 23–28.

Bersani, Leo. 2010. *Is the Rectum a Grave and Other Essays*. Chicago: University of Chicago Press.

Bey, Marquis. 2017. "The Trans*-ness of Blackness, the Blackness of Trans*-ness." *TSQ* 4, no. 2: 275–95.

Breslow, Jacob. 2020. "The Non-essential Transphobia of Pandemic Disaster Politics." *Engenderings* (blog), May 14. https://blogs.lse.ac.uk/gender/2020/05/14/the-non-essential-transphobia-of-pandemic-disaster-politics/.

Brown, Jayna. 2015. "Being Cellular: Race, the Inhuman, and the Plasticity of Life." *GLQ* 21, nos. 2–3: 321–41.

Chaudhry, V Varun. 2019. "Centring the 'Evil Twin': Rethinking Transgender in Queer Theory." *GLQ* 25, no. 1: 45–50.

Chen, Mel Y. 2011. "Toxic Animacies, Inanimate Affections." *GLQ* 17, nos. 2–3: 265–86.

Chen, Mel Y. 2015. "Tranimacies: An Interview with Mel Chen." Interview by Eva Hayward. *TSQ* 2, no. 2: 317–23.

Chu, Andrea Long, and Emmett Harsin Drager. 2019. "After Trans Studies." *TSQ* 6, no. 1: 103–6.

Datun. 2021. Comment on Timeforatincture, "Trans Lesbian?" Mumsnet (forum), June 19, 1:06 p.m. https://www.mumsnet.com/Talk/womens_rights/4229401-Trans-lesbian?msgid=108341318.

Davies-Arai, Stephanie. 2018. *Inclusive Relationships and Sex Education in Schools (RSE): Statutory Guidance and External Providers*. Transgender Trend UK. https://www.transgendertrend.com/product/inclusive-relationships-and-sex-education-in-schools-rse/.

Deliso, Meredith. 2021. "Record Number of State Bills in 2021 Impact Transgender Rights, Advocacy Group Says." *ABC News*, March 12. https://abcnews.go.com/US/record-number-state-bills-2021-impact-transgender-rights/story?id=76401800.

Farris, Sara. 2017. *In the Name of Women's Rights: The Rise of Femonationalism*. Durham, NC: Duke University Press.

Foucault, Michel. 2003. *Society Must Be Defended: Lectures at the Collège de France, 1975–76*. New York: Picador.

Gill-Peterson, Jules. 2013. "Haunting the Space of AIDS: Remembering ACT UP/New York and an Ethics for an Endemic." *GLQ* 19, no. 3: 279–300.

Goshal, Neela. 2020. "LGBT Africans Share Challenges of Life during Pandemic." *Human Rights Watch*, May 19. https://edit.hrw.org/news/2020/05/19/lgbt-africans-share-challenges-life -during-pandemic.

Halberstam, Jack. 2006. "The Politics of Negativity in Recent Queer Theory." *PMLA* 121, no. 6: 819–28.

Halberstam, Jack. 2020. "Nice Trannies." *TSQ* 7, no. 3 (2020): 321–31.

Haritaworn, Jin. 2015. "Decolonising the Non/Human." *GLQ* 21, nos. 2–3: 210–13.

ILGA World (International Lesbian, Gay, Bisexual, Trans and Intersex Association). 2020. *The Impact of COVID-19 on the Human Rights of LGBT Persons, Communities, and/or Populations*. Geneva: ILGA World.

Jackson, Zakiyyah Iman. 2013. *Animal: New Directions in the Theorization of Race and Posthumanism*. Ann Arbor: Michigan Publishing, University of Michigan Library.

Jackson, Zakiyyah Iman. 2015. "Outer Worlds: The Persistence of Race in Movement 'Beyond the Human.'" *GLQ* 21, nos. 2–3: 215–18.

Koch-Rein, Anson. 2019. "*Trans*-lating the Monster: Transgender Affect and *Frankenstein*." *Lit: Literature Interpretation Theory* 30, no. 1: 44–61.

Lewis, Vek, and Dan Irving. 2017. "Strange Alchemies: The Trans-Mutations of Power and Political Economy." *TSQ* 4, no. 1: 4–15.

LGB Alliance. 2021a. "A Letter to the University of Rhode Island." April 11. https://lgballiance.org .uk/2021/04/11/donnahughesletter/.

LGB Alliance. 2021b. "Statement in Support of Professor Kathleen Stock." October 7. https:// lgballiance.org.uk/2021/10/12/statement-in-support-of-professor-kathleen-stock/.

Littman, Lisa. 2018. "Parent Reports of Adolescents and Young People Perceived to Show Signs of a Rapid Onset of Gender Dysphoria." *PLOS ONE* 13, no. 8. https://www.ncbi.nlm.nih.gov /pmc/articles/PMC6095578/.

Murphy, Simon, and Libby Brooks. 2020. "UK Government Drops Gender Self-Identification Plan for Trans People." *Guardian*, September 22. https://www.theguardian.com/society /2020/sep/22/uk-government-drops-gender-self-identification-plan-for-trans-people.

Patrickharviesorganicmuesli. 2018. Comment on 100lbtolose, "Trans Friendly Thread!" Mumsnet (forum), January 23, 2:43 p.m. https://www.mumsnet.com/Talk/womens_rights/3147810 -Trans-friendly-thread?msgid=75044618.

Prosser, Jay. 1998. *Second Skins: The Body Narratives of Transsexuality*. New York: Columbia University Press.

Puig, Krizia. 2019. "The TransAlien Manifesto: Future Love(s), Sex Tech, and My Efforts to Remember Your Embrace." *TSQ* 6, no. 4: 491–520.

Reid, Graeme. 2021. "Global Trends in LGBT Rights during the Covid-19 Pandemic." *Human Rights Watch*, February 24. https://edit.hrw.org/news/2021/02/24/global-trends-lgbt-rights -during-covid-19-pandemic.

Roen, Katrina. 2001. "Transgender Theory and Embodiment: The Risk of Racial Marginalisation." *Journal of Gender Studies* 10, no. 3: 253–63.

Sager, Maja, and Diana Mulinari. 2018. "Safety for Whom? Exploring Femonationalism and Care-Racism in Sweden." *Women's Studies International Forum* 68: 149–56.

Sedgwick, Eve Kosofsky. 1991. *Epistemology of the Closet*. London: Harvester Wheatsheaf.

Shrier, Abigail. 2020. *Irreversible Damage: The Transgender Craze Seducing Our Daughters*. Washington, DC: Regnery.

Stone, Sandy. 1992. "The *Empire* Strikes Back: A Posttranssexual Manifesto." *Camera Obscura*, no. 29: 150–76.

Stryker, Susan. 1994. "My Words to Victor Frankenstein above the Village of Chamounix: Performing Transgender Rage." *GLQ* 1, no. 3: 237–54.

Stryker, Susan. 2019. "More Words about 'My Words to Victor Frankenstein.'" *GLQ* 25, no. 1: 39–44.

Stryker, Susan. 2020. "Institutionalizing Trans∗ Studies at the University of Arizona." *TSQ* 7, no. 3: 354–66.

Summers, Hanna. 2020. "Panama's Trans Community Failed by Gendered Lockdown Measures—Report." *Guardian*, September 30. https://www.theguardian.com/global-development/2020/sep/30/panamas-trans-community-failed-by-gendered-lockdown-measures-report.

Terfragette69. 2018. "TRA Infiltration." Mumsnet (forum), April 12, 9:41 p.m. https://www.mumsnet.com/Talk/womens_rights/3220672-TRA-infiltration.

Tudor, Alyosxa. 2020. "Terfism Is White Distraction: On BLM, Decolonising the Curriculum, Anti-gender Attacks, and Feminist Transphobia." *Engenderings* (blog), June 19. https://blogs.lse.ac.uk/gender/2020/06/19/terfism-is-white-distraction-on-blm-decolonising-the-curriculum-anti-gender-attacks-and-feminist-transphobia/.

Moving toward Radical Love in Organizing Spaces

JO KRISHNAKUMAR and ANNAPURNA MENON

Feminist spaces have, for the longest time, maintained a close link with the idea that the "personal is political" (Hanisch 1969)—referring to the interdependent relationship between the personal self and the political system that the self is based in. Both the personal self and the political self interact, modify, create, and mold each other. While this interaction is claimed to be embodied in feminist organizations, it is often absent in their praxis. In our observations, we note how personal "cis-terhoods" supersede the political "sisterhoods" with a reduction of the political to the personal. In today's world, where an increasing "gender critical" and trans-exclusionary feminism is taking precedence within progressive movements, it is important for people within organizing spaces to take account of our own actions. The objective should be to not replicate the exclusions that we have been subjected to inside our own safe spaces and feminist groups.

Through this article we seek to explore the organizing within leftist feminist groups that we have been a part of and to introspect on exclusionary practices of these groups, specifically those relating to constructs of femininity. We seek to learn and practice solidarity in the intersectional anti-capitalist, queer/trans feminist human rights movements working toward a demilitarized, anticolonial present and future. We analyze our experiences of organizing in political groups that claim to be anti-capitalist, anti-fascist, anti-patriarchal, and feminist but further perpetuate hierarchies of oppression. This can involve relegating the labor of issues of trans/queer rights onto specifically trans/queer people, silencing and/or invisibilizing marginalized folks, prioritizing cis feelings over trans/queer voices, and so on. This article is not written with the aim of focusing on a personal issue; rather it is to draw out the underlying structural problems in a quest for radical inclusion and exploring how to achieve that within the political spaces we occupy.

TSQ: Transgender Studies Quarterly ★ Volume 9, Number 3 ★ August 2022
DOI 10.1215/23289252-9836148   © 2022 Duke University Press

Figure 1. A river of life, inspired by participatory research methods we used to draw out our thoughts on activism that led to this article.

We begin by briefly sharing our individual political journeys, followed by a discussion of our separate and shared experience in a specific organizing space (hereafter referred to as "Space") that we seek to elaborate and problematize. We have visualized our experiences with the graphic (fig. 1) signifying a river of life (Hope and Timmel 1984) to reflect on our individual and collective journeys in the Space we occupied within political organizing groups in the UK. The river originates in the mountains, representative of the expansive work done by resistors before us across movements; since we are not the first, and we will not be the last.

We base our efforts on historical organizing lessons, but we run into similar issues. The river flows into the present day, where all the different individuals who joined the Space at the end of 2019 come together to do everything possible in each of our capacities to fight oppressive systems together. There are barriers along the stream, which we have identified and analyze together through the length of the article and in our conversation; namely, in/visible hierarchies; interpersonal "family-like" relationships; and remarginalizations within "inclusive," "progressive" groups. Our analysis is interspersed by a candid conversation on many of these issues that we had, which we recorded and transcribed for this essay. In the last section, we propose a practice of politics based on creating communities of care to work toward a sustainable progressive movement that expands upon rights for all marginalized communities by talking specifically about the cis-terhood we have experienced and how this affects community building in organizations/social justice work.

Jo: I have been in organizing spaces for not very long, and I was introduced to them because of my combined ability to not shut up about things that bothered me and the speedy realization of my sexual and gender identity. Put together, it was impossible that I would keep quiet about queer and trans rights—they were too close to home. As I kept moving forward through various cities and degrees, I kept getting involved in groups that are collectivizing for political change within the feminist, trans, queer, and sex worker movements.

Anna: I work with groups involving Tibetans and Kashmiris to organize for their rights to self-determination. The people I have had the privilege of working with and learning from/with prioritized an intersectional approach to their politics, and they strongly believed in not speaking for someone, rather amplifying voices to ensure they reach everyone. Since the time I have been politically aware, reflecting on one's own privilege to understand, acknowledge, and be an ally toward other people's struggles has been my approach to become a part of any movement.

* * *

The Space was spontaneously formed to accommodate the growing anger, discomfort, and helplessness in students, academics, and the larger South Asian diasporic community in the UK. They were enraged at the suppression of the protests against the exclusionary citizenship bill proposed (currently, passed) in India, which, for the first time in Indian history, makes religion a criterion for citizenship, thus moving India toward an ethnocracy. The group aimed to collectivize our energies in solidarity with the protestors in India. In addition, the idea was to raise awareness globally about the right-wing authoritarian tendencies being observed in India while also providing material aid for on-ground protestors.

The urgency of the moment meant that the group's foundation was enthusiasm and anger more than anything else, but questions of ideology and practice crept up soon enough as more members joined and more actions were organized. Members noted a centralization of authority within the group in a few cis-women, and one of the author's close interpersonal relationship with them meant she was granted this authority—with limits. The close-knit circle formed new exclusions, defined by the central authority-yielding figures (all cis-women) and trickling down to others, at times accepted uncritically. This issue of centralization of authority was supplemented by the invisibilization of the voices of trans persons.

A meeting was called to discuss these issues in which a cis woman was actively involved in silencing and gaslighting one of the few queer and trans nonbinary members of the group. The responsibility of "fixing them" fell on those who brought up the issues, all of whom were new to the academic/activist circles, and some from historically marginalized groups. When called out, the mediator was accused of "cancel culture" and dismissed. The most shocking fact was that one of the cis women involved decided to leave the Space as her feelings were hurt, which also led to that circle of cis women distancing themselves from the Space without making any attempts to engage with the actual shortcomings of the Space. The Space did not have any measures to ensure the violence was addressed. Instead, group members shared their opinions on a group chat, and the cycle of violence continued in the group chat. A safe space was not established, and the interpersonal nature of the group was not valued.

Cis Feelings and Remarginalizations

Jo: When a group like this falls apart, one would assume that it's probably because there was some explicit transphobic action, or trans-negative action. It is interesting that all of us are pretty "woke," work in intersectional movements, had a lot of experience with different kinds of movements, different kinds of people and had done our own fair share of work to know when we would be hurting people. But even as individuals, even though we were people like that, once we came together, there was just no space for us to grow or learn.

Anna: Since that has happened, I have also thought about it in terms of how we (academics) are. Academia encourages you to develop a particular way of thinking, to create one piece of original contribution to knowledge that we have in our

PhDs, and then you're supposed to defend it for life. Even when you go to different conferences, the attention is on you defending your knowledge. Are we really accommodating other voices, or are we just constantly pushing for our work? I am thinking of a lot of us who work on the same things, within academia, across countries, and how a lot of our frame of thinking remains exactly the same. For example, if they have talked about a particular kind of feminism, they often find the need to stick to that definition. But that's not being somebody who's working in different organizing spaces because you, yourself, as an individual are completely constant and fixed. While this might be useful, it makes us also unable to make sense of our mistakes because we are so busy defending our actions.

Jo: Yes, and academia pushes this need to be an "expert" and often you can be an expert only on one thing, one framework. But also, it gets complicated in my head because then I'm wondering, people will only speak about things they do know something about, and so they keep talking about that thing. Because then otherwise, it is too uncomfortable to walk into a space where you might not know as much about that specific lens. It's just too uncomfortable because you're not an expert in that. The problem is bigger than the individual person.

Anna: Yes, and the systems we exist in, for example, the neoliberal university rewards experts but not "learning." Hence, for it to be acceptable to be part of a movement and be actively learning is often overlooked. The opportunity to listen to many voices to enable that is forgotten—it can be good to be uncomfortable and not to know—it could make spaces, including university, so much more inclusive.

Jo: I'm just largely also thinking that this is an academic problem. A big reason the Space did not work out is because all of us, somewhere felt like we specialized in a certain set of thoughts and specific locations, and we took that for granted. We often get lost in defining, and semantics, in being experts, in creating "one voice," and in an obsession with civility and "politely" disagreeing without letting our organization be messy, fun, and pushing the boundaries of these frameworks we have learned. Our revolutions cannot exist in neat academic frameworks. I'm happy we're talking about that because a lot of the people within "mainstream" activism are often academics, and that affects the way we see rights-based work and our place in it.

*   *   *

What happened in the Space did not occur in a vacuum. It happened after observing patterns of silencing and ignoring some intersections over others. When a meeting was called to discuss these concerns, the violence was invisiblized and couldn't be responded to appropriately. Structural issues of the group when raised were reduced to an "us versus them," with one team advocating for a structural change while the other was feeling hurt. This was followed by multiple attempts by some members to restart these conversations and to engage more critically and with honesty in this space, but these attempts failed, owing to lack of participation. Protecting the feelings of the cis-ter became the priority over the structural issues of the group. The idea of "sister solidarity" that is so inbuilt into cis women, for multiple reasons—physical safety, experience with men, patriarchy—is in reality often limited to "cis-terhood." It is strange that, despite having access to political tools and knowledge, political issues were reduced to a personal "fight," again invisibilizing the experience of trans identities and reiterating a hierarchy in which a cis-person's feelings are prioritized over actual issues that continue to marginalize and silence voices of those who are minoritized (Upadhyay 2021).

The above experience is not exclusive to student or youth organizations, or just anti-fascist ones. The damage that is caused by cis-feminist groups that are not willing to learn and include trans issues in their organizing is serious. Recently, there was a video posted on social media made by a prominent cis-feminist organizing group that interchangeably used the words *intersex* and *transgender* while explaining gender. The videos, used as training materials that were to be shown in rural communities in India, are damaging an already marginalized community by claiming that "people are born male, female and transgender." This is problematic because of not only the misinformation this stems from but also the disinterest with which such statements are made, by not involving and consulting people with these lived experiences (trans persons). After the video was released, transgender people consulting with the organization and trans people outside it asked for the material to be rectified. Comments posted by the trans community under the video have largely been ignored, and the only thing that has been constantly celebrated is "the effort" made by the cis-feminist group by other cis-feminists. The occurrences of popular cis-feminist activists not being held accountable for their transphobic behavior by the women's movement reiterate the priority that cis-terhood takes over sisterhood (Feminist Futures Collective 2021; Sass 2020), even though the material created can have severely negative implications to a group of people as affected by patriarchy as them. The argument goes beyond having trans people working in these groups—even if they are there, they are not given the space or power to ask "higher up" feminists to update their knowledge.

Anna: For a long time, I've been thinking that the politics of guilt never really translates into accountability. And the only ones it's serving is the right-wing in certain ways, because it stops all conversations. People will literally disappear off social media, rather than saying, "Okay, this is what I did wrong. And this is how I'm going to rectify it." And, unfortunately, that has become an easy way out for a lot of people. You turn up again and the world has forgotten, but everything is not okay because you never learned anything. I think we really need to shift the focus from being politically correct to holding them accountable.

Calls have been made to improve these spaces—which are built to exclude trans people who have been assigned female at birth (AFAB) and which do not identify with terminology that points toward women/femmes—but these are met with questioning the movement and the "solidarity women have worked so hard to create." This questions the fragility of the feminist movement and its reluctance to include everyone affected by patriarchy based on inherent differences in how we perceive and construct our personal identities (Olaleye 2020). On the other hand, while on the surface, one chants "trans women are women," there is a discomfort attached to inviting women with a different experience into the space women occupy, and it falls on trans women to constantly prove their woman-hood to the cis-terhood or for that matter to prove "binaryness" for nonbinary, gender-nonconforming people. This discomfort with the other is something we all learn because of our normative existence; but it is not something we can centralize, and ignore when we are trying to build solidarities. We have much to learn from the Black and anti-caste/Dalit movement around the world and in India, specifically on the uselessness of politeness and civility when it comes to questions of creating a messy, but just world (Gauthaman 2020; Zamalin 2021; Newkirk 2018). Our politeness and fear of being confronted with new knowledge, as academics, as activists, is steeped in our insecurity of our own identities. This stops us from having messy conversations.

Power, Hierarchies, and Being "Family"

While the above sheds light on varied constructions of sisterhoods and structures that ensure knowledge and power remains in certain hands, the idea of feminist spaces being linked to family structures is also crucial to our understanding of exclusionary practices within these spaces. Feminist spaces knowingly or unknowingly have started replicating family structures that blur boundaries of consent, power, and access to knowledge based on seniority and parenthood. This possibly happens because we don't critically think about these boundaries within organizing groups, and more attention is paid to getting things done, rather than how we get things done. These "accidental" hierarchies that replicate familial hierarchies don't seem very accidental then, because younger feminists in these groups self-regulate and self-censor, like children do in paternalistic structures, to give space, power, and access to figures in the groups that "know better, have been here longer." It is then in the interest of groups that seek to subvert for these figures at the center (rather, top) of these hierarchies to think about the space they take.

Jo: Imagine making mistakes and leaving a place, backing off because you made a mistake. In this way, people will keep leaving but not do any work beyond removing themselves from that space. Removing yourself from a place where you have hurt someone so that you can give them space, and so that you can move away to do better is important, but with that, the one who has made the mistake should also be doing the work. It cannot stop by moving away. We need to have conversations about allyship not being perfect, about not ever being a perfect ally because that does not exist. We should be comfortable knowing that one cannot be the perfect anti-caste, anti-capitalist, anti-patriarchal, anti-transphobic, and so forth, person out there. The pressure of being the perfect activist breaks down into little moments in organizing circles when you must defend your identity as an activist because that has been attached to you for so long, that you need to defend it with sentences like "I have trans friends." It removes the pressure off me, as an activist, to defend an identity that will obviously change, and it removes the pressure on marginalized people to keep forgiving. The self-flagellating behavior that comes with perfectionism slows the movement because it is, again, centered around *me* and *my* form of activism rather than the larger structural problem. You do your work, let me do mine. Side by side. To be showing emotion, and asking for something to be fixed is not childish, and we cannot have this polite, romantic version of what activism means to govern our spaces. The Space was one collective where I actually made the effort to stay, even though I was the person who was hurt there, because despite the discomfort caused, I really wanted this to work, and the only way was for us all to have a conversation. But even though I stayed, the perpetrators left and nothing was resolved. It has always left me with the question—"how else could this have been resolved?" Moreover, we live in a neoliberal world that makes mental health and caring for it a solely individual thing, without any collective responsibility or action. I believe that, without communicating what went wrong, or how we could make it better, we just "move on" without actually moving on. I am cautious of being a part of any organizing space after this because I need to know we will stop and talk to each other first. That is camaraderie, and activism needs that at its base—not energy, not the rush to fulfil something, but being able to stay in a very uncomfortable space talking to each other and ourselves. As Adrienne Maree Brown (2018) says,

> We will tell each other we hurt people, and who. We will tell each other why, who hurt us and how. We will tell each other what we will do to heal ourselves, and heal the wounds in our wake. We will be accountable, rigorous in our accountability, all of us unlearning, all of us crawling toward dignity. We will learn to set and hold

boundaries, communicate without manipulation, give and receive consent, ask for help, love our shadows without letting them rule our relationships, and remember we are of earth, of miracle, of a whole, of a massive river—love, life, life, love.

Anna: And you're not putting in any effort to explain your departure or its implications. You have raised your voice and said that this is what is wrong in the Space, and that in itself takes a lot of effort, but it didn't change any of the behavior or even get people asking questions. It is very disheartening, our circles are going to be so small, right? We are going to face these people again, and I'm very wary of them reentering such spaces because, in some ways, I know that it's going to be a dead end and it's not going to work out. But how do we deal with this because it is going to happen, and I don't want conversations or the ongoing work to stop because of the presence of this one person. I don't want to give them so much power at the same time as well.

Jo: When I came to the UK, I was contacted to be a part of a collective almost immediately through the people I knew in India. I then stood for an election, met other people in "left" groups, and became part of a collective of students working on university policy. Things seemed ideal, and even my second supervisor was made to seem "perfect" for me by some of these members. After the incident, I also lost my second supervisor. You work with the same people, you have support groups of the same people, you have dating circles of the same people. You all have the same mind wavelength, and when one thing goes wrong, you do not lose just one person, you lose twenty. It's the weird insidious nature of how close these spaces are, how everybody knows everybody. And this is very similar to many marginalized communities—we will be attracted to each other, try to occupy the same spaces, and we end up creating very close-knit groups, and this is further combined with the fear that academics have of losing contacts, reputations and circles.

Offering critiques of communities that we are a part of and often have interpersonal relationships with is dangerous. Dangerous because of the ostracization the world metes out to communities that cannot paint a rosy picture of their struggles, and the ostracization from community members who have rigid ideas of how a community should function—who should have the voice, who should lead, who should be "cancelled."

However, we also know that, just because someone is marginalized, it does not mean that they are not capable of violence. By being paternalistic cis-ters, we end up recreating the same patriarchal structures found within heteronormative spaces. The goal is to ensure that violence does not reproduce itself in a structure that continually ends up shutting down the survivors of that violence. That is on us. We are meant to be safe spaces, safe people, safe events, and safe minds for others of our community.

Radical Spaces, Collectivization, and the Personal Being Political

Jo: What does a radical space mean to you?

Anna: I think in a very simplistic way, it is a place where you can imagine and work toward alternative futures, which has space for everyone you're working with, in simple ways, but at different levels. I think it involves different kinds of work that needs to be done within such spaces to be able to create them because in my research, and outside it, I feel the aspect of imagination itself is, you know, really curtailed. You're always told to think within a particular methodology or do stuff in a particular way. So for me a radical space would mean a space where all of our different realities come together toward a collective goal.

Jo: In your opinion, do you think that before we create a radical space, we need to have conversations on what radical means to each one of us? And what imagined futures mean to each one of us? And what work each one of us wants to do? Does that individuality matter when we are coming into a group? Or do you feel like we should first come together? And then we can discuss the individual listing?

Anna: I don't have a clear answer if the individual should be more important than the group, or the other way around. I think a clear understanding of a collective vision along with your postionality is important. So in the case of organizing against state oppression, while it might be that we are all working toward the same goal, we need to recognize that my experiences and threats as a cis-woman with caste privilege will be very different from a trans person's. If a state attempts to increase control and surveillance over trans bodies and access to gender-affirming health care, that will also eventually implicate increased state scrutiny over my body in the name of "protection" and health care. Hence, if you have that collective vision, it becomes easier to also talk about your own understanding and privileges, enabling us to see where we, individually, can make the most collective impact.

Jo: Yeah, I understand that. It is a big question, and a question a lot of people within organizations we have been a part of fail to address. In my experience, it has never been a linear process of putting either the individual or the collective before the other—it is a conversation to be had to see how these individuals and their individualities make the collective.

Anna: Yeah, then I think what happened with the Space was that people knew there were these different identities, but it was always suppressed for the so-called collective, which wasn't ever collectively agreed to. There wasn't any space to ever have this conversation about what is going on, what each of us was thinking about the individual and the collective. There was always something "more urgent" that came up than us working together as different people. And I felt that was pretty detrimental in the whole process. Like even if we would have had a monthly review, I feel that would have been a space to have these long conversations. This is not to say that a meeting or a circle of reflection is going to solve these big questions, but we need to recognize that these are constant processes that need constant communication. Establishing a space to talk about the things the group is concerned about, and to talk about our identities and processes and personal journeys, gives space to discover the common things that we can build on together.

Jo: So most recently, I've been playing with the idea that there is no such thing as a community or a collective; there are collective actions and community actions you do, keeping the collective in mind. I have been through a lot of unfortunate events within my trans community, involving abuse as well. In this space, you feel as if you can't be hurt, as you're surrounded by similar people. But when you do get hurt by them, it hurts a lot more than it would hurt with anybody else. Because you expect so much more from them, you love them so much more in every essence of the word. So when they hurt you, it hurts a lot more. So, what is community at all? The constant appetite to work with people, constantly question myself and learn, but at the same time, not center my own experience so that I can understand my social location in relation to others'. I do believe that if we work toward creating a better world for those on the edges of the fringes, we will create a better world for everyone else at the same time. For example, make work situations better for sex workers, and all labor groups will be counted within that. Dismantle patriarchy keeping trans people in mind, and patriarchy will be destroyed for everyone else as well.

Anna: My focus has always been more on building solidarities that go beyond performative allyship. I think one of the core concepts of allyship is that you do it all the time, not when it is comfortable and when it suits you. And also, I guess, because of the theoretical work that I do read, and the work I do on the ground, the emphasis is a lot more on building practical solidarity.

To enable this collective work, there might be a need for different methods to deal with the different kinds of violence people bring into community spaces. People hurt people, but they (and we) should have options to deal with that hurt in the form of being accountable to those we hurt, and accountable to ourselves. We know about calling out, and Loretta Ross (2021) speaks about "calling in" and "calling on" people whom we expect better of. Perhaps using a mixture of communication methods like these could open doors to accountability that we did not have before. Having said this, callouts may still be necessary when it comes to exploitative companies and powerful people, while calling in and calling on seems to be a way we could reach out to friends and family that we love, but who are causing harm. The people in the Space believed deeply that they were not transphobic, even if their actions were. Calling out that belief might invite them to reassess and to create a culture of inclusion where they don't feel the need to move away. Radical inclusion takes an immense amount of emotional labor and pressure, especially on those oppressed historically or in particular situations, but it could be a thing we try to adopt on smaller scales so that the fear with which people react to situations in which they have harmed someone can be removed and they can have a conversation. There are always going to be people who do not want to listen, who are racist, casteist, homophobic, transphobic people who may repeatedly harm people. Calling in, on, and out may not work with them, and accountability is a two way street—bigotry has to be excluded from spaces so that others can feel safe. We don't know if any of this is going to work with our groups, but this piece of writing is about trying.

A practice of excluding those unwilling to accomodate any iota of difference to their set beliefs and ideologies, those unwilling to listen and learn, those without empathy for anybody but their kind, those who participate in the active dismissal of the marginalized can create the possibility for radical inclusion.

This is also in alignment with bell hooks's understanding of community, reiterating that "communities cannot be built without conflict" (Brosi and hooks 2012). Conflicts exist all around us, but we should work on developing tools to resolve them with the aim of betterment of the community. Tools can involve something as basic as a sharing circle to a more nuanced manifesto or problem-addressing mechanism or voting for decisions. Resolving conflict should not be understood as having to pick sides, which is precisely what happened in the Space, but a refocus on how to solve it and use that learning to build a better world. We, as organizers, should center those whose voices have been silenced and whose struggles our movements are based on to create communities that embody a practice of care and love for the liberation of all, collectively.

Through this article, we trace our participation in progressive movements within diaspora groups in the UK. We analyze the barriers we observed and experienced—visible and invisible hierarchies of ideologies, gender, age, academic maturity—and study how paternalism and familial structured personal relationships act as a hindrance to tackling discrimination and exclusion in such spaces. Lastly, we dwell on the idea of community and propose a practice of radical exclusion and collective thought to build sustainable and dynamic organizing spaces. The flowing river reflects our ever-growing movements despite the rocks and turns, where we continue to learn, bloom, and wither alongside a perennial river.

Jo Krishnakumar (they/them) is a trans queer researcher interested in all things sex, sexuality, and gender, and how different groups/people experience these wor(l)ds. Their work is informed by their constant learning/unlearning of the privileges they have owing to their social location as a dominant/oppressive caste person while also occupying space as a (mentally) disabled trans person of color. You can find them on their unfinished webspace, www .waytojo.com.

Annapurna Menon is a doctoral researcher and visiting lecturer at the University of Westminster. Her current research project is focused on coloniality of postcolonial nation-states, with India as the case study. Her research interests include postcolonial and decolonial studies and theories, right-wing nationalism, Hindutva, and gender.

References

Brosi, George, and bell hooks. 2012. "The Beloved Community: A Conversation between *bell hooks* and *George Brosi.*" *Appalachian Heritage* 40, no. 4: 76–86. https://doi.org/10.1353/aph.2012 .0109.

Brown, Adrienne Maree. 2018. *We Will Not Cancel Us.* Oakland, CA: AK.

Feminist Futures Collective. 2021. "Call for Accountability in Feminist Circles." *Medium*, May 20. https://feministfuturescollective.medium.com/call-for-accountability-in-feminist-circles -4b0ae9846787.

Gauthaman, Raj. 2020. *Dark Interiors: Essays on Caste and Dalit Culture.* Translated by Theodore Baskaran. New Delhi: Sage.

Hanisch, Carol. 1969. "The Personal Is Political." In *Notes from the Second Year: Women's Liberation,* edited by Shulie Firestone and Anne Koedt, 76–78. New York. https://repository .duke.edu/dc/wlmpc/wlmms01039.

Hope, Anne, and Sally Timmel. 1984. *Training for Transformation: A Handbook for Community Workers.* Gweru, Zimbabwe: Mambo.

Newkirk, Vann R., II. 2018. "Protest Isn't Civil." *Atlantic*, June 28. https://www.theatlantic.com /ideas/archive/2018/06/the-civility-instinct/563978/.

Olaleye, Fopé. 2020. "Dear Cis Black Women, Transphobia Will Never Serve Us or the Goal of Black Liberation." *Gal-Dem*, July 18. https://gal-dem.com/dear-cis-black-women-transphobia-will -never-serve-us-or-the-goal-of-black-liberation/.

Ross, Loretta. "Don't Call People Out—Call Them In." TED Talk, August 2021, 14:19. https://www .ted.com/talks/loretta_j_ross_don_t_call_people_out_call_them_in.

Sass, A. J. 2020. "I'm a Nonbinary Writer of Youth Literature. J. K. Rowling's Comments on Gender Identity Reinforced My Commitment to Better Representation." *Time*, June 19. https://time.com/5855633/jk-rowling-gender-identity/.

Upadhyay, Nishant. 2021. "Coloniality of White Feminism and Its Transphobia: A Comment on Burt." *Feminist Criminology* 16, no. 4. https://doi.org/10.1177/1557085121991337.

Zamalin, Alex. 2021. *Against Civility: The Hidden Racism in Our Obsession with Civility.* Boston: Beacon.

GID as an Acceptable Minority; or, The Alliance between Moral Conservatives and "Gender Critical" Feminists in Japan

HIDENOBU YAMADA

Abstract This essay articulates how feminist, queer, and trans politics in the early aughts have become a precondition for the rise of feminist transphobia in Japan now. On the one hand, mainstream feminists in that period overlooked transphobia in the gender backlash from moral conservatives. On the other hand, a 2003 law on gender recognition for people with GID (gender identity disorder) endorsed the patriarchal system in which only some transsexual people would be recognized. The author argues that these backgrounds allow "gender critical" feminists to oppose what they see as the transgender ideology, forging an implicit alliance with moral conservatives while portraying themselves as being tolerant of people with GID.

Keywords gender identity disorder, moral conservatives, gender critical, Japan

Trans-exclusionary feminism in Japan was first made visible as a response to the decision in 2018 by Ochanomizu University, the country's oldest women's university, to accept trans girls as applicants. Although the increased presence of "gender critical" activists in the Japanese Twittersphere is a recent development, it was the feminist, queer, and trans politics in the early aughts that prepared the ground for current trans-exclusionary discourse. In that period, the gender backlash was provoked by moral conservatives, while the legal recognition of transsexual people was legislated under the name of *seidōitsuseishōgai* (gender identity disorder, GID). The backlash against the notion of gender and the mainstreaming of GID occurred simultaneously; the entrenchment of the two phenomena is crucial because it explains how "gender critical" feminists and moral conservatives

TSQ: Transgender Studies Quarterly ★ Volume 9, Number 3 ★ August 2022 **501**
DOI 10.1215/23289252-9836162 © 2022 Duke University Press

are implicitly allied against what they perceive as the evil ideology of transgenderism, while showing apparent tolerance toward people with GID as an acceptable, "good minority."

The enactment of the Basic Law for Gender Equal Society in 1999 spurred the backlash by moral/religious conservatives. As Shimizu Akiko (2020: 90) points out, it was "a strange predecessor of the 'anti-gender' movements." Its main target was the concept of "gender free," which was promoted by feminists in those days. Being coined in 1995 as a term symbolizing freedom from compulsory gender roles, it was spread by governmental agencies through projects related to gender equality and additionally by feminist scholars who had participated in its dissemination (Yamaguchi 2014: 546–50). Although feminists had multiple interpretations of the term, backlashers understood it to be "a feminist scheme to destroy traditional gender roles" that "aimed for the total erasure of cultural and biological differences between the sexes" (559). They also attacked sex education as a consequence of so-called gender-free ideology. One of the prominent figures was Diet member Yamatani Eriko. In 2002 during a Diet committee meeting, she denounced a booklet titled *Love and Body Book for Adolescents*, which was distributed to junior high school students and contained information about contraceptive pills, for promoting "extreme" sex education. Later in 2005 she joined the project team in the ruling Liberal Democratic Party whose purpose was to investigate "extreme" sex education and "gender free" education (562–63).

The way mainstream feminists responded to the backlash was problematic. In the face of the argument that feminism aimed to deny sexual difference and create genderless persons (*chūsei ningen*), they replied that feminism did not disavow masculinity and femininity themselves and the figure of the genderless person was just an invention produced by backlashers (Ino 2020). They thus disregarded the fact that transphobia and binary gender norms were a feminist concern, too.

The gender backlash coincided with a crucial moment in trans politics. In 1996 Saitama Medical University approved sex reassignment surgery on the grounds that GID was an illness that could be medically treated. The medicalization of trans identity culminated in the 2003 Act on Special Cases in Handling Gender in People with Gender Identity Disorder (hereafter called GID Act), which allowed people diagnosed with GID to change their legal gender in the family register (*koseki*).[1] The koseki system is a national registry of Japanese citizens with a patriarchal structure. Each unit of koseki consists of a father, mother, and child (ren), recording the head of the family (typically male) and each member's parents, spouse, and date and place of birth. It also shows their gender as part of family relationships; every person appears as a father, mother, son, or daughter, instead of a male or female individual. As a result of the development from Saitama

Medical University to the GID Act, GID became a catchall category representing any trans people in mainstream society. Considering that the GID Act, a law on gender recognition, could be progressive legislation in relation to gender politics, the fact that it was passed unanimously without much controversy amid the backlash against gender ambiguity might seem paradoxical. What is remarkable is that Yamatani was a member of the project team for the legislation. It gives us a clue to the paradox: the GID Act was acceptable for moral conservatives. The act contained a "no-marriage" requirement, intended to prevent applicants in heterosexual marriages from changing their legal gender, keeping marriage between persons of the same sex illegal. In addition to this, the act introduced a provision that would exclude trans parents, regardless of whether or not their children were of age. Thus no child requirement became a target of severe criticism from the trans community. Noono Chieko (2004: 11), who was the head of the project team, explained that facet of the legislation by referring to the legal challenges that would result from the recognition of "male mothers" and "female fathers." On behalf of the team, she also expressed concern for the welfare of children of trans people. Ultimately, the no child requirement was added in response to worries expressed by moral conservatives such as Yamatani, who placed a high value on "traditional" Japanese families. Because it was not incompatible with the patriarchal order that the system of family registration embodied, the GID Act could be realized in the time of gender backlash.

The GID Act divided the trans community. It incorporated some transsexuals—those who could meet the legal standards required for GID—into the group of respectable citizens while delegitimizing trans people and queers who were deemed to disrupt the patriarchal order. Trans activists and scholars who were opposed to the mainstreaming of GID and the legal recognition in the patriarchal koseki system declared themselves as "transgenderists" who were marginalized by the medicalization of trans identity. They emphasized that transgender had a contradictory relationship with GID because the former was a term for self-identification while the latter was the specific name of a psychiatric illness. They found in the word *transgender* the grounds for resisting the problematic discursive dominance of the GID category (Yonezawa 2003; Tanaka 2006; Yamada 2020).

All of these conditions—backlash-inciting transphobia, mainstream feminists' inability to address trans issues, and the divide between claims to GID and transgender identities—are replicated in the escalation of transphobia now. Before addressing the ongoing situation, I will expand on two contexts. From 2012 to 2020, Abe Shinzo, who had led the Liberal Democratic Party's project team for investigating "extreme" sex education, headed the cabinet, which revitalized the power of moral/religious conservatives. In addition, *LGBT* began to be brought into the mainstream of society around 2012—almost no substantial changes in official institutions have occurred, though. *LGBT* nonetheless grew in popularity, as it galvanized new consumer demands. Before that time, transgender had been often understood by activists as an anti-GID category. The popularization of *LGBT* (re)introduced the word—*T* in *LGBT*—to the public. Because people were familiar with GID, the *T* was also associated with GID when the mainstream media gave an account of it. Transgender activists and scholars took issue with the conflation, for it meant that GID enjoyed wide currency even when the term was outdated outside Japan. Although their argument had limited influence in mainstream society, *transgender* began to replace *GID* little by little in accordance with the popularization of *LGBT*. However, most institutions tended to acknowledge only GID as a legitimate category. In this respect, the decision in 2018 by Ochanomizu University was significant. It did not rely on the notion of GID but transgender and gender identity, indicating that the university would accept transgenders who identified as a woman but were legally registered as a man (*Kyodo News* 2018). In this sense, the decision represented a paradigm shift in trans politics in Japan: from the medical model of GID to the rights-based model of transgender. That it was based on the latter was important not only because it did not pathologize trans people but also because it explained why it received transphobic responses by online feminists.

The announcement of the decision immediately generated a flurry of transphobic opinion on Twitter. Many feminist accounts began to express their fear that women's safety could be undermined when "men" or "male-bodied" people entered women-only spaces (Hori 2020). By the winter of that year, some accounts brought in "gender critical" stances and vocabularies from the Anglophone world as well as from Korea. They actively introduced to the Japanese Twittersphere transphobic terms, figures, and discourse, including "TRA," "women are not cis," transgenderism as an evil ideology, Karen White and the concern about women's safety in prisons, and the trans dominance in sports. Although a handful of feminist/queer scholars who advocate for trans rights have struggled against the rise of feminist transphobia on the internet, mainstream feminists and organizations continue to be negligent in the ongoing crisis.

One example of the backlash against LGBT people in 2018 shows how moral conservatives utilize the figure of GID to dismiss all people in the LGBT community. Diet member Sugita Mio (2018), a moral conservative who was backed by Abe, published an essay titled "The Support to LGBT Goes Too Far." In it she insists that it is not justifiable for the government to spend money for LGBT couples because they are not "productive," referring to biological reproduction. Notably, she makes one reservation here: she asserts that LGB and T should not be conflated because "T (transgender) is a disorder named 'gender identity disorder,'" while LGB is just a "sexual preference" (59). She expresses her sympathy with the suffering caused by the incongruence between mind and body that people with GID experience and writes that it might be justifiable for sex reassignment surgery to be covered by health insurance. It does not mean at all that she is trans friendly. She condemns the popularization of LGBT as producing confusion in children's gender identity. She also argues that society would be thrown into chaos if anyone could use whichever bathrooms they would like to. In short, she is antagonistic to trans people in general but accords to GID an exceptional status.[2]

This exceptionalization of GID is shared among "gender critical" feminists on the internet. They typically argue that they do not oppose trans people in general because they are indeed supportive of people with GID or transsexual people. They are just against "extreme" transgenderism and "trans rights activists," according to their account. It is unfortunate that some trans people side with this rhetoric. Such a divergence represents the divide in the trans community that the GID Act created. Facing intense pressure by conservatives in the early aughts, feminism did not interrogate transphobia, while the trans movement supporting the law on gender recognition in the patriarchal system did not question the system itself. It resulted in a disruptive divide not only between people with GID as an acceptable minority and transgenders but also between feminism and trans politics. Now in the 2020s, "gender critical" feminists make use of this double divide to portray themselves as tolerant toward trans people while demonizing all trans folks who just seek to live their lives. They are an implicit ally of moral conservatives because they endorse the patriarchal order that the GID Act embodies, and from that order they draw their power to decide which trans should be morally out of existence.

Hidenobu Yamada is a PhD candidate in the Graduate School of Arts and Sciences at the University of Tokyo. Their dissertation focuses on trans politics relating to the medico-legal institutionalization of GID in Japan.

Acknowledgements

I'd like to thank an anonymous colleague of mine for providing how "gender critical" discourse emerged in the Japanese Twittersphere.

Notes

1.   Under the GID Act of 2003, applicants who seek to change their legal gender need to meet five requirements: 1) they are twenty years old or older, 2) they are not currently married, 3) they do not currently have children, 4) they permanently lack their reproductive

ability, and 5) their genitalia appear to be that of the other sex. In 2008 the third requirement was amended to read "they do not currently have minor children." In April 2022 the
age requirement was lowered to eighteen. For further details of the GID Act, see Taniguchi
2013 and Norton 2006.

2. Fujitaka (2021: 177–79) also notes the implicit distinction between GID and transgender
in Sugita's essay as an example of transphobic rhetoric.

References

Fujitaka, Kazuki. 2021. "Posuto feminizumu to shite no toransu? Senda Yuki 'onna no kyōkaisen o
hikinaosu' o yomitoku" ("Trans People as Postfeminist Subjects? Reading Senda Yuki's
'Redrawing the Boundaries of Women'"). *Jendā kenkyū*, no. 24: 171–87. https://doi.org/10
.24567/0002000120.

Hori, Akiko. 2020. "Excluding Whom for What? A Look at Transphobia in the Japanese Twittersphere," translated by Sato Mana. *Trans Inclusive Feminism*, September 4. https://trans
inclusivefeminism.wordpress.com/2020/09/04/hori2019be/.

Ino, Yuriko. 2020. "Feminizumu wa bakkurasshu tono tatakai no naka de saiyō shita mizukara no
'senryaku' o minaosu jiki ni kiteiru" ("It Is Time for Feminists to Rethink Their Strategy
Adopted in the Struggle against Backlash"). *Etosetora* 4: 85–88.

Kyodo News. 2018. "Tokyo Women's Univ. Says Accepting Transgender Students 'Natural.'" July 10.
https://english.kyodonews.net/news/2018/07/a611d4d9b4e1-tokyo-womens-univ-says
-accepting-transgender-students-natural.html.

Noono, Chieko, ed. 2004. *Kaisetsu seidōitsuseishōgai seibetsu toriatsukai tokureihō* (*Reference of Act
on Special Cases in Handling Gender in People with Gender Identity Disorder*). Tokyo:
Nihon Kajo Shuppan.

Norton, Laura H. 2006. "Neutering the Transgendered: Human Rights and Japan's Law No. 111."
Georgetown Journal of Gender and the Law 7, no. 2: 187–216.

Shimizu, Akiko. 2020. "'Imported' Feminism and 'Indigenous' Queerness: From Backlash to
Transphobic Feminism in Transnational Japanese Context." *Jendā kenkyū*, no. 23: 89–104.
https://doi.org/10.24567/00063795.

Sugita, Mio. 2018. "'LGBT' shien no do ga sugiru" ("The Support to LGBT Goes Too Far"). *Shinchō
45* 37, no. 8: 57–60.

Tanaka, Ray. 2006. *Toransujendā feminizumu* (*Transgender Feminism*). Tokyo: Inpakuto Shup-
pankai.

Taniguchi, Hiroyuki. 2013. "Japan's 2003 Gender Identity Disorder Act: The Sex Reassignment
Surgery, No Marriage, and No Child Requirements as Perpetuations of Gender Norms in
Japan." *Asian-Pacific Law and Policy Journal* 14, no. 2: 108–17.

Yamada, Hidenobu. 2020. "Toransujendā no fuhenka ni yoru GID o meguru anbivarensu no
masshō" ("Erasing Ambivalence Related to Gender Identity Disorder through the
Universalization of Transgender"). *Jendā kenkyū*, no. 23: 47–65. https://doi.org/10.24567
/00063793.

Yamaguchi, Tomomi. 2014. "'Gender Free' Feminism in Japan: A Story of Mainstreaming and
Backlash." *Feminist Studies* 40, no. 3: 541–72.

Yonezawa, Izumi, ed. 2003. *Toransujendarizumu sengen: Seibetsu no jikoketteiken to tayō na sei no
kōtei* (*The Transgenderist Manifesto: The Right to Gender Self-Determination and the
Affirmation of Gender Diversity*). Tokyo: Shakai Hihyōsha.

J. K. Rowling and the Echo Chamber of Secrets

GINA GWENFFREWI

Abstract This autoethnographic article attempts to capture the distress of a trans woman in Scotland at the transphobia in the legacy media's coverage of the J. K. Rowling furore in June 2020. Through the use of a frame narrative, the article analyses some of the transphobic elements of Rowling's essay published on June 10, 2020, originally titled "TERF Wars," which prompted an online backlash and a subsequent cycle of negative legacy media coverage against trans people. The article deconstructs two opinion pieces in the *Scotsman* and the *National* that depict Rowling as a victim and trans women as abusive and/or delusional, with an accompanying association of trans women with virtual spaces, set against cis women inhabiting real-world spaces. The newspapers' subsequent, respective refusal to publish counter articles criticizing the opinion pieces is then described, with reference to the legacy media's more general cancel-culture narrative, described by Sara Ahmed as a "mechanism of power." Concluding on the experience of having no personal voice or access to the kind of influence enjoyed by a transphobic legacy media, the article refers to Andrew Anastasia's conception of three modes of transgender voice to identify how only collective action can allow trans voices to be heard and effect change.
Keywords J. K. Rowling, media, furor, trans, *Guardian*

> Those in the outraged online echo chambers might try their best to drown out voices who want to talk about sex, but telling people not to read the world's most famous author feels like a losing strategy. This discussion cannot be ignored.
> —Shona Craven, *The National*

P reserved like frozen eddies in the whirlwind of a moral panic are the words of a national journalist, days after J. K. Rowling (2020) publishes her essay on the threat of the trans rights movement. Shona Craven's (2020) newspaper article, which associates trans identity with online echo chambers and reifies unreality and the hurling of abuse, also crystallizes the kind of "vitriolic media campaigns" in the UK identified by the Council of Europe, "in which trans women especially

TSQ: Transgender Studies Quarterly ∗ Volume 9, Number 3 ∗ August 2022   **507**
DOI 10.1215/23289252-9836176   © 2022 Duke University Press

are vilified and misrepresented" (Chikha 2021). The signals, noticeably outside the UK, have been there for a while: in 2018 the US office of the nominally progressive *Guardian* signs a public letter in protest of the transphobia of its UK editorial line (Levin, Chalabi, and Siddiqui 2018). Acknowledging such events in its *Annual Review*, ILGA-Europe (2021) describes how "anti-trans rhetoric continued to cause serious damage in the UK again this year," adding in reference to the biggest trans-related story of all in 2020, "A prime example is repeated transphobic attacks by author J.K. Rowling, on Twitter and in her writing." All these warnings reinforce what a slew of recent academic studies have also documented, namely, that the UK's legacy media has become something of a safe haven for transphobic voices (Pearce, Erikainen, and Vincent 2020: 685; McLean 2021). Specific to the reporting of the Rowling story in my locality of Scotland, two articles reflect the new moral panic: one by Craven (2020) as the columnist and community editor of the *National*, the other by the *Scotsman*'s deputy political editor Gina Davidson (2020). By comparison to their influence, I am a quiet participant in this story, a recently out trans woman and PhD researcher moved to say something at the hostility I'm witnessing. Days after the articles by Craven and Davidson that delegitimize trans identity, I write and submit counter pieces that get rejected by their respective newspapers. Neither paper runs trans-inclusive commentaries during this time, and no article appears permitted to challenge the framing of trans people as delusional and oppressive. In my distress at being voiceless, I find clarity in seeing the relationship between power and voice.

This is a personal account of the Rowling furor and the media's transphobia, but it is also about voices. Regarding my own, I like Andrew Anastasia's (2014) multifaceted concept of the trans voice as forming a kind of Trinity, as speech-sound, as expression of agency, and as song of collective politicized liberation. The second and third of these pertain to this essay: I want to share a rare act of agency I undertook during an important irruption of anti-trans sentiment in the UK's legacy media, namely, the Rowling story that peaked in June 2020.

My trans voice changes over this time. I watch Rowling's forays on Twitter from 2017 to 2020, and I shrug uncertainly at the "likes" by Rowling of transphobic tweets. I watch the likes mutate into increasingly vicious cycles of statements and reactions between Rowling and those engaged in the online backlash against her. Looking back at this period, I understand I was Rowling's kind of trans person, isolated, quiet, and respectful of concerns. In her essay of June 10, 2020, Rowling distinguishes between the politically voiceless trans individuals who "simply want to live their lives" and whom she in turn claims to love, and the more politically empowered but unhelpfully generalized "trans rights activist" (TRA) movement, which she describes as giving "cover to predators." She is aided by the subsequent coverage of the online backlash to her essay, including the opinion pieces by Craven and Davidson. It is their columns I respond to, their editors who take my trans-inclusive words and bury them.

I have never met Craven, but Davidson is more familiar. She interviewed me a year before the Rowling story over a trans-centered conference I was organizing. My trans voice back then was awkward and unready—barely a speech-sound, let alone an expression of agency or a part of some greater whole. In that interview Davidson brought up a series of examples of TRAs' silencing women whose details I was unfamiliar with. Had I been a researcher then of gender-crit Twitter, Mumsnet, and associated blogs, and been familiar with Davidson's synchronicity with these trans-exclusionary sites, I might have expected her sources and her framing. But still we sat there, two women of not dissimilar ages, cis and trans. It wasn't poisonous, even if I was shocked at seeing her dark reaction when I used the word *cisgender*. It was dialogue, it was "discourse"—wasn't democracy formed from such asymmetrical meetings? Perhaps by meeting me, Davidson could see the gap between real-life trans women and whoever she imagined was typing tweets telling Rowling to "choke on Hagrid's big dick." True to the cute notion so key to liberal democratic principles, I believed a single, momentary dialogue in a café could overcome the daily, incessant messages shared by trans-exclusionists that Davidson seemingly absorbed before and after our meeting. Her coverage of the Rowling story one year later tells you everything you need to know about the failure of my impact.

So one year on from my café-based interview with Davidson, Rowling produces an essay that mixes dog whistles against trans women with the whitewashing of transphobia. Conflating the endeavor of empowering trans people with a public threat, Rowling (2020) says, "I refuse to bow down to a movement that I believe is doing demonstrable harm in seeking to erode 'woman' as a political and biological class and offering cover to predators like few before it."

Associating disempowered minorities with the moral-panic discourse of "predators" or "super predators" (Cox 2020) should signal a red-light warning to any journalist in the global North. Yet it appears that, apart from YouTubers and UK trans charities such as Mermaids (2020), with their published critiques of the essay, no one has the inclination to challenge Rowling's incendiary language. The legacy media instead fixates on the worst parts of the Twitter-based backlash as proof of a trans threat to Rowling, in other words, of a trans threat to people like them. An alignment takes place, as the legacy media consistently allows Rowling, one of their own, to get away with removing trans women from their verifiable position as a vulnerable demographic. In Rowling's (2020) representation, they are a mysteriously influential and politicized subgroup of misogynists, along with the terrorist-inciting Donald Trump and terrorist-associated Incels, but even worse for the access they have: "When you throw open the doors of bathrooms and changing rooms to any man who believes or feels he's a woman . . . then you open the door to any and all men who wish to come inside."

This interchangeability by Rowling of men with trans women is a form of delegitimization that belies her claim of affection elsewhere: hers is a notion of trans at odds with most trans people, reimagining the good kind of trans person as humble, submissive, and content with their exclusion. Her claim of doors being opened, meanwhile, is an act of fear-inciting misinformation, for the doors have been open for a long time to trans women, with no pattern of damage done. Concurrently, and in contrast to the smears, Rowling (2020) whitewashes the trans-exclusionary gender-critical movement: "None of the gender critical women I've talked to hates trans people . . . they're hugely sympathetic towards trans adults who simply want to live their lives." Yet in the same essay, she expresses her admiration for Magdalen Berns, whose well-known transphobic diatribes, beloved by the gender-critical movement (Forstater 2021), include describing trans women as "fucking blackface actors. . . . You're men who get sexual kicks from being treated like women" (Montgomerie 2020). As noted by Natalie Wynn (2021) in her deconstruction of Rowling's social media output of this period, there is plenty of evidence of Rowling's transphobia. All it requires is a journalist with a sufficient understanding of the responsibilities of their public position to challenge Rowling on her use of smoke and mirrors to delegitimize trans people.

Yet a day after the publishing of Rowling's essay, Davidson (2020) produces an article in the *Scotsman* that is a study in escalation, a lesson too in why a journalism that feeds on Twitter is a danger to the public good. The article's title ignores the transphobic content of Rowling's essay and fixates on the online reaction, conflating it with the trans community and making it their responsibility. It is an act with overtones of backlash-based campaigns that make terrorism the responsibility of certain minority groups: "Why Abuse of JK Rowling Is a Problem for Trans Rights Activists." Below the title, Davidson offers her unsubstantiated theory that trans women hate cis women out of jealousy because cis women are the real thing—the setting up of a violent, irreconcilable fault line in trans female identity. Davidson then uses her platform to suggest that, in response to the Twitter pile-on, the natural next step is the rescinding of trans women's rights, regarding their current access to women-only spaces: "Hatred only results in hardening people's minds. Why would any woman agree to share private spaces such as changing rooms or toilets with the same people abusing Rowling?"

I see Davidson's reliance on Twitter to portray trans women as jealous, violent predators as the barely concealed campaigning against my rights. I think again about the café where we met one year before, and the middle-class respectability of it all. I remember we were both dressed in office wear and discussed the merits of the former prime minister Gordon Brown (Davidson for, me more against). I was sipping hot chocolate while conveying my enthusiasm for my conference, she was asking me questions about people I'd never heard of; at other moments, there were intimate questions she asked sensitively, I responded, it was fine. It was a meeting of different people coming together and not totally on each other's wavelength but cordial enough. But what does such a public engagement lead to? It leads to nothing. Still we—the minority—are required to explain, justify, and appease, and by doing so provide the fig leaf of engagement for those journalists who will attack us anyway, at some point in the future. Even if we're the right kind of trans woman, we'll be the exception to their general rule. At what point do we withdraw from such unhelpful engagements, with the realization it was never about dialogue or understanding? Or maybe it was intended to be, but it could never compete with a journalist's lifetime encounters with transphobic imagery, sedimented and revitalized through the online networks they now frequent.

Davidsons's (2019) article about my conference, incidentally, was fine; she even allowed me a final reading with suggested edits. Over the longer haul, our encounter simply couldn't compete with Twitter, just like nothing can compete with Twitter as a delegitimizing source of disinformation about trans people when you're a journalist of the UK's legacy media.

Perhaps my engagement with Davidson allowed me to empathize with her even as she appears to view people like me as a threat. Regardless, I think Craven's article on the Rowling furor, titled "This Is Why JK Rowling's Non-fiction Foray Caused a Twitter Storm," is more hostile to trans identity, not for the content but for the tone. Davidson struck me as being fearful, clinging to a handful of ugly stories about trans people as a sign of things to come in women-only spaces. Her fear seemed real, even if, as an experienced, award-winning senior journalist, she should know better than to fall for antiminority tropes or to think Twitter is a source of truth. Craven's article is similarly one-way traffic on behalf of Rowling but done with a level of contempt toward trans people that almost swaggers in its certainty. Juxtaposing cis people versus trans people as fact versus fiction, as science versus fantasy, and as valid versus invalid, Craven (2020) waxes, "Fortunately for her own sanity, the woman who made up muggles and quidditch and death eaters knows the difference between things that are real and things that are the product of human imagination."

The writing is caustic and smugly one-sided; it seeks only to simplify and undermine one "side" of a manufactured debate. Craven asserts of Rowling, "She knows that sex is determined by chromosomes whereas gender is a made-up set of rules about how men and women ought to be. . . . That's sex as in the real, observable, and immutable difference between men and women." There is so much here that is confident and simple in a high-school-biology manner—these are assertions that reveal no uncertainty or any interest in encountering knowledge beyond her own. The same is true in Craven's open embrace of gender-critical feminism via its surface rhetoric with her quip, "if your feminism isn't critical of gender, you need to go back to square one." It appears not to occur to Craven to interrogate a movement that appeared circa 2017 in direct response to a consultation on trans rights, as if feminism—with the associative descriptor of *gender-critical*—was magically invented in 2017, and that trans-inclusive feminist organizations such as Engender, in existence in Scotland since the 1990s and involved in the consultation stage for the reform of the Gender Recognition Act circa 2017, have never existed.

The manner of the misinformation, in other ways, is uncannily similar to Davidson's. Craven makes no reference to Rowling's predator narrative and the constant misgendering of trans women as the cause of offense for so many. Craven similarly replicates the formula of inoffensive statement versus misogynistic backlash. She asserts, "The indiscretion for which she must be punished is saying that sex is real. . . . What kind of body a person has, not what they might plan to do with it in a 'social bubble.'" Real women, Craven insinuates, have real women's bodies and suffer in real ways, as Rowling has done; trans women exist only in "social bubbles," they don't get bullied, or raped, harassed or murdered, they don't have bodies, and they could never encounter Rowling's experience of domestic abuse. Craven reinforces this framing by listing some of the ways Rowling has suffered, as stated by Rowling in her essay. The framing aligns with what Alison Phipps (2020: 107) calls the "claim to ownership of sexual trauma" by a middle-class-based, cisgender feminism, in which the "designation 'survivor,' and its claim on our empathy and outrage, is withheld from trans women." In her article, Craven continually references Rowling as a victim of abuse. No such framing is afforded to trans women.

Regarding the impact of Craven's words, particularly on the issue of responsibility, one wonders what the journalist—or the editor—thinks are the consequences of the position, taken to a logical conclusion. Legally, it is surely to refuse to recognize that trans people, as virtual people, exist in any legal sense. In Viktor Orbán's authoritarian Hungary, there are laws that recognize only a version of the sex "determined by chromosomes" valued by Craven, and they have in turn legally "disappeared" the trans population. Is this what Craven's newspaper, the *National*, with its call for an independent Scotland, wants for its vision?

Craven's (2020) reference to the echo chamber also plays on my mind, specifically her claim that "the outraged online echo chambers might try their best to drown out voices who want to talk about sex." I have seen it used by other journalists, by arguably the UK's most high-profile liberal mouthpiece in the broadcast media, Piers Morgan (2020). Like Craven, he uses the term to displace trans people—whom he categorizes as "the trans lobby" (101)—along with any other uppity minority; no longer are they citizens but virtual threats. His paranoid discourse, like Davidson's and Craven's when covering trans people, typifies the "anger and fear" that Dag Wollebaek and colleagues (2019: 1) characterize more generally as being "connected to distinct behaviors online." Observe for its furi-ous hyperbole Morgan's (2020: 28, 7) attack on "modern-day anti-free-speech ultra-woke McCarthyism," in which the sources of woe are the "social media echo chambers." They dominate public life, Morgan claims, by gestating "illiberal lib-erals" who become "the modern-day fascists, demanding we all lead our lives in a way that conforms strictly to their narrow world view" (28, 7, 6). Morgan's position encompasses a view of social media as both echo chamber and trench warfare (Wollebaek et al. 2019); what it is not is a concession that trans people suffer just as much on social media as anyone else, and as a disempowered minority, are likely to be particularly vulnerable to Twitter's confrontational dynamics. As noted by Aleardo Zanghellini (2020: 10), sites such as Twitter feature "new manipulative communication practices" including "flaming and trolling," in which bad-faith engagement of discussions acts as cover for harassment and the invalidating of people's experiences or legitimacy—a particularly traumatic form of engagement for those historically disbelieved and delegitimized groups such as the trans community. Outside the UK's legacy media, research reveals how "UK hate crime statistics show a sharp increase in transphobic crimes since 2015. . . . Online abuse is also rising, and many trans people fear for their safety" (Chikha 2021). But this common trans experience of suffering online harassment fails to fit the legacy media's narrative: trans people are always the abusers, never the abused. The articles by Davidson and Craven in this sense exemplify a broader transphobic trend in the UK legacy media that minimizes or omits reference to the suffering of trans people. We are rendered hostile abstractions in a contradictory narrative: trans people are not real, only our violence is real.

The Agency of My Voice

In the days after the articles by Davidson and Craven were published, I write to both newspapers with carefully respectful counter articles that address their respective, problematic issues (Gwenffrewi 2020). Between June 18 and 27, and over a series of twelve emails, I engage with the editing team of the *National* in a bid to have my 600-word article counterbalance Craven's 855-word one. Their refusal to accommodate, and their counter suggestion of a reduced 300-word letter in their letter pages, underscore for me both an insensitivity and a lack of awareness as to what they have done: the dehumanizing and delegitimizing of a vulnerable minority, with a condescending article connecting trans identity with abuse and delusion. Even the offer of a letter is soon withdrawn: they sign off saying that in my demand for a space of a similar word count, I have missed my chance, the deadline for the letter having passed. The responsibility for the newspaper's absence of any counter narrative to Craven's is presented as my fault.

I encounter a much shorter correspondence during the same period of June 22–27 with the *Scotsman* involving four emails, in which I am informed my article has been passed on to their opinion editor, which leads to nothing. By this stage, and after my experience with the editorial team of the *National*, I silently withdraw.

I experience on a personal level the now-famous mechanism described by Sara Ahmed (2017: 226): "Whenever people keep being given a platform to say they have no platform, or whenever people speak endlessly about being silenced, you not only have a performative contradiction, you are witnessing a mechanism of power." Trans-exclusionary feminists like Julie Bindel or Kathleen Stock, and for that matter Davidson and Craven, enjoy regular access to the national media to delegitimize trans identity, while claiming to be silenced by transgender people. Yet the "silenced" ones are elsewhere, known to no one but the gatekeepers who quietly shut them down, if the silent ones have even got that far. Arguably it begins as self-censorship, when you occupy an identity that's disrespected and you assume there is no point in engaging with the institutions of the media, because no one will want to hear you anyway. Then tentatively, when you can no longer keep your silence in the face of constant media attacks, you intervene, only to find out you were right all along and your fragile confidence is dealt a new blow. You're left second-guessing yourself—is it just that you're mediocre, or did you fail to affirm the majority's worldview? Who knows how ubiquitous these modes of silence are for particular minorities? All I know is that, when I tried to come out from the shade and the silence to speak up for trans rights, my voice disappeared, all over again.

I suffered a sense of despair after these interactions for the remainder of 2020. Here is an alternative reality to Anastasia's concept of the transgender voice, "the agency by which an opinion is expressed." I recognized only the illusory agency of my voice: a nameless, unpublished, dehumanized trans woman calling out into an abyss, or standing outside a giant black gate where on the other side public pronouncements were issued against my kind, and all I could do was turn and walk away. It felt as if a history of oppression, and of experience, and of my very humanity, were secrets lost in the echo chamber, and I felt helpless.

Addendum: The Kindling of the Third Element of the Transgender Voice

On August 23, 2021, I see perhaps the last of Davidson, the newspaper journalist, before her departure to work with the broadcaster LBC. In a local story in the *Edinburgh Evening News* that goes viral, the title reads, "Inquiry Launched into Row over 'Transphobia' in Edinburgh Pub" (Davidson 2021). The speech marks around *transphobia* underscore the article's positioning of how transphobia is—perhaps like trans people themselves—potentially not a real thing. Of the story itself, a young trans bar manager in an Edinburgh pub is confronted by a group of trans-exclusionary activists who refuse to leave their table after their booked time expires (Maurice 2021; Stone 2021). The trans-exclusionists have left their anti-trans flyers in the establishment's toilets, the situation for the invalidated trans staff member is traumatic, staff and customers complain of the gender-crit lit, and the trans staff member calls the police to have the trans-exclusionary crowd removed. Davidson's researching of the trans element, with worrying predictability, relies on Twitter, exploiting the trans woman's ironic Twitter handle as "AGP porn addict male"—while ignoring her Twitter handle's *they/she* pronouns—as a justification to misgender her throughout the article with male pronouns. I am one of the many people who make an official complaint about the article's transphobic tone and language and the delegitimizing of the trans staff member. Over the following days, the article undergoes an adjustment, with an editorial acknowledgment that the pronouns of the trans staff member have been corrected to reflect their self-identification.

Finally, it seems I have performed an act that impacts on the journalism of Gina Davidson, by embodying in my action and its consequence the third element of the trans voice, as part of the collective. As documented already, it is the collective voice that those in power fear, the one depicted variously as the "trans lobby" (Morgan) or the "movement" (Rowling). It is also the voice that seems to effect the greatest change.

Gina Gwenffrewi is a researcher and tutor in English literature and queer studies at the University of Edinburgh. She graduated with a PhD in trans studies/English literature in June 2021, with the thesis "Transgender Gaze, Neoliberal Haze: The Impact of Neoliberalism on Trans Female Bodies in the Anglophone Global North." Her research interests include trans cultural production and the way that trans bodies are represented in different media.

References

Ahmed, Sara. 2017. "An Affinity of Hammers." In *Trap Door: Trans Cultural Production and the Politics of Visibility*, edited by Tourmaline, Eric Stanley, and Johanna Burton, 221–34. Cambridge, MA: MIT Press.

Anastasia, Andrew. 2014. "Voice." *TSQ* 1, nos. 1–2: 262–63. https://doi.org/10.1215/23289252-2400208.

Chikha, Fourat Ben. 2021. *Combating Rising Hate against LGBTI People in Europe*. Council of Europe, Committee on Equality and Non-Discrimination, December 17. https://pace.coe.int/en/files/29418/html.

Cox, Chelsey. 2020. "Fact Check: Hillary Clinton, Not Joe Biden, Used the Phrase 'Super Predators'" *USA Today*, October 24. https://eu.usatoday.com/story/news/factcheck/2020/10/24/fact-check-hillary-clinton-called-some-criminals-super-predators/6021383002/.

Craven, Shona. 2020. "This Is Why JK Rowling's Non-fiction Foray Caused a Twitter Storm." *National*, June 12. https://www.thenational.scot/news/18512301.jk-rowlings-non-fiction-foray-caused-twitter-storm/.

Davidson, Gina. 2019. "Transgender Event in Edinburgh Seeks to 'Change Tone' of Debate." *Scotsman*, May 26. https://www.scotsman.com/news/scottish-news/transgender-event-edinburgh-seeks-change-tone-debate-546295.

Davidson, Gina. 2020. "Why Abuse of JK Rowling Is a Problem for Trans Rights Activists." *Scotsman*, June 11. https://www.scotsman.com/news/opinion/columnists/why-abuse-of-jk-rowling-is-a-problem-for-trans-rights-activists-gina-davidson-2881971.

Davidson, Gina. 2021. "Inquiry Launched into Row over 'Transphobia' in Edinburgh Pub." *Edinburgh Evening News*, August 23. https://www.edinburghnews.scotsman.com/news/politics/inquiry-launched-into-row-over-transphobia-in-edinburgh-pub-3355594.

Forstater, Maya. 2021. "A Tale of Two Crowdfunders." *Medium*, June 2. https://mforstater.medium.com/a-tale-of-two-crowdfunders-3fc76abfaed6.

Gwenffrewi, Gina. 2020. "Silenced by The Scotsman." Gina Maya: Edinburgh Trance, July 1. https://www.ginamaya.co.uk/transgender-life/silenced-by-the-scotsman.html.

ILGA Europe. 2021. *Annual Review 2021*. https://www.ilga-europe.org/annualreview/2021.

Levin, Sam, Mona Chalabi, and Sabrina Siddiqui. 2018. "Why We Take Issue with the Guardian's Stance on Trans Rights in the UK." *Guardian*, November 2. https://www.theguardian.com/commentisfree/2018/nov/02/guardian-editorial-response-transgender-rights-uk.

Maurice, Emma Powys. 2021. "Pub Manager Targeted by Sick Trolls after Calling Police on Anti-trans Group." *Pink News*, August 23. https://www.pinknews.co.uk/2021/08/23/i-stand-with-meb-trans-pub-manager/.

McLean, Craig. 2021. "The Growth of the Anti-transgender Movement in the United Kingdom: The Silent Radicalization of the British Electorate." *International Journal of Sociology* 51, no. 6: 473–82. http://doi.org/10.1080/00207659.2021.1939946.

Mermaids. 2020. "An Open Letter to J. K. Rowling." June 12. https://mermaidsuk.org.uk/news/dear-jk-rowling/.

Montgomerie, Katy. 2020. "Addressing the Claims in JK Rowling's Justification for Transphobia." *Medium*, June 16. https://katymontgomerie.medium.com/addressing-the-claims-in-jk-rowlings-justification-for-transphobia-7b6f761e8f8f.

Morgan, Piers. 2020. *Wake Up*. London: Harper Collins.

Pearce, Ruth, Sonja Erikainen, and Ben Vincent. 2020. "TERF Wars: An Introduction." *Sociological Review Monographs* 68, no. 4: 677–98.

Phipps, Alison. 2020. *Me, Not You: The Trouble with Mainstream Feminism*. Manchester, UK: Manchester University Press.

Rowling, J. K. 2020. "J. K. Rowling Writes about Her Reasons for Speaking out on Sex and Gender Issues." Jkrowling.com, June 10. https://jkrowling.com/opinions/j-k-rowling-writes-about-her-reasons-for-speaking-out-on-sex-and-gender-issues/.

Stone, Gemma. 2021. "Doctors Bar in Edinburgh Mobbed by Transphobes." *Medium*, August 23. https://medium.com/@notCursedE/doctors-bar-in-edinburgh-mobbed-by-transphobes-3b4c92f19ce9.

Wollebaek, Dag, Rune Karlsen, Kari Steen-Johnsen, and Bernard Enjolras. 2019. "Anger, Fear, and Echo Chambers: The Emotional Basis for Online Behavior." *Social Media and Society*, April–June: 1–14(c). https://doi.org/10.1177/2056305119829859.

Wynn, Natalie. 2021. "J. K. Rowling." ContraPoints, January 26. YouTube video. https://www.youtube.com/watch?v=7gDKbT_l2us.

Zanghellini, Aleardo. 2020. "Philosophical Problems with the Gender-Critical Feminist Argument against Trans Inclusion." *Sage Open*, April–June: 1–14. https://doi.org/10.1177/2158244020927029.

A Report from LGBTI Philanthropy

EZRA BERKLEY NEPON

P rogressive grantmakers around the world are witnessing accusations of "gender ideology" and related models of manufactured gender panic used as oppositional tools to block, erode, and attack the goals and activities of their grantees. This especially impacts those who fund feminist organizations and groups working for LGBTI human rights. Grantmaking programs that focus on children and youth, sexual health and reproductive rights/reproductive justice, sexual orientation, HIV/AIDS, health-care access, sports, defense of democracy, environmental justice, and other fields are also impacted. Indeed, grantmakers with focus areas that may seem unrelated are called to find common cause, given their shared experiences of opposition from the "anti-gender" movement.

At the same time, progressive funders come under direct attack by those within the anti-gender movement and their political allies whose conspiracy theories often center around George Soros and the Soros-funded Open Society Foundations (OSF) and other progressive grantmakers. For example, a June 2021 article in the *American Conservative* accused OSF of being "highly instrumental in driving gender identity" (Bilek 2021).[1]

In the past five years, progressive grantmakers have developed increasingly coordinated responses to the global anti-gender movement. These responses include research and assessment of the anti-gender movement at global and regional levels; donor peer education through online and in-person convenings and workshops; strategic cofunding and development of new grant funding to support those resisting anti-gender attacks; and coordination across geographic and issue areas through a philanthropic task force.

Background

This is a short field report based on the work of the Global Philanthropy Project (GPP), a network of funders collaborating to expand global philanthropic support to advance the human rights of lesbian, gay, bisexual, transgender, and

TSQ: Transgender Studies Quarterly * Volume 9, Number 3 * August 2022   **517**
DOI 10.1215/23289252-9836190   © 2022 Duke University Press

intersex (LGBTI) people in the global South and East. In 2019–20, GPP's twenty-two member organizations represented half of all foundation funding to LGBTI communities in the Global South and East. These organizations coordinate within GPP to develop a shared research and advocacy agenda toward increasing global LGBTI funding from other foundations, donor governments and multilateral agencies, and high net wealth individuals. For example, our biennial *Global Resources Report: Government and Philanthropic Support for LGBTI Communities* provides detailed data on the global distribution of LGBTI funding by geography, issue, strategy, and population focus, offering a tool for identifying trends, gaps, and opportunities in the rapidly changing landscape of LGBTI funding (GPP 2022). The *Global Resources Report* provides a tool for funders and civil society organizations making the case for funding needs, and it is used by funders in developing and reevaluating their funding priorities.

Founded in 2009, GPP first brought on staff members in 2015. From that point on, the network launched a working group focused on increasing and improving funding to global trans and intersex communities. That working group and the foundations that make up its membership have been instrumental in developing research (e.g., GPP 2019) and donor peer education opportunities to make the case toward these goals, conducting targeted advocacy with private foundations and donor governments, and supporting the development of the International Trans Fund and the Intersex Human Rights Fund.[2]

In 2018 GPP organized a global meeting, "Growing Solidarity: Funding at the Intersection of Faith, Religious Fundamentalism, Human Rights, and Social Justice" (GPP n.d.), bringing together funders supporting LGBTI-affirming faith organizing and those funding opposition to fundamentalist faith agendas. The event was held in Southern Africa adjacent to the biennial conference of Pan Africa ILGA (International Lesbian, Gay, Bisexual, Trans and Intersex Association), a regional network of LGBTI civil society organizations (ILGA n.d.). Growing Solidarity brought together eighty attendees across grantmaking programs focused on LGBTI human rights, sexual health and reproductive rights, and feminist issues to build solidarity, strategy, and momentum around resistance to the use of religion to harm or advance discrimination against LGBTI people around the world. Grantmakers and civil society expert panelists shared stories and information connecting these issues across world regions. For many attendees it was a first opportunity to recognize the scale of the opposition's coordination, beyond the geographic or issue-based focus of their own institution. The GPP also published private research for the convening participants, later developed into a public report: *Religious Conservatism on the Global Stage: Threats and Challenges for LGBTI Rights* (Peñas Defago et al. 2018).

In the next two years, a series of related smaller meetings and donor education events followed, often developed in collaboration with GPP member institutions and/or with allied philanthropic networks including Human Rights Funders Network, Funders for Reproductive Equity, Gender Funders CoLab, Elevate Children Funders Group, Funders' Initiative for Civil Society, and Funders Concerned About AIDS.

These activities led GPP to increase focus on organizing a progressive philanthropic response to the anti-gender movement. In 2020 GPP again initiated private research, which was developed into a public report: *Meet the Moment: A Call for Progressive Philanthropic Response to the Anti-Gender Movement* (GPP 2020a). This report includes a comparative mapping of the funding of the global anti-gender movement and the current progressive philanthropic response. Additionally, we share insights based on comparing global and regional LGBTI funding data as documented in the *2017–2018 Global Resources Report: Government and Philanthropic Support for Lesbian, Gay, Bisexual, Transgender, and Intersex Communities* (GPP 2020b). The findings offer a clear call to action to counter the enormous financial resources are flowing to these anti-rights movements, leveraged into acceleration across global regions and yielding both the attrition of human rights infrastructures and the increasing rise of authoritarianism. Progressive movements and their philanthropic partners are being outspent by hundreds of millions of dollars each year, and the institutions providing that opposition funding have developed sophisticated and coordinated systems to learn, cofund, and expand their influence. We found that between 2013 and 2017, LGBTI movements worldwide received $1.2 billion, while the anti-gender movement received at least $3.7 billion—more than triple the LGBTI funding. Despite this, in our 2020 research looking at the philanthropic responses, we found that the majority of progressive funders did not yet have a focused strategy for this work, and the overall field development in this area was nascent.

The GPP and Elevate Children Funders Group have partnered to develop a number of resources specifically focused on the ways that the opposition, which we are calling "gender restrictive" groups, use child protection rhetoric as a wedge to achieve their political goals. In 2021 we copublished *Manufacturing Moral Panic: Weaponizing Children to Undermine Gender Justice and Human Rights* (Sentiido 2021), which includes comparative analysis of three country case studies (Bulgaria, Ghana, and Peru) and underscores recurring strategies, narratives, and actors, offering insight into how gender-restrictive groups engage in coalitional work across the globe.

The Necessity of "Breaking Silos"

In all this work, the GPP has partnered with other funder networks who see their focus issues as intrinsically connected to issues of gender self-determination. In some cases, the connection is clear. Women's funders, those funding feminist movements, and those funding sexual health and reproductive justice are in the direct line of attack for anti-gender movements whose ideologies align with the most regressive models of biological essentialism and patriarchal visions of women's prescribed social roles. Those funding around HIV/AIDS are well aware of the dangerous roles homophobia, transphobia, and sexism can and do play in blocking or destroying competent public health responses to the pandemic. Many of those funding issues around children and youth have witnessed that LGBTI youth are under attack globally, and at the same time that broader human rights movements are being disrupted by rallying cries to "protect the children" used to attack everything from LGBTI-affirming media to vaccination access to anti-racist education.

For other fields, the connection is not as obvious.

How does this impact grantmakers focused on defense of democracy? GPP has partnered with networks such as Funders' Initiative for Civil Society and Peace and Security Funders Group because donors in these fields are aware that individuals and groups trying to attain or maintain political power, especially in contexts of unstable democratic institutions, are increasingly using the notion of "fighting gender ideology" as a critical component of their campaigns, supporting authoritative, nationalist, and anti-rights political platforms. An example from the *Manufacturing Moral Panic* report: in 2016 a coalition of gender-restrictive and far-right forces successfully mobilized the idea of gender ideology to create moral panic and oppose the plebiscite to ratify the peace process between the Revolutionary Armed Forces of Colombia and the government in Colombia (Sentiido 2021: 52).

How does this impact grantmakers focused on the environment? While this connection may seem the least obvious intersection among our collaborative efforts, environmental funders and the movements they support are indeed impacted by the anti-gender movement. Climate denialism and policy agendas that escalate the global climate crisis are common features of authoritarian governments and those leaning toward authoritarianism. These governments commonly share another set of characteristics rooted in ethnonationalism, state-sponsored homophobia and transphobia, and overall mistrust for the institutions of democracy—together, a perfect storm that undermines progressive philanthropic objectives. Cynical actors in the anti-gender movement, aiming to control power and narrative, often weaponize both climate denialism and manufactured moral panic based in fear of "the other" (whether LGBTI people, migrants or refugees, or other groups) toward their political aims. The *Manufacturing Moral Panic* report explains, "Under the false premise that the United Nations' Sustainable Development Goals [SDGs; see UN n.d.] are part of a neocolonial agenda, gender-restrictive groups in the [Latin American] region are seeking to act against them and oppose environmental policies. Through this kind of messaging, gender-restrictive groups align themselves with powerful actors who have political or economic reasons to oppose environmental regulations in general, and the SDGs in particular. Jair Bolsonaro's government in Brazil is a case in point" (58).

While conversations within philanthropy tend to repeat the necessity of "breaking out of our silos," that truism has been put into action as funders connect the dots between the shared attack and the crucial need for shared response.

A Shimmering Response

In 2021 the GPP hosted the "Shimmering Solidarity: Global Rights Summit," a four-month online convening focused on grantmaker responses to the anti-gender movement and related anti-rights agendas (GPP 2021). The summit served as an opportunity for aligned colleagues to build shared analysis around anti-rights attacks and strategize toward multi-sectoral progressive philanthropic responses. Over 380 attendees participated, represented grantmaking organizations, funder networks, and civil society partner organizations.

Why "shimmering solidarity"? The organizers took inspiration from honeybees, who flip their abdomens upward in split-second synchronicity to produce a wave-like pattern called shimmering in order to repel hornets and other predators. The shimmering mechanism is both sophisticated and magical, demonstrating the bees' remarkable capacity for rapid communication and aligned, coordinated action. Shimmering works by confusing and disorienting opponents through collective movement, making the many appear as one moving body. This self-defense strategy protects the community, not the honey or the queen. Shimmering enables bees to live in hives that are out in the open, and even small-scale shimmering can be effective.

We also looked to honeybees for their cross-pollination function, and for their use of a vigorously democratic consensus-building process while seeking and assessing potential new homes for their hive. We saw all these honeybee technologies as a generative metaphoric space for our work together imagining, exploring, and sharing ideas about our future visions, the paths to get there, and our strategies for undermining the opposition's attack. The shimmering metaphor also helped communicate, in our outreach to potential summit attendees and beyond, that the summit was being organized by queers, that the culture of the event(s) would be creative and collaborative, and that we were rejecting the opposition's narratives about who is or is not part of the "natural" world.

The summit included over fifty sessions on a diverse range of topics. Sessions were categorized into a number of different tracks, including "cross-pollination" or exploration of connections between impacted funding areas; skill sharing including grant-making tools, approaches, models, innovations, and lessons learned; building shared awareness of and resistance to the opposition; highlighting local and regional examples and areas for collaboration; and exploration of how some grantmakers are funding "world building,"[3] narrative change work, and other transformative strategies to develop our visions and movements toward a more just and liberatory future.

What's Next

We are heartened to see a growing number of funders and increasing funding infrastructure with explicit programmatic focus in this area. Building on this momentum, the Global Philanthropy Project has launched a grantmaker task force focused on mobilizing progressive philanthropic responses to the anti-gender movement. In the coming years, additional research and donor convening spaces will be developed in response to task force member priorities.

Ezra Berkley Nepon is senior program officer for knowledge and learning at the Global Philanthropy Project and leads development of the biennial *Global Resources Report*. Nepon is the author of *Dazzle Camouflage: Spectacular Theatrical Strategies for Resistance and Resilience* (2016) and other publications.

Notes

1.   Anti-gender movements often mobilize significant antisemitism in their attacks on those funding LGBTI human rights, trading simultaneously on medieval-era tropes claiming Jewish conspiracies to destroy the "natural family" and Jewish global financial control. Ironically, but not surprisingly, a number of anti-gender attacks have also misidentified top LGBTI funders as Jewish.
2.   IHRF is a program of Astraea Lesbian Foundation for Justice.
3.   Strategies including arts and culture, education, and media.

References

Bilek, Jennifer. 2021. "Foundations Are Setting the Transgender Agenda and Targeting Children." *American Conservative*, June 1. https://www.theamericanconservative.com/articles /foundations-are-setting-the-transgender-agenda-and-targeting-children/.

GPP (Global Philanthropy Project). n.d. "Grantmaker Convening on the Rise of the Religious Right." https://globalphilanthropyproject.org/Events/faithconvening/ (accessed September 29, 2021).

GPP (Global Philanthropy Project). 2019. "Funder Briefings: The State of Trans and Intersex Funding." September 13. https://globalphilanthropyproject.org/trans-intersex-funder -briefings/.

GPP (Global Philanthropy Project). 2020a. *Meet the Moment: A Call for Progressive Philanthropic Response to the Anti-gender Movement*. https://globalphilanthropyproject.org/meet-the -moment/.

GPP (Global Philanthropy Project). 2020b. *2017–2018 Global Resources Report: Government and Philanthropic Support for Lesbian, Gay, Bisexual, Transgender, and Intersex Communities.* https://globalphilanthropyproject.org/grr2017-18/.

GPP (Global Philanthropy Project). 2021. "Shimmering Solidarity: Global Rights Summit." https://shimmeringsolidarity.org/ (accessed September 29, 2021).

GPP (Global Philanthropy Project). 2022. *2019–2020 Global Resources Report: Government and Philanthropic Support for Lesbian, Gay, Bisexual, Transgender, and Intersex Communities.* https://globalresourcesreport.org.

ILGA World (International Lesbian, Gay, Bisexual, Trans and Intersex Association). n.d. "Regions." https://ilga.org/about-us/regions (accessed September 29, 2021).

Peñas Defago, María Angélica, José Manuel Morán Faúndes, and Juan Marco Vaggione. 2018. *Religious Conservatism on the Global Stage: Threats and Challenges for LGBTI Rights.* Global Philanthropy Project. https://globalphilanthropyproject.org/religiousconservatismreport.

Sentiido. 2021. *Manufacturing Moral Panic: Weaponizing Children to Undermine Gender Justice and Human Rights.* Elevate Children Funders Group and Global Philanthropy Project. https://globalphilanthropyproject.org/manufacturing-moral-panic/.

UN (United Nations). n.d. Sustainable Development Goals. https://sdgs.un.org/goals (accessed April 9, 2022).

Toward a Trans* Masculine Genealogy in South America

FRANCISCO FERNÁNDEZ ROMERO and ANDRÉS MENDIETA

Latin American trans* masculine individuals have often been erased from public discourse, both within their societies and within trans studies. On the one hand, within the region, it is frequent to hear that trans* masculinities are invisible. This invisibility or, rather, this erasure of our subjectivities, is directly related to the fact that trans* masculine identities are often not recognized as such and are thus disregarded (Álvarez Broz 2017; Fernández Romero, Torres, and Lenzi 2021). This situation can be attributed both to anti-trans discourses from conservative and progressive sectors, including trans-exclusionary radical feminists (TERFs), and to some sectors that consider themselves allies of a "trans* movement" yet do not address its plurality. Cissexist historical narratives have often also overlooked certain aspects of our histories that are crucial for understanding our biographies and our community-building and political practices.

Within trans* studies, Latin American trans* masculinities have also tended to fall through the cracks. On the one hand, as a whole, trans* studies leans global North–centric (Rizki 2019), similar to queer, gay, and lesbian studies (Pérez and Radi 2019). Moreover, work on trans* in Latin America from both within and outside the region usually focuses on *travestis* and trans women (Radi 2018, 2019; Rizki 2019). Trans* masculine contributions to Latin American trans* rights movements have also been undervalued and at times even unacknowledged.

In this article, we focus on South American trans* masculine existence, especially in the continent's southern region. We begin by recuperating certain historical subjects who are often read by historians through a cissexist framework as examples of "strategic transvestism," a category that suggests that masculine "transvestism" was employed as a ruse to gain upward social mobility.[1] We attend instead to these subjects' narratives, histories, and first-person accounts, suggesting that, rather than examples of strategic transvestism, these subjects are of interest to a broader trans∗ masculine archive. Second, we highlight the narratives, practices, and experiences of individuals who transitioned during or soon after the region's dictatorial period in the twentieth century. In doing so, we suggest differences in the conditions of possibility for the emergence of trans∗ masculine communities and subjectivities, in departure from the contouring force of US national histories. Finally, we underscore the work of South American trans∗ masculine activists from the 1990s to the present, calling attention to their contributions on a local and global scale. Throughout the piece, we draw largely from the research of some of the region's many trans∗ masculine scholars who have emerged over the past decades.

Revisiting the Archive

There are a number of historical archives, notary acts, biographies, and memoirs—to some extent fictionalized—from the eighteenth century to the beginning of the twentieth that suggest the existence of people in Latin America who, though assigned female at birth, lived most or all of their lives self-identified as men, such as Enrique Faver, Amelio Robles Ávila, Antonio Ytá, and Raúl Suárez. These cases have been studied and classified by historians and researchers as women who posed as men or as female husbands despite the fact that one might, from a close analysis of the archive, read these subjects as espousing identifications or practices we might consider trans∗ in the present (Halberstam 1998).

In the specific case of South America, many subjects who might be understood today as trans∗ masculinities, or at least as individuals assigned female at birth who lived as men for the majority or entirety of their lives, have later been classified through a cissexist framework as "women who impersonated men" (examples of this are Abercrombie 2008; González Pagés 2012). These categories have reinforced the central premise of cissexism, which views trans∗ persons as less "real" and "authentic" than their cis counterparts (Cabral 2009; Radi 2015). Especially in recent scholarship on the nineteenth century, masculine "transvestism" has been considered a strategy used to achieve a kind of upward social mobility. Such an interpretation also contributes to denying these subjects' agency.

Although it could be problematic to associate these individuals with trans∗ masculinity during a time when such a category did not yet exist, it is also true that those who wrote or interpreted these stories did not hesitate to label these subjects—who were not allowed to name themselves—as imposters (Martínez 2017; Skidmore 2017; Simonetto 2021). As mentioned above, "strategic transvestism" is one of the most frequent ways of referring to those who might today be named or understood as trans∗ masculinities, given that most historians interpret their "passing as the opposite sex" as a means to achieve power or reap other benefits. In contrast, cultural critics such as Juliana Martínez (2017) reconstruct and criticize this cissexist reading of Faver's life. Following Martínez and reading against the archival grain, we can prioritize these persons' scarce first-person testimonies and how they name themselves (Skidmore 2017) to narrate their histories and recover their trajectories. This is the approach also espoused by Marta V. Vicente (2021), who emphasizes the importance of using individuals' own self-descriptors, while also upholding the utility of terms such as *trans**, to encompass the experience of not living in one's assigned gender across history. In this manner, the alleged nonexistence of trans* masculine histories in South America—or, at best, their limited existence—is strongly linked to the denial of these individuals' practices, narratives, and lived experiences of masculinities.

The first-person narratives and voices of these men appear in the archive, articulating experiences of their lives and desires that contrast with how they are produced, regulated, and inscribed within discourses of power by dominant institutions such as the tabloid press or historiography (Disalvo 2020). Antonio Ytá, whose case has been addressed by Thomas Abercrombie (2008: 6), was "unmasked" (in Abercrombie's terms) and reported by his wife in 1803 for presumably tricking her, as he was actually "a woman dressed as a man." Yet if we look at the sources, we can see that Antonio had not only served as governor of a town in Moxos, Bolivia, while living as a man under that same name; as Antonio himself narrates, he lived as male for a decade until his wife's accusation led him to be examined by the town's doctor and surgeon. Supplementing his first-person account, his mother also provided documents and statements that backed Ytá's position, showing that her son had long expressed, in Abercrombie's terms, a "heterosexual male sexuality" and a "convincingly natural" masculinity (13). If we read Antonio's and his mother's testimonies without cissexist bias, we can claim that Antonio was living as a man many years before any institutional position of power was available to him. Thus, although we cannot elaborate on this further here, there are elements of his account that suggest an alternative reading that does not render him a case of "strategic transvestism."

Another interesting case is that of Raúl Luis Suárez, who obtained his national identification documents in Argentina in the 1910s in which he was officially recognized as a male citizen. As historian Patricio Simonetto (2021) reconstructs, Luis Suárez married Amalia Gómez in 1912 and lived his whole life as a man, even moving through high society and holding prestigious jobs as customs officer. In 1930 his "true sex" (Skidmore 2017) was discovered by doctors after his hospitalization and subsequent death. The press covered the story as "the extraordinary case of [R——] Suárez who pretended to be a man for 25 years" (*Caras & caretas* 1930; former legal name omitted here). Previously, Arturo de Aragón had also been classified by the same magazine as a case of a *"mujer-hombre"* (woman-man; *Caras & caretas* 1906). Like Raúl Luis, Arturo lived much of his life as a man who was known for "dressing well" and for having had "the opportunity to be mixed up in more than one amorous situation with women" (J. Fernández 2012: 114). Yet the magazine's insistence on the fraudulent nature of both of their masculinities reinscribes Raúl Luis and Arturo within discourses of fraud and deception, simultaneously sensationalizing and criminalizing their expressions of masculinity. It also denies the agency they exhibited in constructing various practices and experiences of masculinities.

The stories of Antonio, Raúl, and Arturo are not isolated incidents: they are part of a broader genealogy of what we might read as trans∗ masculine narratives, stories, and histories that have been interpreted through a cissexist viewpoint that overlooks the first-person accounts present in most sources. This manner of narrating these subjects' lives is not only present in writings on the nineteenth or early twentieth century, but it has also persisted when referring to periods when categories such as transexual or *transgénero* had already been adopted by trans∗ masculine communities. That is to say, even self-identification with trans, transgender, or transexual manhood or masculinity has been mostly disregarded by the press (Disalvo 2020) and by some segments of feminist and LGBTQ+ activism, even in the present. In parallel, late twentieth-century trans∗ masculine communities and activism have tended to be overlooked when tracing the histories of trans∗ communities in South America, even in the face of a current increase in interest in the topic. In the following section, we highlight some potential milestones in a trans∗ masculine genealogy of the region.

Trans∗ Masculine Lives, Communities, and Activism in Dictatorial and Postdictatorial South America

The temporality of trans∗ masculine communities varies between and across regions shaped in part by political and historical conditions. In the United States and Canada, the 1970s saw a growth in FTM communities, with the emergence of the first transexual male groups and publications, led for example by Rupert Raj in Toronto or Lou Sullivan in San Francisco (Stryker 2008). In contrast to the United States and Canada, a large part of Latin America was controlled by military dictatorships between the 1960s and 1980s, which established particular conditions of possibility for medical transitions, community building, and political activism. These dictatorships, while at times networked, had uneven national effects on medical transition. For example, in Chile, the government of dictator Augusto Pinochet allowed some individuals to undergo surgical interventions and to obtain legal gender recognition beginning in the 1970s; Fernanda Carvajal (2018) holds that Chilean authorities might have been favorable toward these procedures, as they served to realign or "correct" what the authoritarian regime designated as "deviant bodies" within a conservative moral order. In contrast, in other countries such as Argentina and Brazil, genital reassignment surgeries were illicit under dictatorial governments. Specifically, in Brazil, there existed a general prohibition against what was considered by the military government to be "mutilation" (Neves 2016: 167). In Argentina during this period, such operations were forbidden under National Law No. 17,132 unless authorized by a judge.

This context similarly framed some of the first recorded transitions of men who have self-identified as transexual or trans. In Brazil João W. Nery underwent clandestine gender-related surgeries in 1977 during the Brazilian dictatorship when these operations were illegal. He also acquired male documentation during this time by claiming at a civil registry office that his birth had never been registered as a child. This change in documentation deeply affected his professional life, however: he lost the ability to use his professional degree as a psychologist specialized in gender and sexuality, as it was issued under his previous name, and during the dictatorship there was no legal recourse to change the legal name on his degree (Nery 2011). In mid-1980s Argentina Eugenio Talbot Wright began transitioning socially and medically as a teenager. Although the country's most recent dictatorship had ended in 1983, individuals considered to be sexual or gender deviants continued to suffer harsh persecution at the hands of the police. Talbot Wright reports being frequently arrested during police raids of gay bars for the misdemeanor of dressing as the "opposite sex" (Oliva 2020). Similar regulations were still in force throughout the country until the 1990s and 2000s, although the effects of such regulations have been studied only for trans women and *travestis* (for example, Berkins and J. Fernández 2013).

Travel and the transnational circulation of knowledge was also important in both individuals' lives. Nery (2011) recounts having learned about transexual surgeries on a trip to France, where he read about them by chance in a medical journal he found in a bookstore. Talbot Wright traveled to Chile for gender-related operations, which was also a common practice among trans women to circumvent the requirement for judicial authorization in Argentina. He later attended a university in Cuba, "the ideal for my parents, the socialist country," which he describes as a transphobic society but "not with me, because I'd had surgery and had been 'cured'" (Oliva 2020). According to widespread popular and medical beliefs at the time, transsexuality could be "cured" through surgical interventions to normalize deviant and pathological corporalities.

We know these details through these individuals' later accounts of their own lives, as at the time of their medical interventions they did not widely publicize their trans* status. Both came forth publicly in the 2010s during a time when community activism generated more visibility and rights for trans individuals.

Nery anonymously published his autobiography *Erro de pessoa: Joana ou João* (*Wrong Person: Joana or João*) in 1984. He became visibly trans and an active member of the trans* masculine community only in 2011, when he published an updated version of his 1984 memoir, this time under his own name: *Viagem solitária: Memórias de um transexual trinta anos depois* (*Solitary Journey: Memoir of a Transexual Thirty Years Later*). In Talbot Wright's case, as the son of a *desaparecido* (a political activist kidnapped, tortured, and exterminated by the dictatorial government), he had participated in anti-genocide human rights activism starting in the 1990s, though he experienced resistance from some of the relatives of *desaparecidos*[2] who considered his presence shameful. In the late 2010s he began to share his story with the press and to participate more visibly in trans* activism.

In parallel to these individuals' lives, trans* masculine communities had slowly begun to flourish in some Latin American countries around the turn of the century. Most of the organized trans* masculine groups in the region emerged from the 2010s onward; however, transexual and transgender male activism began to develop in the 1990s within broader organizations. In Argentina Ivo Schuster was part of the country's first transexual organization, TRANSDEVI— Transexuales por el Derecho a la Vida y a la Identidad (Transexuals for the Right to Life and Identity) (see TRANSDEVI 1994). Founded in 1991, this organization advocated for legal gender recognition and for "sex change" surgeries within the country (Butierrez 2021). A few years later, also in Argentina, individuals who identified with transgender masculinity or manhood—including Mauro Cabral Grinspan, whose later career we discuss below—joined lesbian and bisexual activists to create a group called Las Iguanas. They printed a bulletin between 1998 and 1999 in which transgender issues figured prominently, including several articles by *transgéneros masculinos* and references to North American authors such as Leslie Feinberg and Aaron Devor. This publication contains some of the first recorded uses of the words *transgénero* and *trans* in Argentina, which were more broadly adopted by trans* feminine communities only in the early 2000s; up until then, the most common terms in circulation were *transexual* and *travesti*.

Local and Transnational Activism in the Twenty-First Century

In the twenty-first century, specifically trans* masculine organizations began to flourish in South America. For example, Entre-Tránsitos was created in Colombia in 2009; in Argentina, Hombres Trans Argentinos (HTA) was founded in 2010, and one year later, the Asociación de Travestis, Transexuales y Transgéneros de Argentina (ATTTA) created a dedicated space for trans men (ATTTA Hombres Trans); while in Brazil, the Associação Brasileira de Homens Trans (ABHT) and the Instituto Brasileiro de Transmasculinidades (IBRAT) were established between 2012 and 2013. However, many trans male activists from the region are also notorious for advocacy work that reaches across communities and weaves together different geographic scales.

In Chile, for instance, in 2005 Andrés Rivera Duarte founded OTD, Organización de Transexuales por la Dignidad de la Diversidad (Transexual Organization for the Dignity of Diversity), an organization devoted broadly to trans* rights. The OTD worked locally toward achieving human rights for all transexual individuals, and in 2009 it became the first trans* organization to gain consultative status—a status granted to nongovernmental organizations that allows them to have a voice within major global organizations—with the Organization of American States (CLAM 2010). In Argentina the aforementioned Mauro Cabral Grinspan was already involved in regional and global advocacy in the early 2000s, focusing on trans* and intersex issues. He contributed toward key changes in the international human rights system. For example, in 2007 he was one of the original signatories of the Yogyakarta Principles, which are a series of statements on the application of international human rights law to issues of sexual orientation and gender identity. Later, in 2009 he cofounded the New York–based organization GATE (initially Global Action for Trans* Equality, now called Trans, Gender Diverse and Intersex Advocacy in Action). Alongside other organizations, GATE was one of the main driving forces behind the revision of the World Health Organization's International Classification of Diseases, which removed trans* identities from the Chapter on Mental and Behavioral Disorders (Suess Schwend 2020).

These activists and organizations had a local as well as a global impact. In Chile the OTD helped achieve some of the first instances of legal gender recognition without genital reassignment. In Argentina the Yogyakarta Principles were later a key precedent for the country's Gender Identity Law (National Law No. 26,743; 2012), which even a decade later continues to be considered cutting-edge, given that it grants all individuals the right to their gender identity, including depathologized, cost-free access to legal gender recognition and/or transitional health care. Although trans women and *travestis* are most often credited for achieving this law, Cabral Grinspan and other trans men such as philosopher Blas Radi, lawyer Taddeo C.C., and activist Fernando Rodríguez from HTA played crucial roles and were integral to the law's passage.

Also in Argentina, trans men played a leading role in the struggle for trans* reproductive rights and justice. Beginning in the 2010s several activists such as Radi, Francisco Sfeir, and Tomás Mascolo, and organizations such as the Frente de Trans Masculinidades, raised their voices for the inclusion of trans* masculine individuals within the abortion rights movement, which rose in prominence until the National Congress passed a bill broadening termination rights in 2020 (Fernández Romero 2021). Although they did not achieve their goal of being fully included within negotiations around the issue, they succeeded in expanding the language of the bill to include all "persons with the capacity to gestate" in addition to "women" (National Law no. 27,610). In parallel, other trans men sought to make visible the obstacles they encountered in accessing assisted reproductive technologies or pregnancy health care (Mendieta and Vidal-Ortiz 2021).

Final Words

In our home country, Argentina, it is still common to hear that trans★ masculinity is a "new" phenomenon, with at most a single decade of history. But as this piece has suggested, individuals who identify with trans, *transgénero,* or transexual masculinity have existed in South America for at least half a century, and people assigned female at birth have lived in the region as men for longer. That is why thorough research into archives is needed to brush conventional histories against the grain, to expose their cissexist bias, and to enable new narratives of trans★ people's lives and deeds in the past. In doing so, the erasure of their experiences will no longer be reproduced in and by historical accounts. Yet our call for anti-cisnormative readings of trans★ masculine lives extends beyond historical accounts and, indeed, beyond academic scholarship. The urgency of this task materializes in the story of a young Argentinian trans man, Tehuel de la Torre. After his disappearance in early 2021, parts of the press and some feminist organizations have framed the situation as a case of violence against women, or even as a femicide, despite repeated demands from the trans★ masculine community to respect his gender and find him alive. This constitutes an example of the physical, discursive, and epistemological violence that often renders trans★ masculine lives unlivable, ungrievable, and unimaginable.

Although the brevity of this article has allowed us to explore only a few examples of trans masculine existence in a limited number of South American countries, we also hope this brief overview serves as an indication of how the temporalities, spatialities, and modalities of trans masculine existence are contingent on local and regional historical, cultural, and political conditions. Without denying the possible similarities comparative research may find, we believe it is necessary to call into question the universality of trans★ masculine genealogies drawn from global North positions. A deeper exploration of South American trans★ masculine politics would also show how its agenda is rooted in specific circumstances, like any trans★ movement. For example, as we show elsewhere (Fernández Romero 2021; Mendieta and Vidal-Ortiz 2021), the strong presence of trans★ masculine activists in Argentina's reproductive rights movements might not have been possible if the country had not depathologized trans★ identities, thus eliminating forced sterilization. Depathologization itself might not have been a goal of the country's trans★ movement if its health system had resembled the US privatized health-care system, where the loss of insurance coverage for gender affirmative procedures is a concern. Again, this line of research could serve to provincialize analyses of global North trans* masculine agendas, interrogating their own conditions of possibility.

Finally, we have highlighted how South American trans men (and trans* communities in general) not only have been on the receiving end of influences from the global North but also have made key contributions in arenas such as international human rights law and the global field of trans* health. The transnational circulation of individuals, ideas, and activist practices within the region and beyond has played a key role in trans* masculine subjectivities and politics and thus requires further attention.

Andrés Mendieta holds an MA in gender studies from the Universidad Nacional de Tres de Febrero where he also teaches courses in queer and trans* studies. He forms part of the international research project Trans.Arch, "Archives in Transition: Collective Memories and Subaltern Uses," funded by the European Union's Horizon research and innovation program.

Francisco Fernández Romero is a PhD candidate in geography at the University of Buenos Aires, where he also holds a teaching position. He is a doctoral fellow at Argentina's National Scientific and Technical Research Council (CONICET) and a junior fellow at the Center for Applied Transgender Studies. His current research focuses on cisnormativity and ableism in public urban spaces, their effects on everyday life, and trans and disabled activism aimed at broadening access to the city.

Notes

1.   This recuperative intervention is also part of a more extensive investigation framed through the project "Trans.Arch" or "Archives in Transition: Collective Memories and Subaltern Uses" financed by the European Union within the framework of the Horizon 2020 programming under the MSCA-RISE scheme. For more details, see https://trans-arch.org.
2.   In Argentina relatives of *desaparecidos* were one of the main actors demanding the investigation and prosecution of crimes against humanity committed during the 1976–83 dictatorship.

References

Abercrombie, Thomas. 2008. "Una vida disfrazada en el Potosí y La Plata Colonial: Antonio-Nacido-María Yta ante la audiencia de Charcas." *Anuario de estudios Bolivianos, archivísticos y bibliográficos* 2008: 3–45.

Álvarez Broz, Mariana. 2017. "¿Cuánta (des)igualdad somos capaces de aceptar? Formas, mecanismos y relaciones de (des)igualdad en personas trans de la Argentina contemporánea (1990–2015)." PhD diss., Escuela Interdisciplinaria de Altos Estudios Sociales, Universidad de San Martín.

Berkins, Lohana, and Josefina Fernández. 2013. *La gesta del nombre propio: Informe sobre la situación de la comunidad travesti en Argentina*. Buenos Aires: Ediciones Madres de Plaza de Mayo.

Butierrez, Marce. 2021. "Mujer se nace: Karina Urbina y el activismo transexual de los años 90." *Moléculas malucas*, April 19. https://www.moleculasmalucas.com/post/mujer-se-nace.

Cabral, Mauro. 2009. "Cisexual." *Página 12*, suplemento *Soy*, June 5. https://www.pagina12.com.ar/diario/suplementos/soy/1-803-2009-06-05.html.

Caras & caretas. 1930. "Extraño caso de simulación." No. 1.644, April 5. Hemeroteca Digital, Biblioteca Nacional de España. https://hemerotecadigital.bne.es/issue.vm?id=0004693835.

Carvajal, Fernanda. 2018. "Image Politics and Disturbing Temporalities On 'Sex Change' Operations in the Early Chilean Dictatorship." *TSQ* 5, no. 4: 621–37.

CLAM (Centro Latinoamericano en Sexualidad y Derechos Humanos). 2010. "Transexuales de Chile en la OEA." February. http://www.clam.org.br/es/entrevistas/conteudo.asp?cod=6390.

Disalvo, Lucas. 2020. "Desfondar el 'caso.'" *Moléculas malucas*, November 23. https://www.moleculasmalucas.com/post/desfondar-el-caso.

Escalante, Aquiles. 1906. "La mujer-hombre." *Caras & caretas*, no. 407, July 21. Hemeroteca Digital, Biblioteca Nacional de España. https://hemerotecadigital.bne.es/issue.vm?id=0004222779.

Fernández, Josefina. 2012. "Los límites morales de la nación: Una visita al Buenos Aires de 1880–1930 a través de las revistas científicas y culturales de la época." In *Imágenes de la nación: Límites morales, fotografía y celebración*, edited by Josefina Fernández, Alejandra Niedermaier, and Beatriz Sznaider, 13–163. Buenos Aires: Editorial Teseo.

Fernández Romero, Francisco. 2021. "'We Can Conceive Another History': Trans Activism around Abortion Rights in Argentina." *International Journal of Transgender Health* 22, nos. 1–2: 126–40.

Fernández Romero, Francisco, Martín Torres, and Maria Helena Lenzi. 2021. "Presentación al dossier: Hombres trans y transmasculinidades." *Revista Latino-Americana de Geografia e Gênero* 12, no. 1: 259–63.

González Pagés, Julio César. 2012. *Por andar vestida de hombre*. Havana: Editorial de la mujer.

Halberstam, Jack.1998. *Female Masculinity*. Durham, NC: Duke University Press.

Martínez, Juliana. 2017. "Dressed like a Man? Of Language, Bodies, and Monsters in the Trial of Enrique/Enriqueta Favez and Its Contemporary Accounts." *Journal of the History of Sexuality* 26, no. 2: 188–206.

Mendieta, Andrés, and Salvador Vidal-Ortiz. 2021. "Administering Gender: Trans Men's Sexual and Reproductive Challenges in Argentina." *International Journal of Transgender Health* 22, nos. 1–2: 54–64.

Nery, João W. 2011. *Viagem solitária: Memórias de um transexual 30 anos depois*. São Paulo: Leya.

Neves, Benjamim Braga de Almeida. 2016. "Transmasculinidades no ambiente escolar: Laicidade e resistências." In *A política no corpo: Gêneros e sexualidade em disputa*, edited by Alexsandro Rodriguez, Gustavo Monzeli, and Sergio da Silva, 161–78. Vitoria, Brazil: Edufes.

Oliva, Alexis. 2020. "De clandestinidades y disidencias: Eugenio, varón trans e hijo de desaparecidxs." *Agencia presentes*, March 22. https://web.archive.org/web/20200323164839/https://agenciapresentes.org/2020/03/22/de-clandestinidades-y-disidencias-eugenio-varon-trans-e-hijo-de-desaparecidxs/.

Pérez, Moira, and Blas Radi. 2019. "Current Challenges of North/South Relations in Gay-Lesbian and Queer Studies." *Journal of Homosexuality* 67, no. 7: 965–89.

Radi, Blas. 2015. "Economía del privilegio." *Página 12*, suplemento *Las 12*, September 25. https://www.pagina12.com.ar/diario/suplementos/las12/subnotas/10062-951-2015-09-25.html.

Radi, Blas. 2018. "Cómo hacer historia." In *Travestis, mujeres transexuales y tribunales: Hacer justicia en la Ciudad Autónoma de Buenos Aires*, edited by Blas Radi and Mario Pecheny, 169–73. Buenos Aires: Editorial Jusbaires.

Radi, Blas. 2019. "On Trans* Epistemology: Critiques, Contributions, and Challenges." *TSQ* 6, no. 1: 43–63.

Rizki, Cole. 2019. "Latin/x American Trans Studies: Toward a Travesti-Trans Analytic." *TSQ* 6, no. 2: 145–55.

Simonetto, Patricio. 2021. "Raúl Luis Suárez's Smile and the Ruthless Archive." *Notches: (Re)marks on the History of Sexuality* (blog), March 9. https://notchesblog.com/2021/03/09/raul-luis -suarez-smile-and-the-ruthless-archive/

Skidmore, Emily. 2017. *True Sex: The Lives of Trans Men at the Turn of the Twentieth Century*. New York: New York University Press.

Stryker, Susan. 2008. *Transgender History*. Berkeley, CA: Seal.

Suess Schwend, Amets. 2020. "Trans Health Care from a Depathologization and Human Rights Perspective." *Public Health Reviews* 41, art. no 3: 1–17.

TRANSDEVI. 1994. *La voz transexual*, no. 1. Marcelo Ferreyra fonds, Programa de Memorias Políticas Feministas y Sexogenéricas "Sexo y Revolución," Centro de Documentación e Investigación de la Cultura de Izquierdas (CeDInCI), Buenos Aires, Argentina. https:// sexoyrevolucion.cedinci.org/s/la-comunidad-del-archivo/item/2190.

Vicente, Marta V. 2021. "Transgender: A Useful Category? Or, How the Historical Study of 'Transsexual' and 'Transvestite' Can Help Us Rethink 'Transgender' as a Category." *TSQ* 8, no. 4: 426–42.

Erratum for Quincy Meyers, "Strange Tensions," *TSQ: Transgender Studies Quarterly* 9, no. 2 (2022): 199–210.

C. Riley Snorton was mistakenly cited as Riley C. Snorton in the abstract to this article, on page 200, and in the reference list. These errors have been corrected in the print and online versions of this article.

https://doi.org/10.1215/23289252-9612851

DOI 10.1215/23289252-10232750

JOURNAL OF THE HISTORY
OF SEXUALITY ⸻

Established in 1990, *The Journal of the History of Sexuality* illuminates the history of sexuality in all its expressions, recognizing various differences of class, culture, gender, race, and sexual orientation. Spanning geographic and temporal boundaries, *JHS* provides a much-needed forum for historical, critical, and theoretical research in this field. Its cross-cultural and cross-disciplinary character brings together original articles and critical reviews from historians, social scientists, and humanities scholars worldwide.

Articles | Volume 30, Number 1

UNIVERSITY OF TEXAS PRESS | JOURNALS

Printed and bound by CPI Group (UK) Ltd, Croydon, CR0 4YY

13/04/2025

14656483-0005